PIERCING
THE
NIGHT

A Life on the Edge in Post-Amin Uganda
H. EBERHARD ROELL

Order this book online at www.trafford.com/07-0346
or email orders@trafford.com

Most Trafford titles are also available at major online book retailers.

Note for Librarians: A cataloguing record for this book is available from Library
and Archives Canada at www.collectionscanada.ca/amicus/index-e.html

Printed in Victoria, BC, Canada.

ISBN: 978-1-4251-1939-3

*We at Trafford believe that it is the responsibility of us all, as both individuals
and corporations, to make choices that are environmentally and socially sound.
You, in turn, are supporting this responsible conduct each time you purchase a
Trafford book, or make use of our publishing services. To find out how you are
helping, please visit www.trafford.com/responsiblepublishing.html*

*Our mission is to efficiently provide the world's finest, most comprehensive
book publishing service, enabling every author to experience success.
To find out how to publish your book, your way, and have it available
worldwide, visit us online at www.trafford.com/10510*

www.trafford.com

North America & international
toll-free: 1 888 232 4444 (USA & Canada)
phone: 250 383 6864 ✦ fax: 250 383 6804
email: info@trafford.com

The United Kingdom & Europe
phone: +44 (0)1865 722 113 ✦ local rate: 0845 230 9601
facsimile: +44 (0)1865 722 868 ✦ email: info.uk@trafford.com

10 9 8 7 6 5 4 3 2

*Dedicated to the memory of
General George S. Blanchard,
whose faithful encouragement
resulted in this book;*

*and to Debbie, his daughter —
my love till death do us part.*

Thanks...

...to Debbie, for her staunch support, ready availability, and wise counsel throughout the writing of this book.

...to Peter Muth, my fellow-Kraut and friend since age eleven, for his resolute commitment to this project and patient advice hidden in every page.

...to Karsten, a stickler for accuracy and the eye to go with it.

...to Misha, for editing with you, the reader, in mind rather than her Papa, the writer.

...to Margaret Clark, for reminding me of the difference between "brake" and "break" and that it is not "petal to the metal," even for flower lovers.

...to Thaine Norris, my talented friend, for the cover design and layout.

...last yet foremost, to our Father, who kept us and blessed us with a story to tell.

CONTENTS

Introduction...13

Prologue: Under the Gun..15

PART I
FOOTLOOSE AND FANCY-FREE

1. My Early Years..23
2. The General's Daughter...................................35

PART II
UGANDA – MORE THAN JUST SURVIVAL

3. Danger, Disaster, and Destitution 49
4. Learning the Ropes 59
5. Muzungu in the Swamp 77
6. Material Matters Matter 85
7. Bwana Kubwa 95
8. Times of Transition 101
9. A Shake-Down Cruise..................................115
10. Fallen People, Fallen World 135

PART III
RELIEF AND DEVELOPMENT

11. Satisfying the Afflicted.................................149
12. Back to Uganda..169
13. Winds of Change 181
14. Aiding Without Abetting 193
15. The Grass Suffers Again..............................203
16. In Harm's Way 217
17. Sunny but Dark 229
18. Contemplating Contrasts 241

Epilogue: Home Sweet Home 257

APPENDICES

A. Adversity and Blessings................................275
B. Biting the Dust 289
C. One Fancy Ride 299
D. Intergration and Intrigue............................309
E. Unforgettable Arab Hospitality 319
F. Reversals in Asia 331

Final Thoughts 343

INTRODUCTION

Ever since I was a young boy, I dreamed of exotic places in far-away countries. I read adventure stories, like those of explorer Sven Hedin and Karl May's fantasies of courage and discovery. From my early teens on I traveled vicariously with a finger on the map of the world and that far-off look in my eyes, and I determined that, when I was grown up, I would roam all over the globe.

I once flew over Greenland at night and saw the white surface of the world's largest island by the light of a full moon. Just as I pondered what was green about Greenland, I was distracted. There, in the vast, icy emptiness some 30,000 feet below I saw a cluster of lights sparkling like diamonds set in silver – life! I kept my nose pressed against my little window and my eyes riveted on that stark, isolated other-worldliness and watched it disappear as the General Electric engines thrust me toward home.

I thought about the people down there, trying to put myself into their shoes. *How did they end up in that remote place? How do they survive? How do they stay warm? What do they do there? What are their interests? What makes them tick?* And, of course, I would have loved nothing more than to pop in – maybe share a cup of hot reindeer milk with them while satisfying my curiosity.

When I embarked on my first international trip in 1972 – six months of backpacking through Latin America – I could not envision the life-changing effect my travels would have on me. Beyond my fascination with foreign cultures and the burden the grinding poverty I encountered would place on me, I saw the possibilities a practical understanding of the tenets of Jesus the Christ could exert on lives surrendered to Him.

After two international trips as a bachelor and three with my wife, Debbie, the door opened for our involvement in Africa, and we walked through it with gusto.

PROLOGUE

UNDER THE GUN

Peace is not the absence of war,
but the presence of God.
Anonymous

In January of 1986, a defeated army rampaged through our normally tranquil town of Soroti in eastern Uganda. It was like a wounded beast – on the prowl, angry, and menacingly out of control.

On one of those not so peaceful mornings I was startled by a familiar but anxious voice:

"Sir! Soldiers have just broken into your house!"

I whirled around. Our houseboy, Dennis, had spewed out those words, still breathless from running in search of me. His face was stern, but did not express the anxiety revealed in his voice. My family and I had temporarily abandoned our house and moved in with John Mattison, one of my European colleagues. We had joined him on the outskirts of Soroti to escape most of the turmoil inflicted on the hapless population in the center by looting and shooting renegade soldiers.

They were fleeing, all of them, through our town en route to their tribal districts in northern Uganda, having been crushed by a powerful rebel movement that had come up from the south and conquered Uganda's capital, Kampala. Whoever controls the capital runs the country, and for these men the security and tranquility of home was beckoning. There they would quietly disappear into their respective villages or regroup and make a counter-move, if that was what their leaders wanted. For now, at least, they had lost Kampala and, with it, most of the rest of the country, their sense of invincibility shaken. The future would take care of itself.

In those days, Uganda was acting out its African propensity to topple one murderous dictatorship for another. Like the predetermined trajectory of a bullet as it leaves the muzzle of a gun, so, by the forces of tribalism, greed, and lust for power, African governments seem to be predisposed towards coups d'état. In our four years there, we had already been through four – some peaceful, others violent. This was our fifth year and our fifth coup. But perhaps there was hope in this one – at least, that was our hope.

We had left our Fiat in front of the house in our barbed wire-fenced compound. Because looting and car theft were rampant, I had removed the battery and two wheels, siphoned off the gasoline and hidden all in the attic. With that I thought I had sufficiently disabled the car. I had also left the doors of the Fiat unlocked to avoid getting the windows smashed. But I was soon to learn not to underestimate the resourcefulness of a fleeing Ugandan soldier hell-bent on getting home, nor the persuasive power of his gun in the procurement of whatever was needed to achieve that goal. Resistance sometimes led to an untimely death. But that was the last thing on my mind now.

In our absence, four Acholi soldiers had entered our house by breaking the kitchen window. Unsuccessful in their search for the missing parts just five feet above them, they pried open the trunk of the car and removed the spare tire. One down, one to go. Two nuts per wheel instead of four would do. Unbeknownst to me, they had already hooked up a looted battery. Now they were on the hunt for another wheel.

Dennis had found me at the far end of town, and we hitched a ride in an army truck until I spilled the beans and told the soldiers the reason for our hurry. Under the pretext of turning off, they ordered us out. They weren't about to help me confront their fellow looters. We ran the rest of the way, but the looting soldiers were gone – at least temporarily. Panting and perspiring we rushed through the house to identify what might have been stolen. But, other than the broken window, everything seemed to be in order. I was relieved. Memories of a break-in at our Nairobi home years earlier and the attendant loss and mess, as well as a sense of violation, came back to me vividly.

But the armed looters had not left for good. They were focused on only one thing now – our Fiat. Getting to their home district was their singular objective. Once the car was ready to go, well, then there would still be time to look around for other goodies. The Fiat was theirs for the taking, they must have thought, if they could scrounge up a fourth tire. But there was one other obstacle they had not reckoned with.

Like a leading actor backstage and ready to perform his part in an Orwellian drama, I was all pumped and pacing, poised for a confrontation. I had quickly fetched John and some local friends to help me move valuables from the house to a safer location. They were now waiting with me, anxious and grim-faced. Dennis just stood there, stoic, but a concerned look creased his face when the four returned with two Fiat wheels. They looked as though they had been through the wringer – tired and disheveled, and their combat uniforms, anything but uniform, were ripped, soiled, and drenched with sweat. They started shouting from thirty yards away, trying to assert their AK-47-backed authority.

"What are you doing there? You go! We need that car!"

I was not amused, let alone intimidated. I shouted back:

"What do you mean, 'what are you doing there?' This is my house! This is my yard! And this is my car! What makes you think you can just come in here and take it?"

They rolled their stolen wheels past the gate into our compound. I had purposely left it open, because I did not want a closed, much less locked, entrance to become an object of contention. I had to let the intruders save some face by drawing a line in the sand only where it counted – at my car. There the confrontation continued eyeball to eyeball. Amidst the shouting I was aware of the importance of winning the argument on the psychological front. Despite their superior power, I knew that this was not hand-to-hand but head-to-head combat.

They ordered me to sit on the ground, which would have stripped away my dignity and authority and put me in the place of submission. Fat chance of that! I was willing to test the limits of their resolve and made sure they understood that I did not fear them. That would make me equal to them and instill respect. These soldiers were not like their tribal neighbors to the east, the Karamojong. The Karamojong were pit bulls. You didn't mess with them. Our intruders were more like German shepherds. I knew how to deal with that breed. I once backed up a German shepherd that yanked on his chain, snarled, and bared his fangs. I had also confronted menacing soldiers at roadblocks before. These would not leave with our car.

Between our heated exchanges they jabbered with each other in Acholi. At one point Dennis backed off into the house and bolted through the kitchen window. He had understood enough to know that one of them had suggested killing me. As he would put it later: "It got too hot there."

Recalling that face-off, John Mattison wrote to me recently from England: "The hairs on the back of my neck still stand on end at the thought of that experience."

Finally, the most vociferous would-be carjacker made a smacking sound with his tongue, a sign that he was ready to yield. They started to back up, an indication that they were backing down, and I moved forward, chiding them as a father would a misguided son.

Several months later, Harry Garvin, a Southern Baptist missionary, related to me what he had learned from a Soroti Hotel waiter. Three soldiers had discussed in his presence a plan to kill me because I had refused to hand over my car.

Harry's information was news to me. By then, tranquility had returned. Only memories and a diary of the two most dangerous weeks of my life remained. But at that point, like the lingering impressions of a bad dream that teetered on the edge of a nightmare, those lay in the distant past. And, even further back were other, equally memorable events, milestones that prepared me for the rough and tumble of Uganda's volatile years, and experiences that gave me the foundation for an unshakable faith.

PART I

FOOTLOOSE AND FANCY-FREE

1

MY EARLY YEARS

*Remember now your Creator
in the days of your youth,...*
Ecclesiastes 12:1a

I was born in Germany at the beginning of World War II. My father was in Hitler's army and stationed on the Crimean peninsula. While there, he was lucky enough to face the Soviet juggernaut eating caviar and drinking Champaign. My mother was barely coping and caring for my sister, Uschi, and me in a country that was increasingly suffering the consequences of its hegemonic aggression. Admittedly, wars are terrible as they inflict death and destruction and distress on those lucky enough to survive them, and those who wage them unjustly bear a heavy responsibility before God and man. There are occasions, however, when diplomacy has failed to limit tyranny and, for a greater good, a nation must be pounded into submission. That was Nazi Germany – my country of the early 1940s.

We lived in Frankfurt am Main until the tide of the war turned against Germany. My father arranged to house us temporarily in a hunting lodge in a forest near Trier, not far from the Luxemburg border, owned by my uncle and his business partner. That turned out to have been a wise decision, as Frankfurt was carpet-bombed by the Allies. The forest ranger stopped by every few days to make sure we were alright. Mr. Thielen was always dressed in a crisply pressed, green uniform and carried a rifle. To us children he was a combination of Mr. Clean and Superman.

With its tall trees and heavy underbrush that forest held many adventures for two curious kids, and what else was there to do but to explore its dark recesses. One day, Uschi, then six, and I, four, were picking blueberries when we saw something shining through the underbrush. Like Hänsel and Gretel, we sneaked over to have a closer look. We picked our way carefully through the rough and avoided stepping on branches. Their cracking would surely wake up the ghosts or whatever menace might be waiting to pounce.

As we got closer, the shiny something took on shape – mangled shape. It was a plane, shattered into pieces. Wow! The silence of the forest, contrasted by the cataclysmic event that had broken it not too much earlier, really spooked us now. We were scared. I was glad I had my big sister with me. We whispered and looked around. But all remained quiet. There was no sign of the pilots in the twisted wreckage. They must have simply walked away. Boy, had they ever been lucky! They didn't even seem to have been hurt, 'cause there wasn't any blood.

Another time I was hiking among the fields with my father, who was home on leave. How we cherished those precious times with our Papa. It was not often that he could come home to see us. As we sauntered along, we came upon small tin cans and tiny sealed pouches made of silvery paper with writing on it, scattered in the field near our path – food rations for American soldiers. *Must have fallen out of one of their planes*, I figured. *Why were those "Amis"* (our nickname for Americans) *so careless with such precious goodies? Aren't they hungry?* We sampled the contents of some of the pouches right then and there. Boy, were they good! Sweet and savory – flavors little known to our palates. What a find to take home and share with Mutti and Uschi!

Those were lighter moments, but, for the most part, the hell of war haunted us day and night. I remember once hiding with Uschi under a tree in a field when we heard an airplane. We stood with our backs against the trunk, hearts pounding, arms pressed tightly against our sides as if at attention, and facing straight ahead with an upward glance. Maybe we held our breath, too – I don't remember. We had been told that, if we were spotted, the plane would swoop down and shoot us.

"Luftangriffe" (air attacks) were frequent occurrences. To this day I can hear the sirens – warning signals that announced an imminent attack and urged us, wherever we were at the time, to make a dash for the basement or the nearest underground bomb shelter. In outlying areas stood rocket-shaped bunkers made of concrete several inches thick and large enough for three or four people to squeeze into if caught in the open during an alarm. There were slits for fresh air. Through them they could also hear the sirens that blared a second time when the scare had passed. And everyone would breathe a sigh of relief!

Little did I realize in those days, that opposing us on German soil was a young American officer whose life, some thirty years later, would become closely intertwined with mine. It is a testimony to the fact that time heals all wounds, and, fortunately, its march is inexorable. All things come to an end – even hatred and war. And when it was over – well, below is my letter to the editor of our paper, the Daily Camera, of Boulder, Colorado.

I was born in Germany in 1939. In 1944 you Americans dropped a bomb into the house across the street from my house, Schmidtgasse 7, in Gelnhausen, near Frankfurt. Although we were surrounded by two-foot thick stonewalls, we shivered with fear in our basement. Our mouths were wrapped with damp cloths to enable us to breathe, as thick dust had followed the bombing. Our innocent neighbors didn't need such rags anymore. They had become "collateral damage."

Around that time, I remember my mother (my father was in the Soviet Union) taking my sister and me to another neighbors house. A bomb shrapnel had penetrated a wall and the skull of a young woman, who had shielded the body of her new-born with her own. The baby had survived, but the mother lay dead on a bed. I remember innocently playing with lead soldiers, while my mother tearfully consoled the relative who had called her.

We went to a bombed-out soap factory and scraped up what soap we could carry. Goods were tight.

Then a train came and my mother, armed with two loaves of bread, took us to the station. The open box cars were full of old men who should have been at home, reading books to their grandchildren. Tears were rolling down her face as she handed up those loaves to two of the men. We didn't understand. Why was Mutti crying? We didn't know yet what "die Front" meant.

But I remember more: Liberation! No, not from you American "warmongers," but by you from Hitler. As American tanks rumbled through Gelnhausen, no one was allowed into the streets; a precaution against sneak-attacks by German civilians. Well, that proved unnecessary! For leaning out of every window in every house, people were waving anything that could be waved, shouting, singing, rejoicing, as American tank commanders and soldiers received our adulation as though they were returning heroes in a New York ticker tape parade.

Yes, life had not been easy during the war. Still, we were better off than many of our countrymen. My mother had inherited jewelry, silverware, silver table settings and fine linens and had kept furs that my father had acquired from his brother, who was in the tanning business. Since groceries were in short supply, bartering directly with farmers was a way of life. My mother traded those luxury items for hams, potatoes, green vegetables, and lard with pork rind. Open-faced lard sandwiches sprinkled with salt were a daily fare. We also had to suffer a tablespoon of cod-liver oil every day. "It's good for you. It will make you big and strong." And down it went. Even in the immediate aftermath of the war, my father was able to trade some of my mother's inheritance and furs for coffee and cigarettes from the occupying forces. Then, in turn, he exchanged those with the farmers. Our own "coffee" was made from roasted grain. It wasn't Starbucks by any stretch.

After Germany surrendered, we kids were always alert for American troops in the back of their big, green army trucks. When they roared by we chased after them. We had learned that there were rewards for doing that. The soldiers threw out all this wonderful candy we had never known to exist. There was one particular flat, chewy kind that didn't dissolve. I don't know how many sticks of chewing gum we swallowed before we caught on.

We had never seen black men before. We were curious about them. They had gleaming white teeth, and we wondered if their skin color would rub off on white collars. But questions like this didn't occupy our minds for long because we learned very quickly that black GIs tended to be more generous than white GIs. Nobody told us that we should keep such observations to ourselves. For us kids, race was never an issue. In our innocence we just knew that when there were blacks on a truck, our prospects for candy increased. We judged these smiling, uniformed men up there not by the color of their skin, but by the taste of their candy, or better, by the quantity of it. Other than that, they were all the same. Of course, I learned later that that was, unfortunately, not the sentiment in America then, nor had it been in Hitler's Germany. What a triumph it must have been when, at the Berlin Olympics several years earlier, Jesse Owens had kicked his fleet feet into that pompous Aryan attitude of superiority, winning four gold medals, and that right under Hitler's nose.

Though it wasn't nearly as common then as it is today, our parents divorced when I was eight. This wrenching apart of our family was difficult for us. Mommies and daddies belong together, and, inevitably, children become part of the conflict, although our parents avoided playing us off against each other. Uschi and I were awarded, if I can call it that, to my mother. The divorce was amicable, and I remember my father respectfully kissing my mother's hand on a rare visit to our home. He was still a gentleman. He remarried and had two more children but stayed involved in our lives. Though both he and their mother have passed away, Uschi and I have kept in touch with Christoph and Petra, and we try to see each other once a year in Germany.

When I was twelve, I joined the boy scouts. I was so proud of my uniform and that dark blue corduroy beret tilted on my head – now that was something! On some weekends we went to our very own scout house on the outskirts of a village some sixty miles away. What an adventure! I remember listening there to the final of the world soccer cup in 1954, West Germany against Hungary. Yes, Hungary was leading 2-0. But guess who won 3-2!

Our troop had three patrols. Once I arrived ahead of the others in my patrol and found myself confronted by the boys of another one with mischief on their minds. They tied me to a tree and began to taunt me. With malicious pleasure they threatened me with a bucket of water. But they had forgotten to tie up my feet, and before they could dump the water on me I kicked the bucket out of their hands, and they got wet before I did. I guess little incidents like that prepared me for the wilder side of life I was to experience later as an adult roaming the world and facing out-of-control soldiers in Africa.

My best friend was a neighborhood boy named Peter Muth. Peter and I became "blood brothers" by each cutting a finger and holding the wounds together. We were competitive – running, comparing the hardness of our biceps by bouncing pocket knives off them from increasing heights and living out our boyhood dreams in a blanket-tepee in his garden. We were at home in each other's houses, and Worschtebrot (German dialect for an open-faced baloney sandwich) was our rallying cry at suppertime. We became inseparable and vowed to stay in touch for the rest of our lives, no matter where our paths might lead. Within a year his parents moved to

With Peter in Nairobi, 1982 - "Green Machine" in background

Hamburg and our exchange of letters began, one written entirely in Morse code.

As we grew up, we remained faithful to our commitment and stayed in touch. We married the two smartest and best looking women in America. And we both acquired a love for world-wide travel. Over the years we saw each other in England, Kenya, Germany and the United States, and we barely missed each other in Indonesia. We're still in touch today, fifty-seven years later.

In his contribution to an album of memories my wife, Debbie, compiled for my sixtieth birthday, Peter wrote:

> *...new interests – but old competitiveness: a visit to Silver Spring and, almost before you unpack, a Scrabble board becomes the new battlefield and replaces the knives of yore. Years later, in Kenya, a squash court, and battles to exhaustion. I have valued our friendship more than any other. May God give you a happy and blessed 60th, and may he give us many more years in which to dust off those fond memories, meet for the occasional contest, enjoy a Worschtebrot or two and watch our wives become speechless at the sight of two little boys emerging from the bodies of greying men.*

* * *

At seventeen I had an experience that was to change the course of my life. I was not raised in a religious home. God was not part of our consciousness except as the mystical main character of two annual festivals and three once-in-a-lifetime occasions that were steeped in ritual and accompanied by pious verbiage. Nevertheless, at six I was baptized into a name, Heinz-Eberhard, and a church. It should have been infant baptism, but that formality had been delayed by the war. The church happened to be Lutheran because my parents belonged to the non-Catholic half of Germans.

As far as the German government is concerned, its citizens are Christians by virtue of their birth, and, unless your parents belong to that small percentage that adheres to another faith, you are of the Lutheran or Catholic denomination. "Kirchensteuer" is a church tax amounting to about nine percent of the income tax. To avoid paying it you have to formally disassociate yourself from either one. Apart from the faithful who consider this tax their legitimate contribution to their church, even the "unchurched" will often pay up so they and their offspring qualify to get baptized, married, and buried in and through the church. My parents fell into the category of the reluctantly willing, even as we attended services – on some Christmas Eves and, even more rarely, on Easter Sundays.

For me, that was just about the right frequency. In my younger years I found "church" as boring as girls. However, as I got older, my interest in the latter increased, while that in the former remained the same. Religion was for old people, not for us young, adventurous types. Little did I know!

During the latter half of the 1950s in Wiesbaden, I frequented the Christian Serviceman's Center, a home away from home for – no, I didn't really qualify – American soldiers. There was coffee and cake, a reading room – and table tennis. That's what I went for, joined by three other German teenagers. But I also went to improve my English and worked on both for three hours a day, five days a week. On Saturday evenings I attended their Youth-for-Christ meetings, and, again, I didn't qualify – I was a youth for self. God was not in the picture.

To this day I remember the name of a young American soldier and the question he asked me one Saturday afternoon. I was minding my own business, when Gene Shasteen came up to me and started a conversation. At about 5'8" he was my height, with blond hair and blue eyes. He was neatly groomed, friendly, and uncomplicated in his communication. But then, out of the blue, he asked me where I thought I would go when I died.

I had never been posed that question before and remember thinking that, at my age, it was a little early to worry about that. I don't remember the rest of the conversation, but I do remember saying something like "I don't know" even as I was thinking: *Six feet under the ground, and that's it.*

My epiphany occurred on a Saturday evening in 1956 during one of those meetings when, for the first time, the speaker helped me understand what was good about the euangelion, the Good News. I had always believed in the existence of a god, though I had never given him/her/it a thought. That night, the information I received resonated in my brain, captured my heart and began to transform my life – for ever. I discovered God as the loving judge who, entering space and time by becoming that babe in the manger, had Himself paid the penalty I had incurred through violation of my conscience and disobedience to His precepts. The historical Jesus was the Christ who was executed by the Romans. He died for me, so that I might live for Him. I was an unlikely prospect for a life-changing experience. Some of my friends derided my decision and questioned my judgment. A Lutheran pastor, whose views my mother sought about my new orientation, told her that he didn't think it would last very long. That was fifty years ago. A quote by a recent Jewish convert to Christ, mystery writer Andrew Kavlan, in an interview with WORLD magazine (February 10, 2007) fits my experience – "I suspect everyone who sets sail on the sea of faith is a little bit like Christopher Columbus. There are all these people on shore saying, 'Are you crazy? You're going to fall off the edge of reality!' And instead, you discover a new world."

*   *   *

Several years after emigrating to the United States in 1962 I wondered: *How can I travel internationally if I lack the funds for transportation? How about hitchhiking?* (My extensive discussion of this subject below is not an endorsement of this method of travel nowadays. Times have changed. In today's unpredictable environment, hitchhiking is dangerous. But during six months a year for five years in the 1970s it was an intricate part of my life, and for three of those years for Debbie, as well. It enabled us to see the world and prepared us for the tumultuous years we would spend in Africa.)

I quickly learned the art of super-low budget travel. A crisp, clean appearance; standing instead of sitting; looking at the driver instead of off into space; holding up a sign with your destination; hurrying when the car stops; engaging in friendly, meaningful conversation; that was the way to go.

If you saw a couple hitchhiking in Nebraska in the fall of 1975 with a sign that read "AFRICA", that was probably Eb and Debbie Roell. That sign got attention and created interest. A former Peace Corps worker in Zaire, today's Democratic Republic of the Congo, picked us up.

"Are you really going to Africa?"

We were – again. We had an engaging exchange of memories of our first trip and of his own experiences there several years earlier.

A friend of ours from New Zealand once visited us in Colorado. He came up from Central America. His sign read "NORTH POLE." A bit of humor and imagination could get you places.

Hitchhiking was a near cost-free way of immersing myself into an unfamiliar culture. In the setting sun, when thoughts of a place to put up for the night would begin to occupy my mind, the last ride of the day would often result in an invitation to spend that night at the driver's home, especially in poor, rural areas. Since I carried my own sleeping bag, all I needed was a roof over my head and a place to use the bathroom and take a shower. If a humble meal was offered, then that was icing on the cake or, in a day of pervasive junk food, sunflower seeds on the salad. The next morning I would be as good as new.

Thus, thumbs up, as it were, beat flying, busing, and taking the train hands down. Just moving from one city to the next and staying in impersonal hostels, where you never knew if you would wake up the next morning with your possessions still in your possession, was not my thing. There were occasions, of course, when I had to go more out of my way to have a safe night. Yes, I had slept in freezing temperatures in a cornfield in Austria, spent a night in a partially constructed house in Chile and found an unlocked shed at a building site in Brazil, and those were lonely times. Ideally, I would spend the evening with my limited Spanish in friendly chatter with locals and enjoy a comfortable night to boot.

In October, 1972, I ventured on a hitchhiking trip through Latin America, "casi todo a dedo" – almost all by thumb. I chose that continent because I had no oceans to cross, and only Panama's Darien Gap, a track-less and mountainous stretch of jungle, rivers, and swamps prevented over-land progress. For $80 I flew from Panama City, Panama, to Medellin, Co-lombia. From there I thumbed all the way to Ushuaia, a town in the south of an island south of the southern tip of South America and, indeed, the southernmost town in the world. I had left Boulder with $800 and arrived back in Miami six months later with three dollars and lots of memories. I survived the next four days on a loaf of bread and a jar of jam and arrived back home in Colorado in fine fettle.

My second trip took me around the world in *about a hundred and eighty days* and could have been entitled "Planes, Trains and Automobiles" –and trucks, buses, motorcycles, ferries, horse carts, and rickshaws. Back then, I traveled as a *very* lonely Adam, looking for Eve and had no problem understanding why the Bible says, "Two are better than one". She was out there, somewhere, and I was sure that I would find her. After I did, it didn't take me long to realize what a blessing it was not to traipse around alone anymore.

Debbie proved to be an intrepid travel companion. Her let's-do at-titude was complimented by her athleticism and taste for adventure, all of which was to be tested on our first, physically most demanding safari through Southern Europe and North Africa into West Africa. Years later – thirty-one, to be exact – I wrote her a poem. She and I, along with our children, Karsten and Misha, had continued a tradition, started by her father, of writing birthday letters to one another. The night before her fifty-fifth birthday I had still not written anything – shame on me. After she fell asleep, I got out of bed and sat down at the computer, and, with what is here a small glimpse of the future, this is what saved the tradition about an hour later:

> While age my memory may diminish,
> The flame of love will not extinguish.
> My heart's throne you'll not relinquish.
> Twixt truth and folly I can still distinguish.
>
> Far back, in youth, my middle-age, it's true,
> We bucked a trend, the older German, youthful you.
> With trust in God our travels would ensue,
> And two kids later, to Africa we flew.

Again not seeking normal life,
We met with danger, but you, my wife,
Hung in there with me through the strife,
Through dangers, toils and snares so rife.

You persevered through drought and heat.
All hardships you with strength would meet,
And many a guest with joy you'd greet
And faith you found at Jesus' feet.

Our children grew to love our God,
To walk the path the Master trod,
Preferring faith to what was mod.
Approvingly, we gave our nod.

Back home, the Lord gave us success.
You mastered books. My, what a mess!
That paper work, I must confess,
Would have my mind in great distress.

But deftly you dealt with the books,
Master accountant, with good looks.
She sews, she cleans, and then she cooks
Nutritious food. No junk she brooks.

She, that's you, my life, my love,
Just made for me, like hand in glove.
I'm grateful to the One above.
I'm a gray old pigeon – you're the dove.

2

THE GENERAL'S DAUGHTER

He who finds a wife finds a good thing,
and obtains favor from the Lord.
Proverbs 18:22

I met Debbie Blanchard at a small, interdenominational church meeting at the home of friends in the foothills of the Rocky Mountains, just outside Boulder, Colorado. It was a beautiful, sunny September morning. The air was crisp, the sky deep blue, and a six-inch blanket of fresh snow had transformed overnight an Indian summer into a premature winter wonderland. A visitor, who had met Debbie at a Denver sports bar several days earlier, brought her to the meeting. When he had mentioned our little group to her, she had been keenly interested in meeting us and, she told me later, had felt at home the moment she stepped through the door.

We sat in an informal circle, sharing our thoughts, reading from the Bible, singing, and praying. She was off to my right, so not directly in my view. I furtively glanced at her repeatedly, hoping that my interest was not too obvious. Only God would know, and He wouldn't mind – it was He, after all, who had "created them male and female." I knew that she had accompanied a young man who came to our meetings occasionally, but didn't think theirs was a serious relationship since he had never brought her before.

After the meeting we stood in small groups, chatting, and sipping coffee or juice. I felt a hand on my arm. "Eb, meet someone who has just come back from Germany." It was Ruth Bolles, matchmaker par excellence and wife of Dr. Frank Bolles, friends of many years. Debbie and I chatted briefly, then I left her to continue her conversation with Ruth. Still, I kept a discreet eye on her from a distance.

My timid pursuit of her ended when she caught me in the kitchen. I was wearing a muslin shirt with colorful embroidery across the chest. Ruth had mentioned to her that I owned and operated an arts and crafts store in Estes Park, a small tourist town and gateway to the Rocky Mountain National Park. This prompted her to compliment me on my shirt and ask,

"So, did you do that work yourself?"

I was taken a bit off-guard and, with a slightly embarrassed smile, mumbled something about having bought it like that. She was better than I at small-talk, and her initiative encouraged me to contact her later.

But for now I had to relinquish her to her friend and was left with the hope of getting the chance to take her out before long. Her presence at our meeting suggested that she had, at a minimum, some interest in spiritual pursuits. That was important to me. At 5'6" and slender, with her short, sporty haircut, a cute little upturned nose, and beautiful eyes, she seemed to be just what the doctor's wife had ordered. But if her philosophy of life excluded God, then the relationship I envisioned was a non-starter.

I had good reason to be hopeful, though. I was thirty-four and single, and had never seriously dated anyone. I'm sort of an all-or-nothing guy – either a relationship is for real and wedding bells shall be ringing, or I'm playing with emotions and wasting my time. I was looking for a soul-mate, not a stand-in, and Debbie seemed to fit the bill. She was twenty-three, athletic, well-traveled, and available.

On our first date I took her to a restaurant in Denver. I don't remember any details of our conversation that evening except what could have been a defining and thus never-to-be-forgotten question – she asked me how old I was. That was like asking a fat man how much he weighs. Well, I could try to hide my age, but I couldn't run from such a straightforward inquiry. She was shocked. She divulged to me later her immediate thought: "I'm going out with an old man!"

We quickly discovered, though, that we had similar interests. As an "army brat" who had lived in various places overseas, she loved to travel. She had spent her junior year of college studying in France. After graduation she "Eurailed" with a girlfriend through several countries, followed by one year with her parents in Germany. In addition to speaking French, she had a basic knowledge of German and knew a smattering of Spanish. I, too, had done my share of traveling and could get by in French and Spanish. German was, of course, my mother tongue.

I knew that she had some interest in me but couldn't tell on that first date whether or not it was enough to eventually lead to marriage. I was smitten and ready tie the knot but needed to be patient, which wasn't difficult, given my timidity in matters of the heart. But on our second date I decided to throw all caution to the wind. I told her those three little words and, indirectly, asked her the big question: "How would you like to go on a six-month honeymoon around the world?" I was already planning that trip and since she, too, had the travel-bug, I hoped that this approach would work. I figured that, to win a gal like her, a guy like me needed all the help he could get. A round-the-world trip might tip the scales in my favor. Or would it? She thought I was crazy, so I learned later, and graciously wiggled out of that one.

That was tough. Had I miscalculated? I just couldn't understand why she would react so adversely when it seemed so right. But I was still hopeful and would try again. She was worth fighting for. It was my move, but I had to be patient. I had to give her time to think. I am reminded of a merchant who had a shop two stores down from mine. He carried expensive merchandise, and when customers would tell him that they would have to think about an item, Jimmy H. would pull out a chair and encourage them to sit down while they were thinking. But there was no need for that kind of pressure. *Just take your time*, I told myself. And sure enough – patience paid off, and on the third date we were engaged.

*   *   *

Debbie's parents were stationed in Germany with the U.S. military. She first wrote to them of our meeting and desire to get married. We followed that up with a call so I could officially ask for her hand. Naturally, I was nervous. What would they say to this sudden development? Debbie talked first, while I tried to figure out what to say and how to say it. I could tell that, some 6000 miles away, two people had been taken off-guard. Then it was my turn. With considerable trepidation I took the receiver from Debbie. Her father's voice was strong and stern.

"Now, you know this is for life, don't you?" I was elated.

"Yes, Sir!"

What else do you say to a high-ranking military officer who would also become your father-in-law? Actually, we had much in common. He was a lieutenant general in the American army in Germany – I had been a corporal in the German army and now lived in America. Naturally, we saw eye to eye on things.

As the date for tying the knot approached, Debbie and I flew to Luxemburg with bargain-basement Icelandic Airlines. Her mother drove from Germany to pick us up at the airport. Going out of her way like that for us registered with me as a good sign because I knew she was not enamored with the idea of her daughter marrying someone she had so recently met. This relationship had moved much too fast for her. How could Debbie know me well enough for a life-time commitment? And then there was the age difference. A son-in-law twelve years older – "eleven and a half!" Debbie liked to interject – was a stumbling block for Mrs. Blanchard.

Tall, well-dressed, and exuding an air of sophistication, she hid her eyes behind a pair of large, wrap-around sunglasses from the moment we met until we reached her home in Stuttgart, even with a stop en route at my sister's house. I think Uschi was somewhat of a redeeming factor. She is herself elegant and self-assured and lives with her husband in an old ivy-covered house in Bingen, a romantic town at the confluence of the Rhine and Nahe rivers. She put on a "Kaffee und Kuchen" that would have even done a café on the Champs Élysées proud.

Wedding preparations were in full swing. Debbie still needed a dress; I still needed a suit. Invitations went out and an army chaplain was lined up. Flowers were ordered and arranged, and whatever else goes into a wedding about which most of us guys don't have a clue – it was done. Oh, yes, there was the food, of course, but the general, or better, his wife, had a cook and a waiter and a house spacious enough for the occasion. There was also the civil ceremony at the Standesamt, the city registry, before the civil magistrate of Stuttgart/Möhringen with the mayor in attendance. It was official, though not for us, and staid, but necessary. We counted on the Christian ceremony to make our wedding official, but this furnished us with the documentation that proved the government's recognition of us as husband and wife.

And so, ten weeks after we had agreed to spend the rest of our lives together on a September afternoon in Denver, we were married in the general's home on an army base in Stuttgart, Germany. It was November 16, 1974. Major Curry Vaughn, the officiating chaplain, was a big, barrel-chested fellow with a shy smile. He had played football for the U. S.

Military Academy at West Point, my father-in-law's alma mater, so he was an army insider. Through his previous spiritual influence on Debbie he was also a family friend and, what's more, supportive of our marriage. I found that encouraging on our wedding day in my new, classy environment. He, the major, and I, the former corporal, were the lowest ranks in attendance. I had never seen so much military brass in one room.

We spent the first week of our married life in traditional honeymoon style in Uschi's cozy condominium in the Austrian Alps. We hiked in "The Sound of Music" settings and swam in the heated indoor/outdoor pool of the village of Mitterndorf. Debbie was a terrific swimmer and had accumulated many medals and trophies in her summer league. At one point she even had an offer to be trained for the qualifying competitions for the Junior Olympics. Her father had laid out for her what that would mean – more time in the water than on land, I suppose – and, at fourteen, that had been the end of that.

When she now challenged this descendant of the Teutonic tribes to a race, how could he refuse? We agreed on the breast stroke, the only one I knew, and, fighting for the reputation of male chauvinists everywhere, I swam my heart and lungs out – mostly under water, which is supposed to be against the rules - and won by inches. Resting on my laurels or, rather, my life-preserver, I have declined water-related challenges by Debbie ever since.

We also attended a performance of Giuseppe Verdi's La Traviata at the Salzburg opera. It was an elegant affair, and my nice new navy-blue wedding suit was just the appropriate attire – jeans don't quite cut it at European opera houses and concert halls. With that nod to refinement and sophistication, a modest cultural counterweight to our forthcoming free-wheeling hitchhiking tour of West Africa, we returned to Stuttgart and readied our backpacks.

It wasn't the world trip I had promised because we were squeezed for time. My arts and crafts shop in Estes Park was seasonal, and the season wouldn't wait. The shop was located in the bustling center on the main thoroughfare, and the tourist season stretched from Memorial Day to Labor Day. In that timeframe, some three million flatlanders passed through town, mostly from Kansas, Nebraska, and Iowa, but many also from Texas and Illinois. And if we wanted to garner our share of their vacation dollars to be able to go on vacation ourselves, then we had better be back in good time to get ready for the annual reopening.

In those days the phrase "Have a nice day" had just started to be popular – one wonders how good will and courtesy ever managed without it – and with that in mind, I pointed beyond the temporal and transitory by naming the shop "Have a Nice Forever." The top crossbar of the F extended to the end of the word in form of an arrow to illustrate the point – a graphic onomatopoeia. Several years later I met an American tourist in Peru who had vacationed in Estes Park. He remembered the store because of that name. When I started a painting business after our return from Africa many years later, I named it "The Holy Roller Painting Company." Most people got a chuckle out of that play on words, and long after my name was forgotten, that name was still recalled either for repeat business or for recommendation. In business, name recognition is vital, and companies spend huge sums in advertising to get people, for instance, to "just say 'Pepsi' please." My company name served me well and continues to do so in my retirement for the new management.

The shop was a rustic, earthy place. I had hung two silk parachutes to cover a boring ceiling, put down a wood-plank floor to cover cheap linoleum, and hidden the plastered walls behind fake house-fronts, complete with fake doors, windows and curtains, and flower boxes, using barn wood a century old.

I sold some standard items like greeting cards and posters. When blacklights were in vogue, I set up a black-light room in the back and offered garish black-light posters, which sold like hotcakes on a cold winter morning. I was one of the first and, at the time, the best customer of Steve and Susan Polis Schutz, who started in the basement of their Boulder home the now-multi-million dollar company, Blue Mountain Arts. But most of my merchandise was produced by artisans in railed cubicles that resembled the front yards of the fake house-fronts. They made leather goods, silver and bronze jewelry, beaded jewelry, glass-blown figurines, candles, and pottery. The potter worked in the show window – and a show it was. While the other goods were crafted in front of customers inside the store, her turning wheel practically blocked the sidewalk with onlookers, who were then drawn into the store like mice to cheese.

Yes, it was a tourist trap, but a nice one, with a concept unique to the town at the time. I admired the creativity of the artisans, enjoyed watching the customers watching them ply their craft, and yes, loved the jingling of the cash register, also.

When I first thought about this concept, I was in a quandary. I didn't know how to handle payment of their percentages to the artists. A visit to a large ice-cream-and-sweets parlor somewhere in South America solved my problem. There I found the price of the item I wanted on a large billboard at the back wall of the store. Then I paid at the register and exchanged the receipt for whatever I wanted at that price with somebody behind the counter. In my store, I signed the back of the receipt before the customer exchanged it for, say, a purse, necklace, or vase with the artisans. At the end of the month they turned in these receipts for their percentage of the goods sold. And, at the end of the season, I closed up and got ready for my next trip.

So, in another nod, this one to responsibility and due diligence, we would be back dutifully for next year's season. Since there wasn't the time for an extended absence, second best to that promised round-the-world trip was the best I could do for now, namely a five-month hitchhiking tour of West Africa.

* * *

For Debbie's mother, I now realize, it was the worst. She is cultured and elegant and has a penchant for propriety. Our romance was her disappointment. Hitchhiking through parched deserts, snake-infested jungles, and countries run by self-appointed generals with unstable governments, dilapidated infrastructures, and economies on the brink, was not her vision of a honeymoon, especially one in which her daughter was fifty percent of the equation. Now, some thirty years later and with a daughter in her twenties, I can empathize with those fears.

For her part, Debbie was just as adventurous as I and took her mother's reservations in stride. Among four sisters she had been the tomboy, always moving on the double, climbing trees, falling up the stairs, and later, excelling in field hockey as well as swimming.

She was also mischievous and sometimes daring. Once, when her father was serving in Vietnam and the family lived at Clark Air Force Base in the Philippines, she schemed to sneak out of the house to attend a late-night party with her friend, Linda White. She was sixteen at the time and had gone to bed around eleven. After her mother and sister had turned in, she got up, put a wig on the pillow, stuffed other pillows under the blanket, and off she went. Problem was, a sentry on his rounds noticed that the back door was ajar. He woke Debbie's mother and together they searched the house for intruders. When Debbie slipped back through that door in the wee hours of the morning, she saw the glow of her mother's cigarette in the dark of the family room. Suffice it to say, she didn't attend after-hour parties anymore.

My father-in-law warmed up to me quickly and seemed not to worry about our plans. Dad was a pipe-smoking straight-shooter, with erect bearing and a heart for his troops, especially the lower ranks (such as corporals!). One time a soldier from a mechanized unit, under a vehicle with his feet sticking out, was asked by a squatting General Blanchard how life was treating him. "Sir, I am doing fine, Sir, but it would help to get paid on time, what with my family and all, Sir." That soldier had his pay that afternoon. It so happened that the general also made it a priority to pro-

Lt. General George S. Blanchard, 1973

mote German-American friendship, and I was obviously doing my share to contribute to that effort. Furthermore, he reasoned that our trip would make or break our relationship. It did.

*   *   *

The Oldsmobile crept along at a mere 45 mph. I was getting antsy as my mother-in-law drove us to a drop-off point on the world's fastest highway, the Autobahn. Here a BMW will pass a Volkswagen at 110 mph, then veer back into the right lane to make room for the Porsche who, 300 yards back, is already flashing his headlights as he cruises up at a cool 140 plus. The atmosphere in the car was tense, and I knew that it would take Betsy some time to adjust to her daughter's new circumstances – me! Things had moved fast by any standards, Porsche-like – apropos – from a dead stop to a whirlwind romance in only three dates! And now, to top it off, there was this business of hitchhiking through Africa!

It was a cold, drizzly November morning, the kind when one would rather turn over, pull the covers a little higher, and stay snuggled-up in a warm bed. Debbie's mother drove us toward the inevitable moment when good-byes would be followed by waves as her car would disappear in a cloud of spray from passing vehicles, and we would disappear from her rearview mirror.

Parting, as expected, proved difficult, and she ended up driving us farther than planned on the Autobahn towards Switzerland. Inevitably, the point of separation arrived – from my mother-in-law, that is. As her car disappeared in the frantically rushing traffic, a mixture of loneliness and excitement descended on us. The cold, the gray, and the dampness of that morning contributed to the former as our arms were extended towards onrushing cars, driven by mostly suspicious-looking drivers. The thousands of miles and several months of adventurous exploration ahead contributed to the latter. For Betsy, the reality of letting go set in as she was driving back alone. Years later we learned that she had cried all the way home.

So yes, her daughter's marriage to this Kraut did not start on a positive note. But as time passed and our relationship strengthened, she softened. Though she had an aversion to flying, she crossed the Atlantic twice for the births of our two children. Eventually, as she realized that Debbie was happy and that our marriage was going to last, she – the matriarch, who, like a hen had to let go of the chicks she had always guarded – came to accept me as a full-fledged member of the Blanchard clan, and we became friends. In fact, I wrote her years later that, if I were a polygamist, she would be my favorite mother-in-law. Well, I thought it was funny, anyway.

After my father-in-law got his fourth star and became Commander-in-Chief, U. S. Army Europe and Seventh Army, he suggested I write a book about our travels, and I assured him that I would do so right after he had written his. But then I began to write one anyway; "began," because writing books wasn't my thing, though it wasn't for lack of adventures. It wasn't until retirement that I found the time and the inspiration to organize my memories into printable form.

Dad and Betsy, 1977

PART II

UGANDA – MORE THAN JUST SURVIVAL

3

DANGER, DISASTER, AND DESTITUTION

*Truth forever on the scaffold,
wrong forever on the throne –
yet that scaffold sways the future,
and, behind the dim unknown,
standeth God within the shadow,
keeping watch above his own.*

James Russell Lowell

Our friends had predicted that our travels would end once children came along. That prediction proved to be fifty percent correct: Our children did come along, in fact, to well over thirty countries.

In the fall of 1977, in anticipation of the birth of our first child in January, we sold our crafts shop of seven years and bought a house some forty miles down the road in Boulder, home of the University of Colorado. I started a small house-painting business but, influenced by the needs I had seen in my travels, began to look for an opportunity to get involved in Third World relief and development. I was impressed by the fact that, while using His power to meet the physical needs of the deaf, the blind, the lame, and the hungry, Jesus also probed the depth of thinking of his contemporaries: "For what will it profit a man if he gains the whole world and forfeits his life?" (Matthew 16:26a)

Therefore, I was interested in finding an organization that looked beyond man's mere physical well-being and, in keeping with biblical priorities, sought to meet his spiritual needs, as well. Missionary statesman Samuel Moffet expressed it this way: "There is nothing quite so crippling to evangelism and social action as to confuse them in definition or to separate them in practice." That would be my motto, a clarion call to meeting the wants of the whole man – body, soul, and spirit.

Shortly before our son, Karsten, turned two, we stored our furniture in our basement, packed our bags, rented out our house, and moved to The Netherlands to join a Christian aid organization. That was in November of 1979. After our daughter, Misha, was born, the Evangelical Broadcast of Holland (EO) decided to send us to East Africa to help with the start-up of a community center it had built for the Anglican diocese in Mbarara, Uganda. This would be an exciting turn in our lives, we figured, and in that were more prescient than we could have ever imagined.

We began our African adventure in July of 1980 by staying for two months in a small suite at the Fairview Hotel in Nairobi, Kenya. Advertising itself as The Country Hotel in Town, it was a comfortable place on a hill at the edge of city center, surrounded by five acres of tropical gardens – a peaceful retreat that allowed us to acclimate and get ourselves organized for a Uganda still reeling from the aftershocks of Idi Amin's dictatorship. From here, the continent didn't look all that bad. At about 5500 feet, the climate was pleasant, the people were friendly, shops were plentiful and well stocked, gourmet restaurants abounded, and security was acceptable.

On my first solo-trip to Uganda, I got an immediate, eye-opening introduction to that country's problems. I was picked up at the airport with an early model, two-door, metallic-blue Honda Civic. Judging by the way it was running and bouncing, one could tell that it had been fighting for survival many an unfriendly road over many years. It came with a uniformed body guard sporting an AK-47, the Russian Kalashnikov assault rifle I would soon encounter everywhere. My immediate observation: In Uganda cars are expensive, man-power is cheap, and life is dangerous.

Those impressions were confirmed within minutes. We were stopped at several roadblocks manned by foreboding-looking soldiers stuffed into ill-fitting conglomerations of military uniform and civilian clothing. Straps dangling, they carried their AK-47s leisurely in one hand and waved them around as though they were toys, or used them as pointers as though they were sticks. Often they would be directed at you, and, of course, it was always the end from which the bullets exit.

At that time, whites were still few and far between, and I was given the once-over with an expression, friendly though it was, I was to hear in East Africa more than any other: "Muzungu! Howayou?" And thanks to our official-looking armed friend, we were allowed to pass right through without any further ado.

The streets were potholed, dusty, and full of largely barefoot pedestrians dressed in rags. Some of their shirts were so torn, so totally ripped, they were hard to identify as shirts, and I wondered how the owner decided through which holes to put his arms. These survivors of Amin's holocaust moved seemingly aimlessly up and down the middle of the road, hung out on street corners, and shopped at tiny stalls for the barest essentials. Pot-bellied toddlers with runny noses and naked but for grimy t-shirts were playing in the dirt. On wobbly tables some home owners displayed hands of small sweet-bananas, grown in the backyard and offered for a pittance. Garbage was ubiquitous. A few rickety bicycles would pass by, and the occasional speeding, smoke-spewing truck or passenger jalopy would send everybody scurrying. The houses were either semi-permanent dwellings or shops whose corrugated iron-sheet roofs were brown with rust and whose plaster was falling off the walls, exposing the mud brick below.

I spent several days in the capital, Kampala, and stayed at the Apollo Hotel, named after another of Uganda's murderous dictators, Apollo Milton Obote. This luxury hotel of pre-Amin Uganda sat on top of a hill, the grounds sporting manicured lawns and tall, majestic-looking palm trees. It was surrounded by a fence bedecked with colorful bougainvilleas. With its sixteen stories, it overlooked much of the city. Its glory days, when Idi Amin still frolicked in and around its swimming pool, had already passed. Now, the pool was empty except for the brackish remains of the last rainy season. The hotel had only cold running water and for only one hour a day. Whenever I happened to be in my room and water was coming in, I filled the bathtub. There were no bath towels, and my bed had only one sheet. With the air-conditioner out of commission and the temperature around 80 degrees, I dried off the way I used to dry dishes when I was a bachelor – towel-free, naturally.

There was only one key for my room, and I was supposed to return it to reception after unlocking the door. But that door was on the 14th floor, the elevators were not working, and I was not enamored with the idea of being dependent on a valet. The room was one of two booked by my host, a Ugandan government official. After unlocking my balcony sliding door, I saved myself much time and effort for the remainder of my stay by entering my room via his and climbing from his balcony over to mine. Good

Debbie wasn't with me. For a lark in Cairo, years later, I climbed from one of our two balconies to the other on the sixth floor of our hotel. That got me into deep yogurt with her.

It was easy to see that Uganda had suffered catastrophically under Amin and Obote. But despite years of neglect, one could tell that Kampala had been a beautiful city. Built on seven hills like Rome and Amman, it was lush with vegetation and bright with color from jacarandas, frangipani, and flame trees, and bougainvilleas of many hues. It had a pleasant climate with cool nights and bearable daytime temperatures. Though it was a sprawling city, it gave one the feeling of a country town, with traffic noise almost non-existent. The voices of early risers and the swish-swish of the morning ritual of sweeping of compounds were mixed with the crowing of roosters from near and far.

God's creation had remained beautiful – not so man's handiwork. Amin had expelled some 60,000 Asians. Those Indians and Pakistanis had constituted the backbone of the economy, and their departure assured its final collapse. For years, essential services had been neglected in favor of a military build-up. Water pipes were broken and manhole covers busted, leaving gaping holes in streets and sidewalks, just waiting for someone to fall into.

A number of buildings were bombed out in the war of liberation, their rubble randomly strewn were it had fallen. Shop windows were broken as looters had made off with everything that wasn't nailed down – merchandise, shelves, and showcases. Idi Amin had commissioned the building of a large mosque. It was now the unfinished relic of a mismanaged economy. The bamboo scaffolding, falling apart around its tallest minaret, looked from the distance like matchsticks in disarray. Adding insult to injury, that tower, a prominent part of the skyline, left its vertical direction part-way up. The second half was visibly leaning. But, alas, the fame of a Leaning Tower of Pisa would elude it. Adding to the ambiance, stinking garbage was piled high in the streets, and Marabou storks, when not feeding on it, were perched high atop buildings like gargoyles on European cathedrals. They appeared to be deathwatches presiding over a dying city.

There was one barebones but acceptable restaurant. The regular fare was tilapia or Nile perch with posho, a corn porridge, or matoke, a Bugandan staple of steamed mashed bananas. (The Baganda are Uganda's largest tribe; their region is Buganda with Kampala as capital. A single tribesman is a Muganda and their language is Luganda.) Roads were so dilapidated that it was not unusual to have all four wheels hit potholes simultaneously. One street was totally impassable because of a crater that had never been filled in. However, for the time being, that did not matter much since vehicles were scarce. Most belonged to non-governmental organizations (NGOs) such as the U.N., the World Bank, the IMF, and, yes, relief and development agencies.

Still, outside help was slow in coming. In those early days, I would walk around the city all morning to get to know my way around and feel its pulse, which was barely perceptible as the patient was near dead. In those orientation walks I would see not more than four or five expatriates. For the most part, locals slunk about without purpose and stared empty-eyed at the devastation. African cities without blaring music are cities in ruin. That was Kampala, a hodgepodge of morose survivors enduring a bleak, threadbare existence symptomatic of the wider devastation that was Uganda. Violent coups d'état resulting in successive corrupt regimes had confirmed the truth of a Kikuyu proverb, "When two elephants fight, the grass suffers."

I was itching to see Idi Amin's euphemistically called *State Research Bureau* on Nakasero Hill. Of several torture venues, that was numero uno. In it he had killed thousands of purported enemies of his regime, including Uganda's first Prime Minister and first Chief Justice, Benedicto Kiwanuka, and other politicians, civil servants, diplomats, religious leaders, even some foreigners. In the dark of night they were picked up, stuffed into car trunks, and never heard from again. Most of them ended up at the State Research Bureau or at Nile Mansions, another government building, for interrogation, torture, and slaughter. Their bodies were dumped into the Nile. The intake ducts of Owen Falls Dam, a hydro-electric plant at Jinja that supplies Uganda and western Kenya with electricity, had to be cleared continually of bodies. Tens of thousands of Amin's victims were also dumped in Mabira Forest in Mukono district, and the stench from rotting corpses could not be avoided by drivers on the Kampala – Jinja road.

Business-like I strode up to the tall, black gate and informed the Tanzanian soldier behind, that I would like to have a look. He asked for my credentials. Through the wrought-iron uprights I handed him my Colorado driver's license. The color picture must have impressed him – it worked. After he had locked the gate behind me, we started toward the building when he swung around. He returned to his guardhouse to retrieve his flashlight. We descended into the dark, dank void of a basement. He was armed with an AK-47. As pitch-blackness surrendered to the beam of his torch, the thought crossed my mind that I could easily become another victim in these chambers of death. To increase my chances of survival in case he had something unfriendly in mind, I asked for the flashlight and made a point of staying close to him.

Blood was caked on the floor, smeared on walls, and splattered onto ceilings. A ragged shirt here, a flip-flop there. Over the hollow sound of our footsteps I could imagine the screams of the thousands who, right here, had been beaten to death with clubs or hacked to death with pangas (Swahili for machete). A narrow corridor, one end bricked up, a rusty iron gate at the other, had served as a holding pen for those unfortunate souls who would never again see the light of day. Crosses and prayers were scratched into the cold concrete walls: "God, have mercy." Upstairs, doors had been ripped off hinges and left where they had fallen. In the offices, the contents of file cabinets were strewn ankle deep. I picked up a piece of paper: "We regret to inform you that …. died in a car accident."

My mind went back to three years earlier, when Uganda's beloved Anglican archbishop, Janani Luwum, had died in just such a "car accident." Uganda's national television had shown the staged aftermath of the purported crash. In reality, Amin had personally beaten him with a club and then shot him pointblank through the mouth. That had been the seminal event that awoke the world to the fact that the self-appointed "Field Marshall" was not just an unpredictable, quirky buffoon, but a callous murderer. In an attempt to mollify Amin, the Church of Uganda had replaced the murdered archbishop with Bishop Sylvanus Wani, a simple man who was chosen because he was a member of Amin's minority Kakwa tribe and his clan member to boot.

Amin's foray into the Kagera Triangle of northwestern Tanzania in early 1978 presaged the beginning of the end, when President Julius Nyerere fought back, conquered Kampala and sent the tyrant fleeing into exile in Libya. That ended the reign of one of Africa's most notorious rulers, "His Excellency, President for Life, Field Marshal, Al Hadji, Professor Dr. Idi Amin Dada, VC, DSO, MC, King of Scotland, Lord of All the Beasts of the Earth and Fishes of the Sea and Conqueror of the British Empire in Africa in General and Uganda in Particular."

After it had ousted Amin with the help of Tanzanian-trained Ugandan exiles, the Tanzanian army became an occupying force. It erected road-blocks, which, after it left Uganda, remained in place, now manned by the Ugandan army. A tire, a clump of grass, or three or four stacked bricks in the middle of the road meant that soldiers were around, perhaps hidden by tall grass, and you had better stop. Running a roadblock could be deadly.

Its primary or official purpose was to check on the movement of people and goods. However, since these soldiers did not get paid on a regular basis, their secondary, unofficial purpose on these roadblocks was fundraising through extortion. Thus, most soldiers saw in their duty at roadblocks an opportunity to enrich themselves by means of their gun-enforced author-ity. Not having a proper I.D., or being from a tribe out of favor with the government, could result in detention at best, unless handsomely remedied with a bribe.

Greasing palms in these shakedowns was compulsory if you valued your safety. Thus, few African men would refuse to hand over a watch, and few African women would not readily part with a necklace if it were demanded of them. These items would then be donned and shamelessly worn by the uniformed extortionists. Travelers with foresight would keep glittering jewelry out of view and be prepared to part with a few hundred shillings of Ugandan funny-money. Some of us in Christian relief work would hand them gospel tracts in the vernacular instead. They were always welcomed by those who could read and were starved for reading materials. I have no doubt that this literature reminded some of them of the possibly long-forgotten influence of a godly mother or grandmother.

Politically neutral expatriates were not expected to pay bribes and were generally in less danger than Africans for the simple reason that we were highly respected. After all, most of us had left the comforts and relative safety of our homes and come as physicians, nurses, teachers, relief and development workers, and missionaries to serve mostly poor Africans. We were recognized for our neutrality, respected for our industriousness, and admired for our trustworthiness. Still, if we did not give a bribe, locally known as chai, the world's most widely used word for tea, we might have to submit to a search of our vehicles. Perhaps the inconvenience would encourage future donations. This harassment was visited especially upon the soft-spoken and those who exhibited fear.

Rob Morris' experiences proved the point. Rob was a British physician and an old Africa-hand, and he and his family became close friends of ours. Rob was quite antithetical to me. He was quiet to the point of appearing shy and so soft-spoken that I often had a hard time understanding him. But, as the saying goes, appearances can be deceiving.

Once Debbie, the children, and I rode with Rob, Jen, and their children in their Volkswagen bus in search of game in Queen Elizabeth National Park in western Uganda. The area was flat as a pancake, and one could have seen for miles, had it not been for lush green bushes the size and shape of an American Indian hogan or a Mongolian yurt, growing out of the savannah. They were separated by well-worn tracks, about ten feet wide – elephant highways. Sure enough, rounding some of these bushes we came upon a small herd of peacefully foraging pachyderms, adults with two or three teenagers and a baby.

We stopped to observe, but Rob left the engine running in case the matriarch were to charge. But they didn't seem to mind our presence. Apart from the idling engine, the only sound was that of the tearing of thin branches and the occasional snorting. We were mesmerized by these huge, beautiful animals and the quiet interaction between the adults and their young ones. They were like a loving family.

When they moved on, so did we. We would round another bush, and there would be more of them. Rob drove fearlessly among them and brought us closer to those tuskers and their offspring than we had ever been in the wild.

But the soldiers at roadblocks misinterpreted the meekness of his demeanor as weakness, even fear, and made things difficult for him. Since he refused to pay bribes, he often had to unpack his van for a thorough search.

I, on the other hand, figured out early on that I could play those soldiers' game, too, and actually began to enjoy sparring with those guys. I would talk with the young men as if I were their father. Before anyone could ask "Coming from?" and "Proceeding to?" – roadblock-speak for "What have you brought for me?" – I would reach through the window, put my hand firmly on the soldier's shoulder, and then *I* would be the one asking questions. "Is everything quiet around here? Are there any problems? Are you boys behaving yourselves?" Following their compliant answers, I would conclude with "okay," followed generally by a reciprocating "okay," and we would move on. If somebody would ask for *chai*, I would just laugh and say, "You want *chai* already? I haven't even had my coffee yet." He would smile sheepishly, look, at most, at our I.D.s, wave a hand and say "You go, muzungu!" and we would be on our way.

I shall never forget one particular roadblock experience. It was funny but could have been less so had it not been received in good humor. The rack of our Daihatsu carried a box that held our car-top tent and two of three mattresses. It was covered with the same army-green canvas from which we had made the tent. Army green seems to be of the same hue the world over, and for our gear it was an unfortunate color in a country virtually run by the army. But the canvas came only in that one color. The cover was tied to the rack through eyelets with a nylon rope and was periodically viewed at roadblocks with a suspicious upward glance. The box could have easily accommodated several dozen weapons. Trust in the neutrality of the muzungu must have been the reason I was never asked to open it – until one fine afternoon.

I pulled up at a roadblock some thirty miles south of Soroti. It was a typically hot day. A soldier left four or five others sitting on an embankment in the shade of a tree, sauntered up to the car as if on a leisure stroll and told me to pull over to the side of the road. I knew immediately that something unusual was in the offing. He peeked through a back window while shielding his eyes with one hand from the sun's glare. Satisfied that I carried nothing suspicious inside, he directed his gaze up and, making a hand motion, asked me to open the box. That was a hassle, but what is a meek and obedient guest in the country to do?

Stepping onto the spare tire in the back, we both climbed onto the car rack and, while untying the canvas, I had a room-temperature IQ idea. As soon as I had removed the cover and lifted the lid, I grabbed one of the three-foot black tent poles, whirled around, pointed it like a loaded gun toward the soldiers on the embankment and swept it in an arc with a loud "trrrrrrrrrr." For a split second there was stunned silence. The picture froze for a moment in time. The soldier, who had joined me on top to be able to view the box's interior, was equally bewildered. Then everybody broke out in hilarious, leg-slapping laughter, and, for all my trouble and stupidity, I had made new friends.

4

LEARNING THE ROPES

We dance around in a ring and suppose,
but the secret sits in the middle and knows.
Robert Frost

In September of 1980, as Debbie and I were poised to cross the Kenya/ Uganda border with Karsten, now two and a half, and Misha, all of eight months, we were brimming with hope and expectation. We were about to step over the threshold of the endeavor for which we had prepared, uprooted ourselves, and traveled to this continent. Exchanging the comforts and certainties of home and leaving family and friends for the unknown of Africa was less difficult than one might expect, given the excitement engendered by the adventures we envisioned before us. Uncertainty can be exhilarating, and we were to drink from its fountain at times with bigger gulps than we would have, had we always been able to exercise total control.

In addition to transporting the four of us and our suitcases, our trusty Volkswagen bus also carried some of the food we wouldn't be able to scare up in Uganda, carefully hidden from Kenyan customs officials. (Transport of foodstuffs across the border into Uganda was prohibited to prevent commercial smuggling. We, on the other hand, took selected grocery items for personal consumption and had therefore no qualms about skirting that law.) As we started this new chapter, we had no idea that ahead of us lay not only those exciting adventures, but also sobering, sometimes dangerous experiences that would test our courage and commitment. I believe that from the beginning, God revealed Himself to us in a powerful way with an enduring assurance of His presence to steel us for those challenges ahead.

My definition of a miracle is the temporary suspension of natural law. It has nothing to do with an uncanny development of circumstances; circumstances that might be extremely unlikely and therefore considered wonderful, even amazing developments, just fortuitous to some, answers to prayer to others. Only when the physically impossible has occurred can a claim to a miracle be legitimately made. The ax head floating in the Old Testament book of Second Kings is an example of a miracle. Had a fish brought it to the surface, it would not be. Had the fish presented it with the words "Here you go!" it would be.

We had left Nairobi, the "Green City in the Sun," early in the morning on a day that fit that description well. We climbed the gentle slopes of the Kenyan highlands and moved along the 1400-foot-high escarpment of the great Rift Valley, a depression that winds its way for nearly four thousand miles from the Dead Sea to Mozambique. Volcanic Mt. Longonot lay off in the hazy distance, emerging like a mighty cone from the barren valley's expansive bottom. Its rocky sides were riven in vertical lines from eruptions long ago, and its crater was clearly visible. It seemed to follow us as we rounded it for the next three-quarters of an hour. The air was clear and crisp and cool up here. We passed pine forests, logging trucks, and stands with produce such as cabbages and carrots, or handicrafts such as woven baskets and soapstone sculptures for tourists. The vendors were bundled up in sweaters and coats – you might have thought you were in Europe.

But the illusion didn't last long. The temperatures climbed as we began to descend into the hot, dry valley. Lake Naivasha came into view. Then Lake Nakuru, fuchsia pink with over a million flamingoes. Here and there, herds of plump Zebras were foraging near the road. They were obviously camera-shy because they would bolt if you stopped to take a picture.

After a long and mostly hot seven-hour drive over the beautiful countryside of western Kenya, we arrived at the Ugandan border. We were cleared by immigration, customs, and the police on the Kenya side and were ready and eager to cross into Uganda. This place was hot and dusty and smelly and noisy from the many trucks that brought goods from the Kenyan port of Mombasa to Uganda, Rwanda, Burundi, and eastern Zaire, now Congo. But there was more than discomfort and inconvenience behind our desire to get moving again. There was a serious concern: Danger lurked in Ugandan cities after dark. Starting early in the evening, thugs, including soldiers and policemen, would break into houses with their AK-47s, often murdering for nothing more than a radio cassette player, bedding, or for the possibility of finding wads of Ugandan shillings stashed between mattresses. Sometimes they finished a meal still warm on the plates of their hapless victims.

Cars would be hijacked even in broad daylight. One of our acquaintances, John Wilson, the distinguished and respected Ugandan leader of the African Evangelistic Enterprise in East Africa, was killed when he tried to talk hijackers out of taking his car. Similarly, a German woman was shot in such an attempt when she refused to surrender her vehicle. But she survived and drove herself to one of the mission hospitals – the large government hospital, Mulago, was little more than a morgue in those days. Given those realities, we were anxious to reach Kampala, if not Mbarara, before dusk.

It was early afternoon. There was a double-drive chain-link gate across the road leading to the bridge that separated the Kenyan and Ugandan border posts. Rivers may constitute natural boundaries, but I don't think God made them to separate people. Bridges are practical reminders, though, that we still need each other, even if our ability to serve that need is sometimes but grudgingly accepted and strictly controlled by the authorities.

I remember well a bridge I crossed on my trip through Latin America in 1972. It connects El Salvador with Honduras. As of 1969, the two countries had been in a state of war – over a soccer game! I had arrived at the heavily guarded Honduran side the evening before and decided to spend the night there. I erected my mosquito tent on a grassy spot. It was a calm, balmy night, and I slept exceptionally well, guarded by a formidable contingent of heavily-armed Honduran forces. The next morning, as I walked across that bridge, my mind's eye saw the machineguns in my back, even as I focused on the machineguns facing me. *Okay, boys – just hold your fire now! I am neutral! I'm a German citizen! You've heard of Gerd Müller and Franz Beckenbauer? Well, I am their compatriot!*

I also remember the Allenby Bridge over the Jordan River that separates Israel from Jordan. Soldiers were facing each other there, too, and Arabs were strip-searched before being allowed to enter Israel.

Then there was the Victoria Falls Bridge, connecting Zimbabwe and Zambia. That was a relaxed, almost playful place. The railroad car-pulling contest of the World's Strongest Man competition took place there, and, from a tiny platform outside the railing, Misha and I bungee-jumped toward the Zambezi River.

On our West Africa trip, as related in appendix C, our road ended in the Mano River that separated Sierra Leône from Liberia. It had no bridge but canoes still brought people together.

Since the collapse of the East African Community in the mid-1970s, this bridge in no man's land between Kenya and Uganda was much more tightly controlled. Comprised of Kenya, Uganda, and Tanzania, the community had not survived the member countries' political and ideological differences. To keep Uganda's internal struggles from spilling over into Kenya and the depressed Ugandan economy from exploiting the relative prosperity of Kenya, border security had been tightened.

Having satisfied the requirements of officialdom, we were ready to enter the land to which we had committed, but the double-drive gate was padlocked with a heavy chain. I asked one of the officials to unlock the gate so we could travel on. He informed me that the man with the key had gone to lunch. *The man with the key – gone to lunch and with the key?* What was I missing here? Nothing, I was only becoming acquainted with the relaxed ways of Africa.

But to get the full flavor of this situation, one must understand this about 1980s Uganda, if not most of Africa: Lunch can take anywhere from thirty minutes to several hours, and a government worker is likely to be gone for a longer, rather than a shorter period of time. An upper-level official may hang his coat over the back of his chair to give the impression that he is on duty and has just stepped out, but leave for the afternoon, sometimes coming back only to retrieve it at the end of the workday. That was unlikely in this case with a lowly border guard and the pressure of heavy truck traffic, but time was passing, and we wanted to be sure not to get caught by dusk in the middle of nowhere. Kampala was our minimum goal. There we could stay at the fenced and secured guesthouse of the Church of Uganda.

"Well, can you go find the man with the key?"

"I don't know where he went."

"Isn't there another key somewhere?"

"No. We have only that key."

He was stabbing with his finger into the air as he was making his point, and I thought, *One key? What if it got lost? Would you shoot the lock off? Lift the two sides of the gate off the hinges? Get a locksmith from Eldoret, about an hour-and-a-half drive away?* But I was not surprised. The first time I visited Uganda, the immigration officer at Uganda's international airport at Entebbe didn't even have a pen to make an entry into my passport, let alone a stamp. My first good deed in Uganda – I gave him my BiC.

So, here we were with our two children – a toddler and a baby – facing the prospect of spending the night in this poor excuse for human habitation. We weren't even sure there was a hotel with the promise of some comfort. And even if there had been one, there was no way our car with our "personal effects" – two words that were border jargon for your stuff – would have survived the night untouched. A night watchman would happily walk away from his job if he could do so with a couple of suitcases full of our duds.

Sleeping in the car wouldn't be safe either, so that the only escape from our predicament would have been a return to the nearest Kenyan town, Eldoret, some sixty miles back on a road fit for a tank. Clearly that guardian of the gate, possessor of the key to our deliverance from major inconvenience, had better get back here and soon.

Suddenly, just as I was expressing under my breath my disbelief at this situation, my first negative thoughts of this mission, I heard a clanging sound from the direction of the gate, some thirty feet away. The lock was still locked, but the chain had separated from the lock, and the two loose ends were dangling and rubbing against the metal of the gate. Nobody was near the gate. There was no wind, let alone an earthquake. The chain – at about three inches per link, the size commonly used on gates – had been loosely wrapped. I don't know that it had broken, because I didn't see a broken link on the ground. Nevertheless, it was quite the event and an encouragement to our deflated spirits. Chastened, I uttered a quiet "Praise God" and turned to the officer:

"Sir, God has broken the chain." (Technically that might not have been the proper description, but I wasn't worried about the details then. Nor was he.) "Would you please open the gate?"

That hot afternoon reinforced a lesson: God's timetable, not unlike that of Africans in their more relaxed culture, is unpredictable. He is sovereign above all speculation, unfathomable in His wisdom and abundantly merciful in the revelation of his power.

Coming back down to earth, we still didn't make it to Mbarara that day. But we got beyond Kampala and spent the night in a secure compound with the bishop of Masaka, the Right Reverend Christopher Sen-jonjo, eighty-five miles from our goal.

We arrived at our destination the next morning and moved into a three-bedroom concrete house built on Ruharo Hill, just outside Mbarara, by a former missionary, Dr. Algie Stanley-Smith. Dr. Smith had been the first man to translate the Bible from English into Lukiga/ Runyankole, the tribal language of our own Ankole and the neighboring Kigezi district in the southwest. A narrow, red-earth lane, lined on both sides by huge Eucalyptus trees, led from the main road past the compound of the bishop of Ankole, the Right Reverend Amos Betungura, on the left and the community center on the right. Our house was next door to that, and between it and the old, red-brick Anglican cathedral that stood squarely at the end of the road, was a nursery school. Mbarara High School was behind the cathedral.

Here is what Debbie wrote about our new home in our Christmas letter in 1980:

> *Mbarara is a quiet and peaceful town of 15,000, surrounded by green, rolling hills. Our community, Ruharo Hill, located some three miles from town, is even quieter with some fifty houses spread over two square miles, overlooking fertile fields and pasture, most of the land belonging to the Church of Uganda. Since traffic is practically nil, a village atmosphere prevails. We have a daily parade of longhorn cattle in front of our property, and chickens and goats are plentiful.*
>
> *Our accommodations are quite western, with a spacious house* (I think she must have expected a one-room mud hut) *and large yard surrounded by a tall hedge for privacy. The vegetable garden is already producing; flowering shrubs and fragrant frangipani trees add to the beauty of the setting.*
>
> *We have had to adjust to some inconveniences, common to Africa and, particularly, to post-war Uganda: We lose electric power for hours and, sometimes, days at a time. When mealtime comes, we are challenged to switch gears from a four-burner stove with oven to a one-burner paraffin cooker. Our water is pumped in from the town but reaches us only for about fifteen to thirty minutes every three days, looks like weak tea and probably comes straight from the river.*
>
> *Grocery shopping is a real adventure, everything sold in open-air markets coming straight from farm or garden: meat off the carcass;*

fresh fruit and vegetables; and grasshoppers and flying ants when in season. Fresh milk is delivered daily and must be boiled. From the cream we make butter once a week.

Nobody ever seemed to hurry here. When you met somebody on the way, there was always time for an elaborate greeting and inquiry about, yes, even the well-being of the cattle, which emphasized their importance in the culture. The Banyankole are pastoralists, and their long-horn, chocolate-brown cattle – commonly referred to simply as "the animals," as though no others existed – are their most precious earthly possession. Here a man's wealth is not measured by the money in his bank account, but by the number of his "animals." The daily parade of longhorn cattle Debbie referred to consisted of some two dozen well-fed animals that moved by our house at around five o'clock on the way from their pasture to their corrals. Their progress was accompanied by the sound of their hoofs on the hard-earth lane, snorting, and the monosyllabic prodding of their herder. The "cowboy," as young as eight, would walk bare-foot behind the cattle, and move stragglers along by slapping them across the hindquarters with a long stick.

Predictably, milk is an important part of the Banyankole diet. One of our friends in Mbarara, Verinah Rujoki, lived on nothing but milk until she was six years old, and she seems to have weathered that one-dimensional diet just fine.

The Ankole cow's milk is richer than that of our cows and tastes as though the animal has been through a fire. In the absence of refrigerators, the milk is stored in a black, decoratively carved wooden container whose interior is smoked by setting it upside down onto the opening of a clay pot in which a certain type of grass is burned from a side opening. The rising smoke permeates the wooden bowl's interior, and the resulting preservative effect is absorbed by the milk and gives it, together with the smoky flavor, a longer "shelf life."

Years later, Dave Glaze, a friend from my church who accompanied me on one of my visits, fell sick when he drank more of that milk, given to us by well-meaning friends, than he could stomach. The problem was exacerbated by the omnipresence of cooking fires, and it took him several days to overcome his newly-acquired sensitivity to smoke.

As Debbie mentioned in her letter, water was a problem both in quantity and quality. We had to boil and filter all that we used for cooking or drinking. I would take advantage of heavy downpours by showering behind the house in my swimming trunks. We also caught the run-off from the corrugated-iron-sheet roof in two fifty-five-gallon drums after I had fashioned gutters from the community center's left-over steel roofing. A good downpour would fill them both. We could get by on ten gallons of water a day, while still keeping ourselves socially acceptable. To conserve, we flushed the toilet with dishwater and went by the motto, "In the land of heat and sun, we don't flush for number one." That, too, was socially accepted.

With the nursery school next door, Karsten, then nearly three, had no lack of friends. These children had never seen a playground, didn't even know there was such a thing, and it was my pleasure to wow them. I built one in our yard with eucalyptus poles. There was a tire swing and a regular swing, a seesaw and a ladder leading up to a railed high walk that ended at a metal slide. That slide had been welded for me with materials from the community center by a neighbor and friend, Polly Bamutungire, whose father, William, was the diminutive, bespectacled diocesan treasurer. The slide ended in a sand box for a smooth landing. In a country with only home-made toys, such as balls made from rags or plastic and cars ingeniously fashioned from wire with soda bottle caps for wheels, our yard

A busy playground

became a regular place for the nursery school's recreation. Later, in Kenya, I built another playground with bamboo and wire. The slide proved a bit hard on the gluteus maximus.

Some of the things Uganda lacked were bad, so that was good. For example, hard as it may be to believe in our sue-happy nation, frivolous law suits. That meant that I did not need to carry a million-dollar insurance policy to protect us in case of an accident on our playground. Moreover, no parent, aware and approving of their child playing on our playground, would have dreamt of suing us in case of an accident, even if that foolishness had been possible. As for insurance, in those early days I was not aware of any being available for anything anywhere in the country.

I realized quickly that my most useful role at the community center was only as point-man for my employer, the Evangelical Broadcast of Holland. The bishop had hired a teacher from Mbarara High School as my assistant. Adonia Kabarema was in his mid-thirties, an innovative man with valuable knowledge of the ins and outs of the Ugandan government apparatus as it affected the establishing and running of our programs. A tailoring school, a carpentry school, a secretarial school, a medical clinic, and a library had to be registered with the appropriate authorities. Yes, I knew my strengths, but I was also aware of my weaknesses, reluctant though at times I might have been to acknowledge them, and it was my pleasure to let Adonia use his experience to handle the bureaucracy. Since he proved to be more qualified for that work than I, I helped him as needed, rather than the other way around.

I was delighted to involve myself in more practical tasks for the benefit of the community. I converted a dump truck, left from the building of the community center, into a more useful vehicle by raising its two-foot sides and back with a grid of readily available Australian eucalyptus poles, the type I had used in the construction of the playground. Whenever I went to Kampala, either with that truck or our Volkswagen bus, I would bring the mail for the East Ankole district from the main post office. The book of Proverbs says, "Like cold water to a thirsty soul, so is good news from a far country." (25:25) Ugandans could use all the good news they could get, and if I didn't bring the mail, the people of the district went without for weeks at a time since the postal system had no vehicles to move it. The average haul would be twenty to thirty mail bags, released to me because of trust in my white skin upon signing a simple form.

In addition to lacking the initiative to discourage thievery and robbery by going after the culprits, the police department lacked transportation. I don't know which lack came first, but "to serve and protect" was not a priority. As in the rest of the country, the attitude here was rather lackadaisical. With our VW bus and my enthusiasm for supporting law and order, combined with my availability to help in the pursuit of robbers, the police gained renewed incentive. It was another small, practical way I involved myself in the moral rebuilding of the area in my sphere of influence.

On several occasions I had the opportunity to observe their method of interrogation. The philosophy was simple: Make them talk by dispensing a generous beating with a three-foot piece of 12 or 14 gauge electrical wire. Once the pain is greater than the desire to withhold information – the cases I witnessed involved low thresholds – common sense kicks in for the common good. "A whip for the horse, a bridle for the donkey, and a rod for the back of fools." (Proverbs 26:3)

Since there was no regular transport for the roughly three miles from Ruharo Hill into town, I also started a minibus service with our Volkswagen. It was free of charge and left three times a week at 7:59 a.m. I thought that such a precise departure time might make a point about punctuality, an unknown concept there. And I *did* leave on time and started the return trip at 9:59, as well. When consideration is given to those who disregard timetables and are inconsiderate of everybody else's time and activities, tardiness is encouraged. It has been said and is consistent with Christ's purposeful and ordered life that, while He was never in a hurry, He was also never late. We can all write that into our appointment books.

Shortly after our arrival I had to leave for Uganda's "Wild West" – the north-eastern district of Karamoja. Like the Banyankole, the Karamojong are a pastoral people. Their young warriors are known and feared for their ruthless cattle-raiding of neighboring tribes, such as the Sebei to the south, the Iteso and the Acholis to the west, and the Turkana and Pokot across the eastern border in Kenya. To the north was the Sudanese border, with slim pickings. The Karamojong's five clans – Matheniko, Jie, Dodoth, Bokora, and Pian – also raided each other.

Idi Amin had tried to stop the practice. He had also attempted to force them to wear clothing, but, as "tried" and "attempted" would indicate, had failed on both accounts. Except in Karamoja's few population centers, the men, especially the young warriors, would wear nothing more than bone earrings and occasionally still a lip plug, and the women wore only skirts of crudely tanned animal hides and colorful bead necklaces.

The Karamojong were a tough and dangerous lot and had no qualms about killing anyone standing in their way or posing a threat. They possessed between thirty thousand and forty thousand AK-47s and millions of rounds of ammunition, most of them looted from the armory in Moroto, Karamoja's capital, after the chaos that followed the overthrow of Amin. These young men were fierce warriors and expert marksmen and, with their new-found fire power, had successfully resisted any further attempts at civilizing them. To re-supply themselves with weapons and ammunition, they engaged in arms-smuggling and would trade their stolen cattle with weapon dealers across the borders in Kenya and Sudan, even as far away as Somalia.

In a lighter moment it occurred to me recently that the United States government could benefit from the Karamojong's prowess in its fight against the Iraqi insurgency. We wouldn't even have to arm them. Just promise them a cow for every terrorist killed, and they'd be off and hunting. Imagine a hoard of wild and naked men running through Iraqi cities. The insurgents would be so horrified, they would come right out into the open and engage them in battle. Round up them Herefords.

On a more serious note – I just learned that the Ugandan government is planning to further arm the Karamojong and send them to fight the notorious "Lord's Resistance Army" (LRA). Founded in 1986 by an Acholi voodoo priestess, Alice Lakwena, as "The Holy Spirit Movement," its avowed aim was to overthrow the then newly-established government of Yoweri Museveni and run the country by the Ten Commandments. That goal was, and continues to be, one of the most hypocritical justifications ever for inhumane behavior.

Many Acholi soldiers of Okello's recently defeated army followed Lakwena, believing she had magical powers. They died by the thousands as they trusted her assurances that smearing shea nut or engine oil on their bodies would make them impervious to bullets. After their defeat, she fled by bicycle into Kenya, where she enjoys the protection of the UN and the Kenyan government in a refugee camp.

Her cousin, Josef Kony, took over the bloody guerilla campaign with the remnant of that ragtag army. He operates out of southern Sudan, abducting children from northern Uganda, particularly from the Acholi tribe, and wreaking havoc on the population. Some of the children are forced at gunpoint to kill their own parents. They are marched to rebel bases, where the boys are trained to fight and the girls are forced into sex-slavery. On the march, those who cannot keep up are forcibly beaten or hacked to death by their fellow captives. Some starve on the way, while others have been known to drink their own urine to keep from dying of thirst.

Then, hardened by mind-boggling cruelty, the boys, turned savage beasts, return to abduct children themselves, and the cycle goes on. This conflict has killed over half a million people and displaced a million. Some 20,000 children have been snatched from their homes, and between 4,000 and 5,000 have escaped, most scarred forever psychologically. Run the country by the Ten Commandments?

Nowadays, every evening masses of children, known as "night commuters," walk from their villages to towns and sleep on verandas or in shelters to avoid abduction. In Acholi's capital Gulu alone, an estimated 12,000 – 15,000 shuffle in for a relatively safe night. The next morning they return to their schools or homes – that is, if they still have homes and families to go back to.

I have no doubt that the Karamojong would be up to the challenge to fight this embodiment of evil. And while their cruelty is not as arbitrary as that of the LRA, arming murderers to fight other murderers does not sound like a good idea to me. (This also disqualifies them from the harebrained idea of fighting the Iraqi insurgency.)

Like the Masai of Kenya and Tanzania and many lesser-known tribes, the Karamojong's main diet consists of milk mixed with the blood of their cattle, which they draw by piercing a vein in the cow's neck with an arrow and catching it in a long gourd. To make cheese they add some of its urine. Meat is reserved for special occasions, as they will not easily part with an animal. They know each one by name and can pick it out of a herd of hundreds. To us, they all looked alike.

The Karamojong are also hygienically challenged, and word was out that no self-respecting mosquitoes would sting them. But now, many were dying, not from malaria, as so many Africans do, but from a drought that had killed much of their beloved cattle and whatever crops they had planted.

* * *

The EO had purchased grain within the country, which we now delivered for distribution to a Catholic mission in northern Karamoja near the Sudanese border. I accompanied the driver of a large hired truck. The rainy season was upon us, and the dirt roads in the wide open savannah were in terrible shape. There were large, muddy patches that had immobilized numerous vehicles. In the process of getting shoveled out or pulled out by others, the road became deeply rutted and the thick, sticky, black clay was churned up – a near impassable mess.

After we had gotten stuck three times in the span of about a mile, each time accompanied by laborious work to get mobile again, I asked the driver to let me try my luck. Having fought the road most of the way, he was most willing, and we switched places. During a two-year stint in the German army, my driving lessons had been on a big, four-wheel drive truck that required double-clutching. Now I welcomed the challenge, though I understood that there is only so much you can do given the conditions of the roads. With my more aggressive approach and perhaps quicker reactions, everything went fine for several miles, though I had a few close calls. But then, coming over a hill, I saw a section of churned mud about the length of a gridiron that resembled a plowed field, and I knew I was in trouble. There was no way around it, as I did not want to get into the even softer grass-covered earth on either side. I had only about 200 yards to gain speed, but that muck, like gravel on a run-away truck ramp, sucked the momentum right out of our moving mass. We were hopelessly mired.

Before long, a passing Land Rover took a message for us to the Catholic mission. A farm tractor was dispatched with a large trailer and about eight young, lean Karamojong, the only ones I have ever seen unarmed and fully clothed – well, with shorts, anyway. Appreciative of the food for their people, they displayed a generous amount of enthusiasm with the energy to match as they loaded most of the sacks onto the trailer and pulled us out with the tractor.

Many nations were involved in staving off the ravages of the drought. Once there were eight of us from seven nations sitting around a table in our hotel in Moroto. Among them, the French airlifted some of our grain with a Puma helicopter into even more remote areas. The Dutch had flown high-protein biscuits into Entebbe International Airport with their carrier, Martin Air. When a corrupt Ugandan government tried to charge them landing fees for the free food destined for its own starving people, the

Dutch threatened to fly it all back. Eventually Uganda relented. Later, I found the biscuits for sale on the black market in Karamoja. It's easier to talk about foreign aid than to deliver it successfully. But more about that later.

Meanwhile, Debbie was left alone with a toddler and a baby, both in diapers and none of the conveniences we in the West take so much for granted, such as a regular supply of water, and "Pampers," which were but a memory from, it seemed, a different planet. There was no "pampering" in Uganda of any kind. When she learned through a messenger that I would be gone an additional week, she seriously contemplated returning to Kenya, if not straight home. But she remembered a Bible verse about giving thanks in *all* circumstances and decided to start with that.

Early the next morning the bishop brought Jackline to be our house-girl, and in the afternoon the electricity came on, and, simultaneously, water began to fill our tank in the attic. It was just the relief she needed. Jackline proved a gem. A Tutsi by tribe, she was of Rwandese origin but born in Uganda, fine-featured and slender, with a delightful disposition and a good command of English. She loved the children and became a faithful helper for the duration of our time in Mbarara.

We hired Stephen, a married man with several children, to be our gardener. He was a small man and walked with a pronounced limp from polio. Peter Muth, my boyhood friend, had sent money to be used as I saw fit. I bought two wheelchairs that changed the lives of two disabled people; one, a 65-year-old woman who could only crawl while dragging her legs, the other, a 21-year-old polio victim who was also lame in both legs. With the balance I bought an Indian "Hero" bicycle for Stephen. He was so overwhelmed with gratitude for a gift he could have never afforded, he dropped to his knees before me, raising his clutched hands, as if I were a god to be worshiped. For all the life-changing good that bicycle brought into Stephen's life, for a short period it also was a magnet for trouble.

One night, at around eleven – we were fast asleep – there was a knock on our bedroom window. Startled I sat up.

"Who is it?"

"Sir, they have stolen my bicycle."

It was Stephen, and it hadn't been theft – it had been robbery. Three men had surprised him in his home after dark and taken the bike at gun-

Stephen with his new bike

point. But they had a problem: Stephen knew one of them. I was confident that we could catch these men, and we wasted no time. I quickly got dressed. *It will be an interesting night*, I thought.

Since Mbarara was more peaceful than Kampala after dark, we jumped into our van and raced to the police station in town. There was no traffic and only a few people could still be seen in the black shadows of the night. As I walked in, a burly officer gave me a knowing grin; he recognized me. But that didn't change the situation. The blue-uniformed federal police, whom I had helped so often, could not reciprocate because they had only two men on duty that night.

Just as Stephen and I had decided to get some young men with pangas (machetes) to flush those guys out of whatever hut they were hiding in, he remembered on our way back the brown-uniformed district police, stationed just up a hill. I didn't even know they existed; they kept such a low profile. But with increased hope we drove up there.

They were ready and willing and gave us a four-man escort armed with two old carbines, and together we chased those robbers through banana plantations and mud huts most of the night. We were aided by enough moonlight to allow us to make our way safely, i.e. as safely as is possible in the pursuit of armed thugs. I remember at least one occasion when one of the officers demurred just long enough for me to storm ahead into an abandoned hut. I was too presumptuous and foolish to hesitate. I moved right in. In the course of our time in Uganda, I would yet make sure, albeit unwittingly, that I would appropriate a good share of God's infinite grace.

The stillness of the night was interrupted by the police making inquiries through locked doors. Sometimes the occupants, fearing that we were bandits ourselves, would let out a sustained, high-pitched scream to alert their neighbors. I would calm them by informing them that I was the muzungu, the white man whom they knew or had heard about. My non-African accent assured them that I was telling the truth. That gave them confidence. They opened their doors without hesitation and provided whatever information they had in now hushed tones.

By 4 a.m. we had success. We were handed over one of the robbers who had been hiding in a hut – a squatty, stocky, barefoot guy in just a pair of ripped shorts. I never learned his relationship to the people in whose hut he had sought refuge. Never mind – we had our first man. True to their modus operandi, the police slapped him around a bit while jabbering what I assumed was anything but sweet nothings. Then they tied his hands behind his back with a vine. Knowing that cooperation was the only way out of a beating, he led us to a bush, mumbled something, and nodded. One of the policemen reached in and came up with an AK-47. He test-fired it once into the quiet of the night, and now two bullets were missing from the magazine. We had one of the robbers, and the others wouldn't be far behind. It had certainly been an interesting night. Now, it was time to get some sleep.

Even without the telephone, word in Africa spreads fast. At midmorning, the principal of Mbarara High School stopped by our house with news. At a village market, some thirteen miles down the road, two men had been arrested trying to sell a "Hero" bicycle. Stephen and I rushed out there with two policemen, this time with our federal guys, and, after he had made positive identification of both robbers and his bicycle, we brought them back to Mbarara. We had our trio.

Several days later a woman, who had heard about the arrests, came and identified those three as the killers of her husband – which explained the unaccounted-for missing bullet.

A welcome bi-product of that exercise was the safety of Stephen's crops, which had been subject to frequent theft.

"They fear me now," he said with obvious pride.

But when there was another disturbance in his area, he brought the bike to "sleep" at *our* house.

5

MUZUNGU IN THE SWAMP

The reports of my death are greatly exaggerated.
Mark Twain

Stephen arrived for work one morning with a painfully self-conscious grin and blurted out, "Madam, have you heard? They've found a muzungu floating in the swamp!"

I had not returned from Kampala the night before as planned. Since I was unable to reach Debbie, she did not know what the hold-up had been. In one of the world's most dangerous countries at the time, that could conjure up all kinds of scenarios, the least-scary of which would attribute our delay to a problem with the vehicle we were using. That truck had broken down numerous times before.

In our five-month-hitchhiking trip through West Africa in the winter of 1974-75, we had learned to expect the unexpected and dismissed it with a cynical "*WAWA*" – West Africa Wins Again. Though in some respects more advanced, East Africa, just like the other side of the continent, suffered from intervals of economic setbacks caused largely by incompetence, corruption, and coups d'état. And Uganda had just reached the end of such a debilitating cycle. Spare parts were difficult to come by, and maintaining vehicles with duct tape and rubber bands proved, predictably, unreliable. Additionally, telephones, apart from those in post offices, weren't working – so what's a wife to do? Trust God and wait.

Driving is perilous in many Third World countries. Not only are roads often narrow and poorly maintained, but drivers can be utterly reckless, and whatever traffic rules there are, will often be minimally enforced in towns, and not at all in rural areas. Uganda was no exception. One missionary lady was involved in a tragic accident in Tororo, in the eastern part of the country. A truck driver had chosen to drive on the wrong side of the road – in Uganda that meant on the right – because it was less potholed than the left. As the truck was barreling towards her, she thought the driver would not turn back to his side of the road. She moved right at the same time as he moved left. She did not survive.

Mbarara lies 170 miles southwest of Uganda's capital, Kampala. Connecting the two cities is a two-lane road that crosses the equator – prominently marked with two white-painted circular concrete structures on either side of the road – passes five reed swamps, and winds gently through a lush countryside of grasses with isolated compounds of mud huts or semi-permanent houses amidst lush banana plantations. At the halfway point is one of Uganda's largest cities, Masaka, situated by Lake Victoria. As you get closer to Mbarara, you see the occasional herd of Ankole cows grazing peacefully – idyllic scenes.

At one time the road was paved, but, after years of neglect, the second law of thermodynamics had taken its toll. Now the asphalt had crumbled away from the edges toward the center to such an extent that in some places only about a two-foot wide irregular strip reminded motorists of more travel-friendly times. Compounding this problem was a drop-off of up to three inches at the line where the blacktop had been worn away. Whatever had remained of the original road had succumbed to the usual wear and tear – potholes.

Given these conditions, drivers sought to keep the wheels of at least one side of their vehicle on whatever pavement had survived. At the narrowest points, one driver would have to surrender the paved part to another and drop down onto the rutted roadbed. Juggling for position became a game of chicken, and, in the vehicular version of David versus Goliath, the latter generally won. Thus cars surrendered the right-of-way to trucks and buses, but army truck drivers would let everyone know unashamedly that they were kings of the road, often plowing right down the middle and hogging whatever pavement was left. Sometimes the game turned tragic when neither driver was willing to give. But there were also the universal problems of excessive speed and miscalculation when passing.

One day the bishop sent me with a pastor of the Church of Uganda, the Rev. Raboni, and a driver to Kampala to pick up medicines, relief food, and second-hand clothing. It would be a load big enough to require the use of the converted dump truck.

Raboni, as many called him, was about 5'6," a quiet and serious man, with a calm, reassuring demeanor. He was jut-jawed and had a pronounced forehead. A medical assistant, he had a remedy for whatever ailed you – an injection. If you had a runny nose, you got an injection; a cough – an injection. It seemed people loved that needle and simply didn't feel treated unless they had been injected. Whether he had inured them to this form of care, or whether their unquestioning acceptance had encouraged him to discard other forms, I don't know. But it seemed to have worked frequently enough – either in reality or, as a placebo psychologically – that it became the accepted method of treatment. His patients certainly liked him and appreciated his service.

We had finished our official business in Kampala and had loaded eighty-four bags of mail at the main post office, an unusually large number. Then I picked up a new Peugeot 504, sent from England for the bishop. As we started back toward Mbarara, Raboni and I were following the truck. We had agreed to take a young woman from our district, who had asked for a lift. She was in the truck, keeping the driver company. At the outskirts of Kampala I stopped at a village market – about a dozen stands side by side, lining the road. Those markets were always colorful, with fresh fruit and produce from nearby trees and fields. I bought papaya and mangos and chose from among neatly balanced stacks of nine oranges the one that looked best.

About twenty percent of Uganda's land surface is covered by lakes, rivers, and swamps. As mentioned earlier, there were five huge reed swamps on our stretch of road between Kampala and Masaka – with a good potential for cultivation. But the only one in the whole country partially utilized for growing rice is near Tororo, in eastern Uganda. Known as the Kibimba Rice Scheme, it was a Chinese-Ugandan cooperative project and covered over 1700 acres. It was neglected for a long time, but has been rehabilitated under the ownership of a Ugandan-Indian family.

About ten minutes south of the market, a straight stretch of the road went right through the middle of one of those swamps. As we sought to catch up with our truck, we could already see from the distance that there had been an accident. People were swarming around the scene. My heart began to pump in overdrive as I envisioned the worst. The lack of well-equipped and properly staffed healthcare facilities, especially in a rural setting such as this, complicated the treatment of injuries and disease and often, very often, led to what in the developed world would be considered unnecessary death.

A public-service mini-bus – known locally by its Swahili name, "matatu" – loaded with fifteen to twenty passengers, had attempted to pass an Indian-made Tata truck just as our truck was closing in. I don't know if the poor condition of the road had contributed to the accident or if it had just been a case of "pilot error." (Drivers of public vehicles were known as pilots.) But passing on the uneven surface was a risky maneuver at any time. There had been a collision, and somehow all three vehicles had plunged into the swamp on the same side.

Down the embankment pandemonium reigned as survivors stumbled through the reeds in two to four feet of water, trying to rescue those trapped inside the partly submerged matatu. Goods were scattered everywhere, including the mail sacks. Some of the injured had clambered onto the road and were walking around in a stupor. I took them immediately to a dispensary located in an Irish convent nearby. Amazingly, our truck driver was not hurt and was helping wherever he could. Raboni's training was particularly useful now. The girl we had given a ride didn't require immediate attention, although small shards of glass from the shattered windshield covered her face and glistened like snowflakes in the afternoon sun. Amazingly, her eyes had not been injured, and her pain seemed bearable.

Villagers had rushed to the scene and joined the uninjured in an effort to lift the matatu off the victims trapped under water. The more seriously injured were hauled up the embankment to the side of the road. There was crying and groaning mixed with calls for help. So far I was not aware of any deaths. Shortly after Raboni's and my arrival a Tanzanian army truck stopped. The soldiers commandeered another matatu to take some of the injured to the convent and transported others with their own truck.

The German government had built a hospital on the grounds of the convent years earlier. But it was partially destroyed in one of Uganda's wars and then, with a generous lack of foresight, looted by the villagers of the area. It had never been rebuilt, ostensibly for that reason. Now there was only the small dispensary and one nurse among the sisters, but they all kicked into high gear and doctored as best they could with salves, bandages, splints, and words of comfort. I tried to help at the dispensary, but with no stomach for blood and close to passing out twice, I returned to the scene of the accident.

The principal from a nearby high school had arrived with a school truck and several strong young men. With their help we saved all of the mail and most of the other goods from opportunists ready to pounce on anything unguarded. Some items were soaked, others, remarkably, had stayed dry. We hauled them up the embankment, loaded them into her truck, and took them to the safety of the convent.

Because of her foresight, initiative, and practical help, I authorized the principal to salvage whatever she would find useful from the church's demolished truck. It turned out later that the diocesan leadership back home did not agree with my decision, assuming the truck could have been repaired. It was difficult to accept the total loss of an uninsured vehicle. But as their man on the spot, I was more familiar with the situation. With the scarce resources in Uganda at that time it would have taken days, if not weeks, to launch a rescue attempt of the demolished truck. On the other hand, some villagers had already arrived with wrenches and other simple hand-tools, eager to strip it as soon as we were gone. They would be all over it like vultures on carrion. In those days, when a simple rag or a sheet of paper had value, imagine what the pillaged truck parts would bring in Kampala or even Masaka. Except for the frame, nothing would go to waste, because everything had value, even the metal siding of the body, which would be pounded into cooking pots. Our trashcans in America would have been goldmines in the Uganda of the late 1970s and early 1980s.

The principal was grateful, and I understand that she was able to retrieve the wheels, the engine, and other valuable parts. I had made the right decision.

Back at the dispensary, I learned that the seriously injured had been stabilized and taken by the army to Kampala for further treatment. The army's help could not be taken for granted. Under Amin and Obote, both northerners, such assistance in the south and west might not have been so readily forthcoming. Six bodies had been recovered – tragic – but the death toll could have been much higher.

We spent the night at the sisters' convent in comfortable beds with clean sheets. We relished a delicious, home-cooked meal, and Raboni and I rounded out the day by joining them in songs of praise, in prayer and reflection in a beautiful worship service in an equally beautiful chapel. After dealing with trauma and death, turning our thoughts from our fragile, temporal selves to the One who gives us life and purpose was an uplifting experience. It was a fitting end to a day I shall never forget.

*   *   *

It was the following morning that Stephen brought the tragic news to Debbie. When I had not returned home the night before, she had become anxious and had committed to God the uncertainty of my whereabouts and well-being. In child-like faith and confidence she had entrusted me, the children, and herself to the God who had already taken us and would yet take us, as the song says, "through many dangers, toils and snares." She had gained peace in the knowledge that He was in control. Thus, she was positioned to face tragedy as well as triumph and able to keep her composure when the morning started with Stephen's devastating report.

She went immediately to the diocesan office to find out whatever they knew. They had also heard that the dump truck had had an accident, but nothing more. Canon John Rujoki, husband of Debbie's friend Verinah, promptly rode his motorcycle to the post office in Mbarara to phone Kampala. Perhaps the provincial office of the Church of Uganda would know something.

Meanwhile Debbie received a significant piece of information from two independent sources: I was not supposed to be a passenger on the returning truck because I had been given the job of driving the bishop's new Peugeot back. Still, a muzungu floating in the swamp when very few wazungu lived in the area – we were aware of only one other white male in the vicinity of Mbarara – was grounds for worrying. What if, WAWA-like, there had been a delay in the arrival of the car or a hang-up with customs, both good possibilities? Either one would have likely put me back into that truck.

At the convent, meanwhile, we were still busy with activities related to the accident and wouldn't be leaving until early afternoon. There was no way I could communicate with Debbie, and I had no idea that word of the accident had already preceded us. I was blissfully ignorant of the fact that to passing vehicles – if there were any at the time; I hadn't noticed – I would have stood out like a Golden Retriever in a kennel full of Black Labs. Had I noticed, I would have expected word of the accident as well as news of my survival to reach Debbie via the diocese.

But apparently none of the messengers had seen me, or, perhaps unaware of a concerned white family, none had thought of reporting the survival of one of its members whom they could readily identify.

Shortly after midday, Raboni's wife, Joyce, arrived at our house. She was distraught and, upon seeing Debbie, dissolved into tears. There had been an accident, she had heard, and everybody had been killed. (Those African drums must have been out of tune.) This apparent confirmation of Stephen's report in the morning made Debbie only more resistant to giving in to despair at news not confirmed by eye-witnesses. She comforted Joyce as best she could, believing that rumors of my and her husband's death were greatly exaggerated.

At around three in the afternoon, a small car pulled into our compound. Debbie did not recognize the two white women who came to the front door, but interpreted their smiles as good news. After brief introductions, they asked whether she had heard from me.

"No!" she answered. "Why do you ask?"

"Well," came the reply, "he spent the night with us, and we just wanted you to know that he is most assuredly on his way."

6

MATERIAL MATTERS MATTER

It is not the man who has little,
but the man who craves more,
that is poor...
Socrates

..., but, as Socrates indicated, they – the material matters – are overrated. Nevertheless, craving for more is universal. In developed nations, aspirations for material possessions are generally on a more sophisticated level than in Africa's underdeveloped nations, multi-millionaire-despots being the most obvious exception. With greater affluence come greater expectations. But whether in Africa or America, whether we aspire toward a pair of leather shoes or a new automobile, yearnings for bigger, better, and newer are rarely satisfied. As soon as one coveted item is acquired, a new object of desire, like the proverbial carrot, is dangling in front of our minds' eyes. For the formerly barefooted African it may be a bicycle now and, after he has acquired one, a motorcycle becomes the next target.

On the opposite end of the spectrum, one needs to look only at the extravagance flaunted by American movie stars, entertainers, and top-flight athletes. Mike Tyson, the former heavyweight boxing champion of the world, earned over 300 million dollars in his short career. By the time it came to a screeching halt, he had spent his fortune on luxury cars, custom jewelry, Siberian tigers, and a 48,000-square-foot, 37-bathroom mansion and was in hock for over thirty million dollars. Ecclesiastes 5:10 "He who loves money will not be satisfied with money, nor he who loves wealth with his income; this also is vanity." Or, as Lee Iacocca is said to have stated more bluntly, "Here I am in the twilight years of my life, still wondering what it's all about... I can tell you this, fame and fortune is [sic] for the birds."

Admittedly, Uganda's destitution was severe. There were genuine needs spread across a wide spectrum of the population. However, the country's biggest problem was not lack of consumer goods but the manner in which a large percentage of its citizens went about acquiring them.

One of the most frequently used words in our early days there was "looted." Everybody talked about looting. This had been looted, and that had been looted, and it could have just been stolen, or taken at gunpoint – not that it made a lot of difference. Favorite loot were "luxury" items such as radio cassette players and bicycles, as in Stephen's case, but more basic items such as cooking pots, blankets, and clothes would do as well.

Some of those items were looted several times since looters would also be looted. Windows and doors, plumbing fixtures, timbers and corrugated iron sheets were looted from bombed-out or abandoned houses in towns and suburbs. Even copper wiring was dug out of the concrete walls of the destroyed homes of the affluent. Everything of value – and almost anything had value – was subject to looting. One Ugandan refugee in Nairobi told me that even his wife had been looted. He laughed when he said it, so he didn't seem to be all that heartbroken about it.

Most Ugandans measured the state of their economy not by the value of their stocks or the number of unemployed. Their barometer for national affluence and poverty moved with the availability of two simple white granular commodities: sugar and salt. When they talked about sugar, times were not bad. If it wasn't available, they just settled for "dry chai," meaning they drank their tea without sugar. Later, in times of plenty, Ugandans would make up for the earlier shortfall by putting up to three heaping tablespoons of sugar into a cup of tea. That was their dessert – their meal was then complete. But when shortages in Uganda were acute, the subject of conversation became that other white commodity. When people talked about the high price or total absence of salt, times were tough.

Once, after the fifth and final change of government in our five years in Uganda when order was returning to the country, I visited Angus Newman, a British employee with the World Bank's agriculture department, in the Soroti Hotel. Suddenly there was a commotion outside. Army vehicles roared in, came to a screeching halt, and disgorged soldiers who were obviously on a mission. Guns at the ready, they dispersed to the four corners of the property. We knew immediately that an important government official had arrived. As I was leaving the hotel about half an hour later, I came upon a number of military officers grouped around a central figure in the lobby. The man had alert eyes, full cheeks, and a smooth, round face. He was animated and spoke with conviction, gesturing as he focused on the faces of those around him. He was obviously trying to convey an important point to these men. I was passing and had barely said "Good morning," when I recognized the man as President Yoweri Museveni. He was wearing the same green army fatigues as the others in the huddle, but the face was unmistakably his. I whirled around and, through a gap in the group, stretched out my hand.

"You must be Mr. Museveni."

He laughed as he shook my hand, and said, "No, but I know that fellow."

Yes, and I knew that fellow also. *Must be his way of being coy*, I thought. I had heard him say one key word – sugar – and knew that the president was talking about the economic progress made under his government. Uganda, the "Pearl of Africa," as Winston Churchill had called it, was making a come-back.

But that was yet several years in the future. Now salt was the talk of town. The economy was in ruins. The Ugandan shilling was practically worthless. Coins did not exist, and the highest denomination was the 100-shilling note with a value, at one point, of ten U.S. cents. Imagine going to a shopping mall with nothing but dimes! Of course, there were no malls to worry about. Once nighttime security was restored and you could take a family or a group of friends out to dinner to one of the handful of elegant restaurants in Kampala, you carried a briefcase or, to draw less attention, a daypack or a brown paper bag with filthy notes, reeking of tobacco and rubber banded together in bundles of 100 – ten dollars each bundle. Credit cards would not be accepted until much later.

Uganda's illegal black market kept the economy limping along. The value of the Ugandan currency fluctuated greatly, but, for the most part, it was in a downward spiral. The official exchange rate early on was seven shillings to the dollar. The black-market rate was nearly twenty times that. And without foreign exchange, imports of consumer goods would come to a standstill, and people could not leave the country since the Ugandan shilling was not accepted outside its borders.

With all the factories dilapidated or destroyed, most consumer goods were imported. Some of the exceptions included lumber, bricks, and unprocessed foods, because they were produced or grown locally without the need for foreign inputs. Uganda's fertile soil and abundant livestock had prevented greater catastrophes under two near-successive tyrannical regimes – Amin and Obote II.   Therefore, thankfully, there was always food.

There was also plenty of money – it just didn't have much value. Anyone who would exchange his foreign currency at the official rate would not be able to sustain himself unless he had unlimited funds to pour down the drain of nation-wide corruption. I heard of an expatriate Roman Catholic priest who, perhaps trying to live by the rules or still new to the country, had tried to change money at the bank. The tellers started bidding for it. "I'll give you...!" Everybody wanted foreign exchange. Once I exchanged money at the black-market rate with an officer of the bank in his office. He wanted to send his son abroad for further studies.

Even the Kenyan shilling that, outside Africa, had little more value than Monopoly money, was coveted and considered legitimate currency on Uganda's black market. When crossing the border from Kenya, you would be inundated with young money-changers holding big wads of Ugandan shillings, eager to defraud you, often just a few yards from specious government officials. (They probably got their cut!)

When changing with them, you wanted to be sure you knew the going rate. You also wanted to keep your money tucked away safely until you had counted what you had bargained for, unless you were hard up for adventure, were a fast runner, and could handle the guy once you caught him. I changed frequently at the border, but when in-country, I changed with our trusted Indian business sources. They, in turn, trusted us and would readily accept our checks drawn on U.S. bank accounts. And yes, the Asians had started to come back and, with foreign exchange obtained through money-changing, were beginning to get the economy rolling again.

The subject of the Asians' trust of us foreigners reminds me of an incident that happened in Kenya. Debbie was shopping at a supermarket in downtown Nairobi. She had filled her cart, only to discover at the checkout, after frantically rummaging though her purse, that her wallet had been stolen. The sympathetic Indian store-manager, shaking his head from side to side, told her that there was no problem. "It's quite alright. Just take the groceries with you and bring me the money tomorrow." He had never met her.

* * *

In much of the world one or the other spouse does not come free. In India, the bride's family must pay the dowry, most commonly in the form of 22-karat gold jewelry that, though worn by the bride, belongs to the husband. In Africa, on the other hand, there is a bride price to be paid by the husband-to-be or his family. That, obviously, is not true of Asian families there who, like Latinos in America, continue to maintain the culture of their country of origin.

The bride price is a way for the parents and members of the extended family to get remunerated for the investment they have made in the young lady's upbringing. Even when the parents, perhaps out of Christian conviction or because of their love for their future son-in-law, are not interested in exacting a bride price, grandfathers and grandmothers, uncles and aunts may say, as I've heard it said, "Let me also eat," food being only a metaphor.

I have had the privilege of observing two Ugandan bride-price negotiations. One involved my close friend from Mbarara, Eldad Kateshumbwa, as the potential groom. Eldad was a slender, smallish, dark-skinned man of the Hutu-related Bairu. His bride, Eunice, was taller than he, light-skinned and of the Tutsi-related Bahima. The former are the farmers, the latter the cattle keepers.

In Rwanda, the Belgian colonial masters had exploited distinctive differences between these tribes by drafting the aristocratic Tutsis into government service and using them to rule the majority Hutus. In Uganda, the British had employed a similar strategy – similar, in that they used one tribe to help them run the protectorate of some twenty-five tribes – but they chose the Baganda, the country's largest. Yet now, though tribalism was still a big problem in Uganda and the main source of all the upheaval, the distinctions between the Bahima and Bairu had largely disappeared, and they lived together peacefully as one tribe, the Banyankole. That was significant, as in Rwanda, only thirteen years later, the tribal relatives of the Bairu would slaughter up to 800,000 of those of the Bahima and moderate Bairu.

Eldad's and Eunice's marriage reflected that remarkable unity, as did, in fact, that of the bishop – Amos Betungura was a Muiru; his wife, Constance, a Muhima. Moreover, both of our friends came from respected, Christ-honoring families and were themselves committed Christians. They were well educated, having graduated from Makerere University, one of

Eldad and Eunice Kateshumbwa and Rev. Raboni, medic

Africa's most reputable institutions of higher learning. Eunice's brother, who was still studying there, was Uganda's chess champion at the time. Still, education and modernity aside, they had to go through the traditional channels of bride-price negotiations.

On a prearranged day I drove several of Eldad's older, influential relatives and acquaintances to the home of Eunice's parents in their remote village. As instructed by the elders in the car, I stopped outside the compound and turned off the engine. We waited. It was peacefully still. There was light chatter, some in English, some in Runyankole, but nothing in particular about the reason for our being there. These men had done this before – they were old hands at bride price negotiations.

We had been seen by family members, but they were obviously not in a hurry as we were left sitting. Nobody acknowledged our presence, let alone asked us to wait a bit longer. *How badly do you want our daughter?* seemed to be the unspoken question. Perhaps it was part of the psychological pre-bargaining process. You don't show anxiety or excitement.

Patience is a virtue that was left out of me when I was formed in the womb. (Must've been my mother's fault!) But I had become better at it since arriving in Africa, and I remained, if outwardly, my serene, amicable self.

After about twenty minutes we were invited into the compound and escorted into a large, perhaps twenty-four-by-twenty-foot, temporary shelter with four-foot high walls and an open-rafter thatched roof. The floor was covered with a carpet of freshly cut grass. The walls were lined with low-slung wooden chairs and backless school benches, and for every fourth or fifth chair and every second bench there was a coffee table decorated with a vase of freshly cut flowers on a doily.

Marriage was a communal affair, and this furniture had been borrowed from several households in the neighborhood. Neither Eldad nor Eunice was allowed to be present. The atmosphere was saturated with tradition – Tevye of "Fiddler on the Roof" could have related well – and the air was thick with the formality and decorum of the occasion. Events such as this confirmed to me that graciousness and dignity are not byproducts of wealth and power. In fact, not infrequently, they produce just the opposite – arrogance and brutishness.

Standard gifts were a gomas for the future mother-in-law – a traditional gown with a six to eight-inch-wide, finely embroidered matching silk sash from China. A conzo was for the father-in-law – a traditional, white, sparsely embroidered, ankle-length robe, often worn under a suit jacket.

The negotiations involved other payments. In this case, although both families were relatively well off, it helped that Eunice's parents were favorably inclined toward Eldad and appreciated his spiritual commitment. Three cows and 15,000 Ugandan shillings ($125 at the time) were an acceptable package. The successful negotiations were followed with long, formal speeches by both relatives and friends.

Then an elaborate meal was served. Though a total outsider, I had been graciously received. But it was not until that point, apart from initial greetings, that I was included in conversations. I was impressed by that. As a muzungu, having become accustomed to being front and center of interactions in the village, I was impressed by their unhindered affirmation of their culture. To be able to witness this event was at once an uplifting and humbling experience, one that is as fresh in my mind today as it was then, over twenty years ago.

In those districts where cattle represent the wealth of the tribesmen, they are the logical and primary payment. In Karamoja, when raids were successful and rains sufficient for pasture, a strong young warrior would be chosen to fling a stone as far as he could. All the cows that could be driven single-file to the point of impact would constitute the bride price. (I understand that, nowadays, an AK-47 might be included in the dowry expectations.) In other areas the number might range from two to six cows. (Curiously, in my experience, *cows* were always the objects of bride price negotiations. There must have been sex-discrimination against bulls!) However, in our early days, when Uganda was in turmoil and goods were hard to come by, the family of a young man might have had to pay one to three cows, 10,000 – 15,000 Ugandan shillings, maybe a goat, five pounds of sugar, a case of soda, and a jerry can of gasoline. The goat might provide the meat for rice-pilaf at the wedding. The sodas would be the drinks for the bride and groom and their immediate families at the wedding feast.

Gasoline was often unavailable except on the black market, where it was for sale in five-gallon plastic jerry cans or soda bottles. On the economy the price jumped from seven shillings to 81 shillings per liter. One missionary physician in Kampala, who was paid in Ugandan shillings, probably via official channels and at the official exchange rate, told me that when he filled the tank of his Volkswagen Beetle, he exceeded his monthly income. Kampala's robbers must have known of his predicament. The doctor's home was inside the hospital compound. After a trip into town, as he was waiting in his car one early evening while the gate keeper unlocked and removed the chain, two men relieved him at gunpoint of the offending vehicle.

We bought the fuel for the Dutch-built community center in 55 gallon drums at the Royal Dutch Shell terminal in Kampala. Once, the speaker of the House of Parliament, the Honorable Francis Butagira, at the time of this writing Uganda's ambassador to Washington D.C., came to the community center for gasoline for his Mercedes so he could return to Kampala. (Imagine Nancy Pelosi coming to your house for fuel.) Since I was able to help the speaker, he gave me his business card. "If you ever need help, come see me." And he jotted a note on the back. Since I had always tried to behave and never needed to redeem it, I added my own brief message on the back and gave it to a Ugandan acquaintance who worked with the Navigators, an international, interdenominational para-church organization. He had repeatedly applied for a passport but, unwilling to pay a bribe, had been rejected every time. That card worked magic. Within two weeks and with no payoff under the table, both he and his wife, a physician, had passports. It helps to fuel the right people.

We made two shopping trips to Rwanda because Uganda was still devoid of some of the basic consumer goods we take so much for granted here in America. In Kigali they were about two and a half times more expensive than in Nairobi, but the trip was three times shorter, and Rwandan roads were better than most in East Africa.

If Kampala was the shooting capital of Africa, then surely, Kigali must have taken the prize for day-time thievery from cars with foreign license plates – like ours. One day we parked downtown, doors locked, windows up. Within ten minutes we returned to find the little triangular front passenger window open and the main window rolled halfway down. A Belgian man came out of his office behind us and told us that he had chased the would-be-thieves away. "Merci beaucoup, Monsieur!"

I went into a bank in the city center. Because of the heat, we had left the driver and front-passenger windows rolled down. Debbie was sitting in the passenger seat, and the children were playing in the back. Karsten decided that he needed more room and set our overnight bag onto the driver seat. Suddenly this guy walked up on Debbie's side, rattled the door handle (and her) and shouted, "Laver la voiture?" (Wash the car?) With her distracted, his accomplice reached through the window on my side, and the bag was gone, replaced by a sick feeling in our stomachs.

As a result, we had to spend some of the money with which I emerged from the bank minutes later on some of the necessities we had just lost. That stop had yielded diminished returns. But we were left with enough money to splurge on lunch at the hotel that would become a rescue center during the Rwandan genocide thirteen years later and the focal point of the motion picture "Hotel Rwanda," *Des Milles Collines*.

7

BWANA KUBWA

*He was like a cock who thought the sun
had risen to hear him crow.*

George Eliot

[Marian Evans Cross]

When signing guest books, some of Africa's most notorious rulers –
perhaps like other, more deserving political heavyweights – will claim for
themselves two opposing pages. Like those pages, empty except for the
oversized scrawl of their names, their larger-than-life lives are devoid of
positive content as they selfishly suppress the people they claim to serve.
This is a short but, in keeping with that dichotomy, sufficiently long chapter devoted to His Excellency, Dr. Apollo Milton Obote.

For twenty-three years, Milton Obote cast a long, dark shadow over
Uganda. Following independence from Britain in 1962, he became Uganda's first prime minister. In 1966 he began his first term as president after staging a coup that ousted the first president, Kabaka (King) Edward
Mutesa II, Buganda's monarch, and drove him into exile in London.

In January of 1971, Obote attended a British Commonwealth Conference in Singapore. While there, he, in turn, was ousted from office by his
Army Chief of Staff, Lt. General Idi Amin and spent the next nine years
in exile in Tanzania. In late 1980, the Uganda People's Congress, Obote's
party, won a disputed election that returned him to power until the Acholi
general, Tito Okello, overthrew him in 1983.

Obote fled into exile in Zambia with a number of his cabinet members
and most of the country's hard currency. His second regime had been particularly brutal. Some estimates put those killed during his two reigns at
over 500,000, most of them from the Bantu tribes of the southern, central,

and western parts of Uganda. On October 10, 2005, at eighty years of age, he died of kidney failure in a Johannesburg hospital.

If there is any equity to life, any fairness, then there has to be a reckoning after death. An afterlife in which evil men such as Obote, Amin, Saddam, Pol Pot, Hitler, Stalin, Mao, Genghis Khan, Nero, and other tyrants of history are held accountable befits our concept of justice. How on earth could those monsters annihilate over a hundred million people and then blithely waltz out of life and escape accountability? God forbid! Life itself would be a capricious monster. Let no one be so certain, except in their own uncertainty.

*   *   *

Shortly after Obote's return from exile in Tanzania, Bishop Betungura asked me to drive him to a meeting with the ex-president. Paulo Mwanga was the current head of the Military Commission, a care-taker government. Though a Muganda by tribe, he was preparing the way for Obote, the Langi, who was in the process of planning his second comeback.

Ugandan bishops didn't drive themselves to official functions in those days. They had their designated drivers, and generally purple Church-of-Uganda flags that matched their white-collared purple shirts fluttered from the front fenders of their cars. Those appendages gave them the aura of authority that would help them through Uganda's many time-consuming and at times dangerous roadblocks. Appearance was everything, and authority was understood by everybody. Now, instead of ambling up with thoughts of "What can I get here?" the soldier might just snap to attention, click his heals for a crisp salute with his fingertips at his forehead, palms facing out, and it would be "Sir" this and "Sir" that.

Thankfully, times have changed all that, and with increasing stability in most parts of the country, roadblocks have become largely a thing of the past, as have the Anglican Church's flags and chauffeurs.

For some reason, Amos Betungura's regular driver was unavailable, and I was a convenient and most willing replacement. I had already met Mwanga, a bullish looking man with thick glasses and a Rolex watch. Now I welcomed the opportunity to meet Uganda's second ruler after independence.

The reception was at Government House, a large, state-owned villa, used for hosting visiting dignitaries. In the spacious living room, at the apex of a horseshoe-shaped seating arrangement, stood a big, overstuffed chair reserved for the guest of honor. From there the chair sizes decreased with the decreasing status of the invited guests and ended up with backless school benches. One chair was reserved for the bishop right next to Obote. Perhaps because I was the token white man, I got to sit just two chairs over from the "bwana kubwa," (Swahili for "big man") – other drivers would have had to wait outside. On a coffee table before him was not coffee, but a bottle of wine and a glass and the customary white doily under a vase with flowers. In the course of the evening, Obote would finish that bottle all by himself.

Milton Obote was about 5'10" and slightly built. He was a handsome man with chiseled features and medium-length hair which he parted on one side. He was very dark-skinned, and an African acquaintance made a disparaging remark to me about that after the meeting. Like Obote's other hosts, he was a Munyankole, a Muntu (Swahili for person), with brown complexion.

In the West, we are hesitant to talk about skin color, because that has often been the focus of discrimination and abuse. In an effort not to offend the sensitivities of minorities, we have developed unwritten laws for acceptable communication. Black Americans used to be referred to as "colored people" and before that, as "negroes." Today those terms are considered racist. In the nuanced world of political correctness, however, "people of color" is, at the time of this writing, perfectly fine, even considered enlightened, perhaps because it includes other non-whites. That white, too, is a color seems to be of little consequence.

The now-widely-used term "African American" is also considered proper, even though, by implication, it ignores large African minorities of Arab, South Asian, and European ancestry. For a couple of years we had a neighbor in Colorado who was a second-generation Namibian of German ancestry – a *white* African American." We also had a neighbor of Indian ancestry, who was born in Kenya. She would be an "*Indian* African American."

Africans have no qualms about referring to somebody as "that black one" or "that brown one." With their smooth skin and creamy brown color, Ethiopians and Somalis have, in my opinion, the most beautiful complexion in the world, and most whites seem to agree when they go to the beach and bake in the sun in token bathing suits, glistening with lotions. Ethiopians don't seem to be unaware of their external blessing. This anecdote is attributed to them: "When God made man, He put him in the oven but took him out too soon. That was the European. He made another batch which He left in too long. That was the African. The third batch He made just right. That was the Ethiopian." Even the Bible asks, "Can the Ethiopians change their skin, or leopards their spots?" (Jeremiah 13:23a) No, and why would they want to?

Racism in the West has its counterpart in tribalism in Africa. A Langi friend of mine, Alfred Otim, once told me that, during his studies at Makerere University when Obote was in power, one of his classmates, who belonged to a Bantu tribe, had threatened him with, "You wait until we are in power. Then we'll kill you."

At the time of that meeting in Mbarara, no one imagined that within a year, out of that very town, a Munyankole (Museveni) would arise to fight a four-year guerilla war against the presiding Langi (Obote) and, through his own coup, eventually succeed in ousting Obote's Acholi successor-through-coup-d'état (Okello) from power. (Alfred survived his classmate's threat, but many didn't.) Such are the tribalism-inspired vicissitudes of African political life. Nepotism and tribe-favoring treatment often follow an election, and, on a larger scale, Nilo-Hamitic or Bantu tribes will generally benefit economically from the election of one of their own, as well, to the neglect of the others. That, in turn, creates resentment and, eventually, revolt followed by suppression and all-out war, setting the stage for the next coup d'état.

Most invited guests bowed low at a respectful distance and mumbled a few hesitant words of greeting. Those of higher social status and bold enough to step forward to shake his hand would do so in typical East-African fashion when acknowledgement of one's lower social standing is called for, by placing their left hand on their right forearm. Their right would remain open and barely touch the big man's hand as a further sign of deference. Some brought gifts, including a calf that was led right into the room. Obote accepted it by meeting it half-way across the room and putting his hand on its head.

Then followed the eloquent speeches in which Ugandans are so proficient. For this famous, or more precisely, infamous visitor most speakers assumed an ingratiating posture – the torso slightly bent forward, legs and feet at attention military-style. Amazingly, Obote himself didn't give a speech. Perhaps he was not inclined to preach to the choir. His time would come, and for now he contented himself with being admired and adulated. The assembly could have been the setting of a late-period Rembrandt: most of the attendants half hidden in the shadows, with a burst of light and colorful palette focused on the guest of honor, bold brushstrokes capturing the focused, reverential mood.

As is common in Ugandan society, those consumed with self-importance will not look at those of lower rank while communicating with them. Obote had paid more attention to the calf than to his welcoming hosts – he barely looked at those wallowing in self-abasement. This was his way of further removing his exalted self from the hoi polloi groveling before him, and it confirmed to them the appropriateness of their obsequiousness.

When I had a chance to engage him, I asked him in what field he had earned his doctorate. I knew that it was an honorary degree. Some say it was awarded to him after he had made a speech of several hours at the United Nations headquarters in New York; others, that it was conferred on him by Indira Gandhi on a state visit to India. But whatever the history, I wanted to hear his response.

"Well, you see," he replied, "I'm a diplomat."

And that was that. He was indeed.

8

TIMES OF TRANSITION

For everything there is a season,
a time for every matter under heaven:
Ecclesiastes 3:1

Our days in Mbarara were quickly coming to an end. The community center was up and running and soon, so were we. We had made many friends, and, other than the thugs I had helped put behind bars, we knew of no enemies. Bishop Betungura gave us a farewell party in the dining room of the community center. The starting time was to be seven o'clock. But punctuality was an alien concept in much of Africa. At such functions, invited guests customarily arrived between one and one-and-a-half hours late. I remember an occasion when the diocesan secretary was typing at 11:15 a.m. a program that was to have commenced at 10:30 a.m. So, being aware of this cultural phenomenon, we appeared an hour after the planned start-up time. Imagine our surprise and embarrassment when we found the place humming with people. They had been invited for one-and-a-half hours earlier than we.

In August of 1981 we moved to Nairobi into the fully furnished townhouse of missionaries with the Church of Christ, who were going on home leave. It was convenient not to have to set up a household with our limited funds. Moving back into a modern city – with regular electricity and water, working telephones, post office boxes, fully-stocked grocery stores, fine restaurants, hotels with swimming pools and affordable memberships, a sizable community of other expatriates, and increased safety – was simply wonderful, especially for Debbie. In Mbarara she had been largely confined to our house with few friends, limited communication to the outside world, and without some of the most basic conveniences.

I began to work for a media organization related to the EO. Its purpose was to communicate through existing channels, as well as through new ones we hoped to develop, the good news of God coming upon this planet in human form. The director, Leo Slingerland, was a tall, burly former law-enforcement agent from Holland with a kind heart and an easygoing demeanor. While most private residences in Nairobi's suburbs had signs on their gates that warned prospective burglars – and there were many – "Mbwa kali!" ("Mean dog!"), Leo, who had chickens in his yard, amused the neighborhood with a sign that read "Kuku kali."

The organization was squeezed financially, and, after about six months, Leo replaced me with a local man who was more affordable than an expatriate with a family. That made sense to us; so we said our good-byes, but had no inclination to leave Africa. There was too much need and opportunity not to immerse ourselves productively and contribute to the aspirations of this continent.

It has been said that when God closes a door, He opens a window. I really wanted to continue to be involved in relief and development, but then not one, but several windows opened in another field. By way of an acquaintance in Colorado I met Kenya's Chief Inspector of Schools, the second-ranking official in the Ministry of Education. Through him I was given the opportunity to teach religion classes in Nairobi high-schools and hold devotionals for student bodies. That was a welcome opportunity to influence young minds – up to six-hundred at a time.

Many of these young people came from religious homes, but, just the same, for a majority God was not part of their thinking. I eschewed sanctimonious talk and made an effort at introducing God into the issues that occupied their minds. If I could convince them of the historical reality of Christ, from the virgin birth to the resurrection, then I would have come a long way towards bringing them to a new understanding – Christianity, not as a religion or philosophy that is largely handed down impersonally from one generation to the next like an heirloom and, therefore, perceived as irrelevant to one's daily affairs, but as life-giving reality as relevant to them as food on the table and a roof over the head.

I also sought to communicate that God is not a kill-joy accepted by weak minds, and that a life with Christ is not lived in la-la-land. Rather, I presented it from my own experience as a life of rational balance, adventurous discovery, and fulfilling involvement. If I could be the catalyst that would set them seeking Him who can transform a stale existence – like a chemical substance that changes a colorless, bland liquid into a colorful, bubbling one – then I would have accomplished my mission. That done, there would be plenty of opportunity for them to get acquainted with Him, since Christ was accepted and honored widely in Kenya. Starting them on that path was my hope.

Meanwhile, after four-and-a-half months, our acquaintances for whom we had been house-sitting, returned from home leave just as another missionary family took their furlough and went overseas. We moved into their home with our few belongings. Their compound was surrounded by a high wall with glass shards embedded in the top – the local form of razor wire. The house also came with a German shepherd. In a society that is given to an inordinate fear of dogs, that pet was a bonus. Her bark was so ferocious that anything in the house automatically became anathema to a would-be burglar.

We discovered also that, despite the security devices in and around our house, safety was not assured. After only a few nights in our walled compound, it became apparent that we had a fox in the chicken coup: Our night watchman had stolen the side-view mirror from our car.

Another time, another car, another side-view mirror. I had gone to lunch and was parked at the main post office in downtown Nairobi. As I returned, and before the Toyota Land Cruiser came into view, I recognized the blaring of its alarm. I rounded the corner, noticed the coveted object missing, and saw three young men strolling away from the car. When I challenged them, they started fleeing in different directions. I picked one – must have been the smallest one – and gave chase. Immediately others joined, shouting "Huyo! Huyo!" – "There he goes! There he goes!" The thief pulled out an ice pick and started stabbing at passers-by who tried to stop him. The chase went one block up Kenyatta Avenue, right on Muindi Mbingu Street and past the Six-Eighty Hotel, back down Kaunda Street, over a low wall into the Holy Family Cathedral compound, back over and across City Hall Way, down into and through the Moi Garden Restaurant and, through a back door, up a flight of stairs into the adjoining compound of the Jomo Kenyatta Conference Center. Whew! I'm out of breath just remembering it.

As the first chasers dropped off, other pedestrians joined the pursuit. For them, this was a welcome distraction from the monotony of a midweek afternoon. Exhausted, the thief hurled the ice pick as far as he could and surrendered to an agitated vigilante crowd. Before I reached him, the first blows were already landing, and I knew that, without intervention, he might well be killed. Thievery in Nairobi was dangerous business, and periodically, with a gruesome picture to prove the story, the newspapers would report that yet another thief had been beaten to death.

I hovered over the crouched guy like a hen over her chicks and shouted for the wild pugilists to stop. I remember one man landing a crushing blow into his face right under my outstretched arm. Finally they stopped, and one of them joined me in taking him to the police headquarters a few blocks away.

There he was made to sit on the floor, which was an ominous development for him, as it implied guilt and made him more vulnerable, as I was about to witness. One of the officers was standing at the counter, writing a report when we arrived. Upon hearing what had happened, he turned around, asked, "Who? This guy?" and slapped and kicked the sitting man. Then, as if nothing had happened, he returned to his report. No Rodney-King repercussions here! No mirror, either – one of the thief's accomplices had gotten away with it.

*   *   *

The Bible says that the love of money is the root of all evil. The world turns around money. A good share of time is spent earning it and much of the rest of time, it seems, spending it and talking or thinking about it. And there never seems to be quite enough of it. When we left the EO, we left a salaried position, and ironically, as we considered our next step, we, too, became preoccupied with the thought of money – how would we manage so far from home, family, and friends without an income we could count on each month?

Initially we lived on our savings. As they dwindled, we knew it was time to consult with the leadership of our home church about our immediate future. We had been in Africa two years and felt it was time for some rest and recuperation and to introduce Karsten and Misha to the land of their heritage. Perhaps we could stay long enough for them to exchange their African/British accent for an American one. So, when our hosts returned from their furlough of four months, we sold our "yellow submarine," an old four-wheel-drive Subaru station wagon, and put the proceeds toward airline tickets home.

We were gone three and a half months, of which we were about five weeks in Europe. The rest of the time we spent in the U.S. where friends from our church furnished us with accommodations and a car. We thrived on the renewal of relationships and were encouraged by the assurance that the church that had sent us out initially into a salaried position, would now continue its support of our involvement in Africa financially, as well. Although we had no obligations, our R & R was packed with activity, particularly in Colorado. We had many friends to visit and stories to tell. Karsten and Misha enjoyed their time, too. He learned to ride a bicycle, and she learned to swim, and before we knew it, our home furlough was up. It ended the way it had started, with visits to Debbie's family on the East Coast.

It's never easy to bid good-bye to loved ones for long absences, especially when the destination is not known for stability. But we knew the ins and outs of the territory and felt assured that, with God, we were "in good hands," as it says in the advertisement of what the British call appropriately an *assurance* agency. Our confidence was infectious and helped in the parting.

It was to be tested, however, as early as on our return flight. We flew with Sudan Airways, popularly known as the "In sha'Allah ('If Allah wills') Airline," but that day "Allah" hadn't willed. The plane developed hydraulic problems, and instead of landing in Frankfurt and being received by my sister, we landed at London's Heathrow Airport and were received by four fire engines that raced alongside our plane, blue lights flashing. The delay discombobulated our schedule, but gave us another opportunity to see Peter and Marilyn Muth for several days before flying on to Frankfurt. We had already visited them in their home in Chorleywood on our way to the States.

Originally, we had been scheduled to fly from Frankfurt to Nairobi via London, also with Sudan Airways. But, call it providence or credit that nebulous "good luck," that flight had already been canceled back in May. It had been scheduled to depart London on Saturday, July 31, arriving at Jomo Kenyatta International Airport on August 1, 1982 at one o'clock in the morning – not a fun time to reach anywhere, especially with a two and a four-year old. At two o'clock, the Kenya Air Force launched a coup attempt from Embakasi Barracks, just a few miles from the airport near Airport Road. We were told later that cars and buses had been shot up and scattered all over the highway. Had that flight not been canceled for whatever reason two months earlier, we might well have found ourselves on that road for our last adventure.

It had taken considerable persuasion, then, to get us rescheduled on Sunday's flight – which was also cancelled, because Nairobi's airport was closed due to the coup attempt just then in progress.

As if all this confusion had been Sudan Airways' fault, the airline redeemed itself by booking us in Business Class on the first available flight two weeks later with Lufthansa out of Frankfurt. However, the upgrade was not entirely free. Sudan Airways lost my toolbox, chock-full of valuable new tools, on the London – Nairobi leg. The refund was another case of "in sha'Allah." Despite several letters to its offices in Khartoum with copy to IATA, the International Air Transport Association, Sudan Airways never reimbursed us.

The timing of our return could not have been more convenient, as we were given the opportunity to house-sit yet again, this time for a Norwegian couple. Inge and Åslaug Tveite worked for a Norwegian aid organization and, within days of our arrival, went on home leave. Theirs was a modern white-washed stucco house with a red tile roof. It had a large, manicured garden and a stucco-wall enclosure. We felt as though we belonged to the prosperous diplomatic community, a welcome illusion if it doesn't go to one's head. And we stayed there, as in the two previous Nairobi residences, rent-free and enjoyed the continued services of a gardener and an askari (Swahili for soldier or night-watchman).

Since we had sold our car before our departure, we needed to find a replacement. It had to be a used one, on the lower end of the price scale. Cars in Kenya were expensive because of an import duty of up to 150%. To increase one's prospect of getting anything reliable, it was imperative to buy one from a departing expatriate. That limited the choice considerably, even more so because the cars of foreigners were typically of the higher-end variety.

I scoured the newspapers. We could only afford to spend between $3000 and $4000, but there wasn't much in that price range. However, wishful thinking made me linger longer on an ad for a Fiat that was decidedly beyond our means. Hoping against hope, I contacted the owner, who turned out to be the manager of Pepsi Cola, East Africa. It was his wife's car, and they were relocating to Greece. I met him for a test drive of the yellow 1976 Fiat 124, 5-speed with only 34,000 miles on the odometer. It sported a powerful engine and had large, comfortable, white, imitation-leather seats. And it was in good shape. Its value had been set at $5500 by the Kenyan Automobile Association. I informed him that our budget did not allow us to exceed $4000, but he was not prepared to accept that – not yet, anyway. We exchanged business cards, and he told me that the car would be ours if they hadn't sold it in nine days, the day before their departure.

The possibility of that happening was remote, as he was running ads in two papers, and his asking price was reasonable. I was hesitant to wait that long, given the distinct possibility of being disappointed nine days hence and having to start looking all over again.

That evening in our living room I had an idea. Karsten was four-and-a-half years old, and I decided to tap into his child-like faith. Sitting on the couch together, I pulled the seller's card out of my pocket and explained the situation to him. Then, with my arm around him, we both prayed. I remember the scene clearly, but I don't remember where Debbie and Misha were at the time. Must have been a guy-thing. An hour or so later we put the children to bed, too early for Karsten to learn about the telephone call that came later that evening – nine days earlier than had been conditionally promised.

Before the Tveites returned, we located a rental property that was ideal for us. It was a two-bedroom stone house in Nairobi's Westlands area, just three blocks from the house we had occupied before we moved into the Tveites' home. It had a large living room and big windows opening up to a lovely, spacious yard. It was located at the end of Mimosa Road, a narrow, unpaved, hedge-lined lane. There was a large lawn, front and back, with a drive around the house and mature trees along much of the property's perimeter. One of them had a big fork about twelve feet up. It was well suited for the tree house I later built for the kids with bamboo from stands on the property. The place was fenced and had small servant's quarters and a shed. It belonged to a Somali businessman who didn't speak English. If smiles had been enough, we would have had a solid contract. As it was, he had several adult sons who readily obliged by drawing up an agreement.

The tree house

Getting hooked-up to the telephone network was a frustrating, time-consuming effort, as we would not compromise our convictions by paying the customary bribes. After three months and persevering visits to the telephone company, we were finally successful. But our name did not appear in the telephone book until we returned to Uganda two years later. For that failure, the local version of the AT&T of the twentieth century compensated us by leaving our name in the telephone book for three years after we had been disconnected and had left the country. At one point we even made it in bold print to the top corner of the page. We were famous!

The house came with an askari, whose fearsome weapon was his voice. His job was to scare potential thieves away and to open the gate for us and visitors. Some of Nairobi's askaris were Masai who carried spears and knew how to use them. Those who could afford it, hired Securicor, a night-watch company. Their askaris were connected by radio to their buddies waiting in small pick-up trucks that were parked in the vicinity. Banks also employed Securicor. You could readily recognize their guards. They wore blue uniforms, blue motorcycle helmets with upholstered leather neck protectors and carried baseball bats.

Burglaries are most common during the rainy season because heavy downpours suppress noise. One stormy night I decided to check on our askari. There was a heavy downpour, and lightening shooed away the darkness at regular intervals. How anyone could sleep through the thunder claps is beyond me, but it turned out to be no problem for our man. He had curled up on the floor of the shed near the house. The next morning I fired him. Since he rejected the termination by showing up the next evening and refused to leave when I ordered him to, I carried him outside our front gate, set him down and bid him good-bye. He picked up a rock just large enough to handle with one hand and threatened to hurl it at me, but didn't quite have the courage to part with it.

There was good reason for employing askaris, as burglaries, especially of white and affluent black homes, were common. But with or without them, we never had a problem at that house at night. That is not to say that we were never burgled.

We had a membership for the swimming pool at the beautiful Serena Hotel, about a ten-minute drive from our house. Following an outing there one fine Sunday afternoon, we pulled into our driveway. We could see immediately that something was wrong. There was an item on the step by the side door that hadn't been there when we left. It turned out to be my Sharp Intelli-Writer, a simple word processor and forerunner to today's personal computer. The lock on our wooden side door had been busted. We had had visitors.

We jumped out of the car and ran through that door, hearts pounding. The place was a mess. Clothes were strewn on the floor, drawers yanked out and some items dropped on the way out. We must have surprised them. They had been picky – looking for more expensive items. They had grabbed most of Debbie's jewelry, such as she had, had taken my three suit jackets and had made off with the power cord to the Sharp and, probably, with more than we could identify and therefore didn't really need.

We were grateful we had returned to our burgled house when we did. We had heard of places that had been totally cleaned out. Our feelings were ambivalent. It was almost like Christmas finding all the things that had *not* been taken. Debbie and I were excitedly pointing out individual valued items that had been left, when Karsten proudly showed us his most prized possession and exclaimed, "Look, they didn't take my soccer ball!"

His worries were gone. Ah, the innocence of a child. But we felt violated. *Aren't things like this supposed to happen to somebody else?*

One thin gold necklace that had survived the burglary had more than one life. Before we learned that it was not a good idea to sport glittering jewelry in poor countries, Debbie was sitting in a mini-bus right by an open window. As it pulled away from a busy stop, a thief reached in and grabbed a hold of the necklace. Although it opened, it slipped through his hand, and dropped onto Debbie's shoulders. Debbie turned just in time to see, with a measure of satisfaction I am sure, disappointment creep over his face. Fortunately, she paid for the lesson with just a minor scratch on her neck.

We decided to hire a gardener who would double as an askari in our absence. Marengwe was the son of a fine Christian man who had worked at the Mennonite Guesthouse at the entrance to our Mimosa Road for over fifteen years. Stability, dependability, and friendliness were his inheritance. And friends gave us a Labrador puppy. We hoped he would quickly grow into a ferocious watchdog. But no such luck! Apart from his black coat, the only thing he would shortly have going for him would be his size. Africans had told me that, all else being equal, black dogs are feared more than others. He had four white paws, so we called him Boots. Misha thought he was her baby and would carry him around until he wiggled and nipped her ear.

At the time of the burglary we didn't own much, but we were happy. Karsten had his bicycle and soccer ball, Misha had her dolls, and we all had our moving boxes to sit on around a table that never lacked. We slept on foam rubber mattresses on the floor and had a comfortable couch and some chairs from a garage sale held by homeward-bound expatriates. As Socrates testified, "Having the fewest wants, I am nearest to the gods." We agreed with him – for the most part.

In addition to our small church back home, Debbie's parents became our regular supporters. Our budget was tight, but we managed. Like the Apostle Paul, we had learned to live in plenty and in want. We never suffered privation, and we never asked anybody to "pray about supporting us financially."

Meanwhile, unbeknownst to us, something else was brewing back home. Through a church in Alexandria, Virginia, a wealthy businessman heard about us and used our availability to channel, on his behalf, funds and roofing materials that I would buy in Kenya to a church in Tororo, Uganda. Since Tororo was on my way to a new part-time involvement with an American couple working in emergency relief and development in Soroti, I considered the purchase of the goods and a more complicated border crossing a small price to pay for the opportunity to help in another benevolent endeavor. It's been said that you can't "outgive" God. We gladly helped out, expecting nothing back, but, as it would turn out, that help carried its own unexpected reward.

One day Debbie and I received a letter from John A. informing us that he and his wife, Leslie, were coming to East Africa to inspect the work they had funded in Uganda. We met them for the first time at the Nairobi Intercontinental Hotel. With a solid build and a square chin, John had the appearance of a middle-weight boxer or football player – maybe a running back. Leslie was obviously accustomed to the finer things in life, and while she was chatty and had a pleasant personality, she exuded what we later heard described as "old Virginia money."

By that time we had come into "old Africa money," and had been able to buy proper chairs for our dining room, so that we were not shy about inviting them for dinner. I collected them at their hotel. John was dressed business-casual, but Leslie looked spiffy in our humble home. After supper, John looked at me across the table and said matter-of-factly:

"Eb, Leslie and I have talked and decided to send you and Debbie $1000 every other month. This money is not to be for your needs, but for your wants."

After I picked up my chin and went through the responses I thought appropriate after such a surprising announcement, I said something about putting that money towards a four-wheel drive vehicle, which was actually a need, not just a want. The next day, John and I were in downtown Nairobi. He skimmed through the advertising section of a newspaper and declared, "Eb, here are three Land Rovers for sale. Why don't we buy those? One for you, one for John O., and we'll find somebody else for the third one."

My chin didn't drop this time – I was becoming accustomed to pleasant surprises from someone for whom money was not an issue. I told him that Land Rovers are expensive in consumption and upkeep and that I would like to hold out for a four-wheel-drive Daihatsu.

"When you find one let me know, and I'll wire the money."

Within six weeks an acquaintance put hers up for sale, John sent $12,000, and we had our all-terrain vehicle. That generous gift notwithstanding, John faithfully kept his original promise until we departed from Africa. Someone once said that "God's work done God's way will have God's supply." In our case, I don't know about the middle-part of that statement. I'm sure that we ran more on mercy than on merit, but that's just it – as the song says: "'tis mercy all, immense and free, for oh my God, it found out me."

9

A SHAKE-DOWN CRUISE

Hitch your wagon to a star.
Ralph Waldo Emerson

The Daihatsu proved to be a godsend. With the endemic instability of the continent, I knew that, if ever a violent coup were to shut down the airport and wreak havoc in the country, this vehicle could become our mobile refuge, a means of escape from Kenya or Uganda, even from the continent. I looked at it as a vital link to the outside world and set about to outfit it accordingly.

One of the uncertainties in large parts of Africa is availability of fuel. That was the first problem that needed attention. I decided on a welding shop owned by Sikhs, those turbaned Punjabi Indians who share the same last name, Singh (lion), and, in East Africa, tend to work in engineering-related professions. Indrajit designed and had his top African welder, Stephen, make a fuel tank that was fitted under the driver's seat and connected to the main tank under the passenger seat with two hoses, one on top, for filling from the overflowing main tank, the other at the bottom, for leveling the fuel in both tanks. He replaced the front bumper with a platform with four-inch-high rails. It carried two metal jerry cans on the outside and a toolbox in the middle. Now I could drive nearly a thousand miles without refueling and could carry more tools than I knew what to do with. He made a roof rack that extended over a foot beyond the windshield and carried a second spare tire at the front underneath.

I outfitted our Daihatsu with a car-top tent that Debbie sewed from over forty feet of canvas. To accommodate my claustrophobia, we added two skylights and two side windows made from clear German vinyl. For cross-ventilation she made five mosquito-net-covered openings with rain flies that could be raised and lowered from the inside. She did a superb

The car-top tent ready for the night

job and, alluding to my deficient designing skills, called it our cut-and-add project. In game parks we could get up at sunrise, climb "downstairs" and go on a game drive without taking the tent down. With the size of our mobile home, we blended right in with the elephants.

The rolled-up tent, along with two of our three foam-rubber mattresses and eight black tubular tent poles ranging in length from two to four feet, was stored in a box that covered the width of the car and was about four feet long. The sides were ten inches high, and the front was hinged on top to the lid and on the bottom to the floor of the box. A frame with a built-in ladder was attached to the back of the lid, lay on it when it was closed and swung free when the box was opened. It came to rest on the rail of the front platform that carried the jerry cans and toolbox, supporting the open lid, which became a horizontal extension to the top rack over the hood of the car. The double-hinged front of the box, along with three inches of the lid, rested on the front end of the rack. The eight sockets for the tent poles were welded into the rack and fastened into the box.

Like the roof rack with the open box, the tent was nearly twelve feet long and accommodated us and the children comfortably. The mattress for the rack behind the box was wrapped in canvas and, during the day, rested on a sheet of plywood that spanned and covered the two sideways-facing benches behind the driver and passenger seats. There it doubled as a playing surface and bed for the kids, who were sometimes joined by a sleepy driver. For privacy we had hung curtains in the back windows. At night, the mattress completed the floor for the tent on the roof rack behind the box, and whatever was on the rack, mostly luggage and, sometimes, additional fuel and fresh water, both in plastic jerry cans, was moved onto the

The car-top tent opened up

plywood platform below. The retrofitted Daihatsu was our Swiss-Family-Robinson contraption on wheels. It was practical, efficient, user-friendly, and above all, it worked.

We took this outfit on a shake-down cruise of three-thousand miles around Lake Victoria, going from Kenya to Uganda, Rwanda, Burundi, Tanzania, and back to Kenya. The trip was remarkable for its diversity – going from left-hand traffic in Kenya and Uganda, to right-hand traffic in Rwanda and Burundi and back to the left in Tanzania; from potholed roads in Kenya and, with the added nuisance of roadblocks in Uganda, to easy travel on the smooth roads of Rwanda and Burundi; from English in the three East African nations, to the francophone countries of the two former Belgian colonies in Central Africa; from the ready availability of fuel and food in Kenya, Rwanda, and Burundi, if at a price, to scarcity in Uganda and Tanzania. The one shared characteristic of all five countries was the deference of their people toward us.

Away from the cities we were, of course, the objects of curiosity. What we would call gawking is considered observing in some cultures – meaning there is nothing wrong with it. Since every culture defines for itself what are appropriate and inappropriate expressions of curiosity, the uninitiated in foreign lands can be made to feel uncomfortable, at times even violated.

Once, after a day's journey in Burundi, we set up our tent for the night near the top of a grassy hill. The sky was blue, the air was still, and all was quiet. There was no sign of life around. But then, out of nowhere it seemed, people began to show up. They lined up in a semicircle at about twenty paces and quietly, or with hushed comments, followed our every move. It seemed they didn't have a care in the world, but they had time – lots of time. No jobs to go to, no dental or hair appointments to keep, no kids to pick up from school or take to soccer practice. Their lives seemed unencumbered and exuded spontaneity.

We had parked just off the road on public land, so we were not a bother to anyone, nor, for that matter, was there a sign of hostility on their part. But, understandably, in this rural area, with no television, movie-theater, concert hall, or soccer club, we were the happening of the month, if not the year – a little white family with their green and yellow house on wheels – and who would want to miss that? Since no one came forward to talk with us, we assumed that nobody could communicate in either English or French, and they seemed content to watch us aliens with our strange habits and equipment from the distance. We didn't have any candy or chewing gum or other such tokens to share and decided to leave the initiative for more personal contact up to them.

Our car-top tent would have been a curiosity almost anywhere in the world, but then we began preparing supper with our *Camping Gaz* one-burner stove. Now that was something! I hadn't sent my wife half a mile or more to collect firewood and carry it back on her head. I had taken a tin can, opened a pouch hanging from my belt and removed a red gadget with shiny metal sandwiched in between. With my Swiss army knife I had effortlessly opened the can. Now, Debbie prepared our soup on a fire coming out of a fist-sized canister. When our table was set, we sat down and said a prayer of thanksgiving. As we started to eat, as if in response to a whistle, our observers began to leave. And when they departed they meant business – there were no stragglers left behind. In the culture of this particular tribe, the start of our meal was the point at which further scrutinizing would have been impolite. We were glad to note this inhibition and respected their collective sensitivity to their own cultural constraints. It helped us accept their earlier gawking.

At Lusahanga we arrived at a "T" in the road and were misled by a sign that was turned around. Unfortunately, it turned us around, too, a fact we were to discover a bit late. We hadn't thought of double-checking our directions either with the map or against the position of the sun and didn't have our Rocky Mountains to help us distinguish east from west, north from south. In this lightly-wooded area one had to choose to go either fifteen miles north to Biharamujo from where a road turned off to the east, or fifteen miles south to Nyakanazi, where another road turned off, also to the east. The two roads started off parallel at about thirty miles from each other, but then gradually led ever further apart – one angling north, the other south. We had followed the sign to Biharamujo, but, in fact, were going to Nyakanazi.

In a deserted part of this savannah, not yet knowing that we were on the wrong road, we came upon a bridge that spanned a dry creek bed. It was severly damaged, with an array of loose timbers scattered where once a drivable surface had been. It looked as if a tornado had ripped them up, whipped them around and dropped them – just like that. Three or four trucks were parked on either side, their drivers waiting for whoknowswhat.

To this day I can't imagine what they could have hoped to accomplish by just sitting there. This bridge might not have been repaired for months!

We got out of the car with a wave to the truck drivers, whose curious looks said as much as, *"So, now what?"* And that's what we were thinking, too. We didn't cherish the idea of turning around. We had done that once, in Morocco on our trip through West Africa, when we had been told, falsely as it turned out, that the border to Spanish Sahara was sealed. That had forced us to return to Spain and to sail via the Canary Islands to the southern tip of Spanish Sahara from where we entered Mauritania. Sure, I had grown more mellow and accepting since our hitchhiking days, but backtracking still didn't hold much of an appeal to me.

As we looked at the tangle of heavy beams that lay scattered across a stable sub-structure, it occurred to us that we might be able to line them up parallel and, hey, if Evel Knievel could jump umpteen cars with a motorcycle, we could certainly drive some forty feet across a broken bridge on those beams. They were, doubtless, sufficiently strong to carry the weight of our vehicle.

Debbie, as game as ever, and I went to work moving the rough-sawn timbers. At eight to ten inches wide they approximated the width of railroad ties, and their length spanned the sturdy supports. We laid out two lanes, spaced to match the distance of the wheels from one side of the car to the other. As we worked, the truck drivers remained by their rigs. Although we knew that these men customarily speak English, they were, like our visitors the evening before, uncharacteristically aloof and watched askance from the distance.

Since most trucking companies in East Africa are headquartered along the predominantly Muslim-inhabited shores of the Indian Ocean, most of them are Muslim-owned and their rigs Muslim-driven. Perhaps that explained their reticence to engage us because, in their eyes, women are not supposed to do "men's" work.

On our second trip in 1975, Debbie and I were given a lift by a Muslim trucker in the Sudan. In the vast, empty western desert, with no particular road or track to follow, we came upon a group of Hadendowa Beja, whom the British referred to as the Fuzzy Wuzzies. They became famous under the Mahdi by defeating General Gordon at Khartoum. There was a log, and, with this wild-looking bunch watching, Debbie and I got on and rolled each other off, lumberjack style. After a lot of laughter and jibberish

Debbie with Hadendowa Beja

that expressed their approval, they wanted to try. My turn came first, then I asked Debbie to have a go with them. They really got into the game as my athletic wife knocked them off, one by one. Everybody was laughing at their buddies coming off that log – except our driver. He came up to me and told me that I shouldn't let her do that, since she could break a leg. Well, perhaps he feared for us, as those mop-haired, wild-looking guys carried swords under their robes or daggers under their armpits. Perhaps their sporty demeanor could change. But we survived, as did Debbie's legs, as did, most likely, the drivers prejudice.

I don't know if Debbie's hauling of the timbers with me was the reason for these truckers' distant demeanor. There was hardly any traffic on that road, and it must have taken several days for even that small number of trucks to accumulate. I would think that after waiting in the loneliness of that deserted place they, too, would have considered us a welcome distraction and gone out of their way to interact with us.

Debbie and I double-checked the spacing and sturdiness of the beams. Then we took Karsten and Misha to the other side. I got down on hands and knees to scrutinize once more the alignment of my two driving-surfaces. Satisfied that all looked good, I returned on the tangle of beams and got into the vehicle – the moment of truth had arrived.

Debbie bent down low, no, not to pray, though that might have been a good idea, but to have an unobstructed view of all four wheels on their narrow supports from her squatting position. Then she directed me across. In four-wheel-drive-low I crept forward, allowing the engine to move the vehicle just above stall-speed. I kept my eyes fixed on her, and my feet resting lightly on clutch and brake. It was reassuring to know that, although the timbers were not bolted down, the car would not plunge into the riverbed below if a wheel rolled off one of the tracks. There were still too many timbers randomly scattered for it to just fall through. But it could get wedged between them, and it would be a major job to get it back onto the track.

I stopped a couple of times and checked how I was progressing on the two narrow lanes. The wheels sat squarely on both, but the alignment ahead needed to be slightly adjusted. Other than that, things looked good, really good.

At last I was across and thought triumphantly that he who laughs last, laughs best. But I pretended to be my humble, unassuming self and flashed a friendly smile as we waved good-bye to the truckers. They nodded and waved back. Perhaps we had given them incentive to work together and rebuild the bridge with the available materials. But then, apart from the risk of driving those multi-ton rigs across, that was, no doubt, beyond their call of duty.

The book of Proverbs says that pride comes before the fall. In our case – my case – it was more a sinking feeling as we began to arch ever further south: We were on the wrong road. We were heading toward Dar es Salaam instead of Arusha and the Kenyan border beyond. That sign had pointed us in the wrong direction!

Now, having crossed the bridge, we were even less inclined to turn back. *There must be a connection between those two roads.* Our Michelin map showed a thin red line snaking north and linking them, and it appeared to be still ahead of us. But finding its counterpart in the real world of turned signs, broken bridges, and lack of people to help you find your way proved difficult. After a few miles we came upon what resembled a ghost town. With just a handful of houses, the place seemed deserted. There wasn't a soul in sight. Going by the distance we had traveled since crossing the bridge, we thought the elusive road might be in the vicinity.

Between two dilapidated buildings there were about thirty feet of road that ended abruptly in grass and shrubs. Upon further inspection, though, we discovered that that piece of road seemed to continue as an overgrown dirt track. That red line on the map was sage green in the real world. It was camouflaged well. Underneath the three-foot-high grass the track was approximately ten feet wide and made the dirt road we had been on look like a superhighway.

It was mid-afternoon as we ventured off the road, about the time when in an other world commuters begin to brace themselves for rush-hour. Our hour here was anything but that. We started moving forward in first gear, the front rack pushing down the grass. Intermittent bushes on either side, like roadside poles in Colorado ski-country, told us the layout and direction of the track ahead. For a while there was no problem – until we drove with our right front wheel onto an anthill, invisible in the tall grass, while the left one sank into a mud puddle. With the three extra jerry cans of fuel and two of potable water, plus other gear on the top rack of the car, not to mention our tent box and the rack itself, we were sufficiently top heavy to flip, as if in slow motion, onto our side.

It was one of those situations in which your mind tries to reject reality even as your mouth acknowledges it with a despairing, "Oh, no!" The kids in the back sat on the window that was still intact, Debbie on the door. Looking up at me, she wondered why I hadn't fallen on her. I had tightened my grip on the steering wheel, wedging myself between it and the back of my seat.

As I shut off the engine, a sense of foreboding gripped me and in a split second all kinds of questions raced through my mind. Could the engine leak fuel and its heat ignite it and fire envelop the car? Can we right it by ourselves? Will I be able to drive it? One question I didn't have: Where is the nearest AAA? I pushed my door up and emerged from the vehicle like a tank-commander from the hatch of his Abrams, just not as triumphantly. Debbie handed the kids up and grabbing my hand, followed them. Karsten was laughing and Misha was crying – which made a lot more sense. Debbie was composed, and I felt stupid, although I was not aware of having done anything wrong – other than not driving on a paved road with proper signs pointing the way to a Holiday Inn with international TV News and Sports and a restaurant with a steak dinner and ice cream for dessert.

Amazingly though, not only was none of us injured, but the car had suffered no damage, not even a broken left side-view mirror. Thank God for guardian angels and the soft earth and thick grass that, though being the cause of the accident, made amends by cushioning our fall. Misha recovered her composure quickly and, like her brother, began to think that this was more fun than a visit to an amusement park. (I am making that up – she had never seen one.) I remember Karsten sitting on the back wheel and spinning around. He had created his own.

Debbie and I, on the other hand, were concerned – engine oil was leaking slowly, and we had only an extra half quart. There was no time to lose. While we unloaded the rack, we contemplated our predicament. We were in a deserted area, and it might take most of the day, perhaps even longer, to find help. Using the carjack would require building ever higher supports and changing angles with materials not readily available. But the more we could tilt the vehicle with the jack, the easier it would be for Debbie and me to push it the rest of the way. However, our best prospect lay in the possibility that two bicycle-pushing men we had passed earlier had not turned off, but were still heading our way. Failing that, perhaps our next best prospect was to disconnect the manual winch from the front of the car, tying it to a nearby tree and cranking the Daihatsu up by the rack. Would the rack hold? Maybe, if we raised the car as high as we could with the jack, and then "Jane" would crank, and "Tarzan" would lift from the other side. Meanwhile, oil was still leaking.

A pedestrian appeared, seemingly out of nowhere in that desolate, wooded place, walking in the direction from which we had come. And yes, soon the two men we had passed caught up with us. I don't remember any of the three speaking a word of English, but our situation spoke for itself. They communicated with each other in Swahili. Welcome to Tanzania! We felt at home with our first interaction with East Africans since leaving Uganda.

Together we righted the car, and, while they supported it, I got in and drove it off the anthill and out of the hole. Much to their delight we gave them each an American dollar. I don't think they were ever able to exchange it even if they had found a bank, as African banks generally don't change anything below a ten-dollar bill. They would probably just pin, what for them was the equivalent of a day's wages, to a wall in their homes. That dollar was doubtless as close as they would ever get to America.

I added the partial quart of oil and found that we were at the "add" mark. Not bad! It was enough to make it out of that desolate place. At about two-thirds of the way to our goal, the road to Arusha, our trusty Daihatsu got high-centered in a place where the tires of heavy trucks, somewhere between the time of the Battle of Hastings and then, had cut deep ruts into soft earth. But, akuna matata – not to worry, our bicycle-pushing friends caught up again soon, helped us reverse and pointed to a place some twenty yards back, where some intrepid drivers with greater foresight than I, had veered off the road and bypassed the ruts through the bush.

Third time's a charm, except, in this case it was a tree. We followed that short detour, but just to make certain that it wasn't to be our day, were yanked to a stop. *What on earth is that?* Because of the tall grass I hadn't seen anything and whatever it was, it was under our car now. (I'm sure Gary Larson could have come up with something for his "Far Side" cartoons here.) We were already in four-wheel drive, but we couldn't go forward or backward any more than we could go sideways.

Biting flies were stubbornly seeking landing space wherever our skin was exposed. Sweating and itching, I crawled through the thick grass underneath the car. My eyes focused on the culprit – the root end of a four-foot piece of tree trunk. It was some kind of hardwood, perhaps ironwood, because one of the roots, only about two inches thick and eight inches long, had embedded itself in the undercarriage and made a dent in the floorboard.

Never leave home, if it is in Africa, without your Swiss army knife. With the razor-sharp saw blade I cut off some six inches, which set us free again. With that final obstacle removed, we were back on our way to civilization, such as it was.

A similar Swiss-army-knife-rescue experience occurred in southern France shortly after our marriage, only that we weren't stuck with a car, but in a room. We had requested and been given a room for the night in a Catholic compound. We locked the door and got ready to sleep when Debbie perceived the call of nature. The toilet was just down the hall, but there was a locked door – our door – in the way, and it would not unlock. Try as we might, with the key in a little bit, all the way, or somewhere in between, it would not budge the bolt. We were prisoners in that room.

To set us free I took the lock apart with my knife. The next morning we left a note of explanation and two dollars for compensation for the inconvenience we had caused. Now I can own up to the fact that, instead of giving Debbie a diamond ring for our seven-week engagement, I had given her a Swiss army knife. In neither situation would the former have gotten us unstuck. The latter was considerably cheaper, too.

*   *   *

The remainder of our trip included the Serengeti National Park and Ngorongoro Crater for some of the most spectacular wildlife viewing in the world. The Serengeti is Tanzania's best-known wildlife sanctuary and sports the "the big five," elephant, rhinoceros, cape buffalo, lion, and leopard (the hippopotamus is sometimes substituted in the count for the leopard), as well as many other species of plains game. Coming from the Speke Gulf of Lake Victoria only a few miles away, we entered the Serengeti on the west-side through a trackless corridor of wide-open grasslands. Very little game is to be seen there, which was probably just as well. Predators follow their prey, and we almost got into a situation where we didn't need their company.

We were moving along happily, looking forward to communing with the wilder side of nature and oblivious to the fact that the lush grass, because of that wilder side, had received a generous downpour and was now getting soggy. Our Daihatsu didn't have the shift-into-four-wheel-drive-on-the-fly feature, and, by the time we noticed that I was driving in a veritable swamp, it was too risky to stop and get out to engage the front-wheel hubs. I feared that even four-wheel drive might not get us going again if we stopped. (Another "Far Side" moment on the far side of the Serengeti?) I also hoped we could pull through without shifting down, as that would create a further loss of momentum.

The car began to labor, the RPMs ground dangerously low, and the engine's sound approached a lower octave on the musical scale. What if we got stuck? No trees for winching ourselves out, no branches nor rocks to put under the tires for traction. We might have to wait for several days before help would come our way – the corridor was about ten miles wide, with no traffic as far as the eye could see.

I remembered a German "overlander," who got stuck with his Mercedes Unimog in the sands at Tan Tan, southern Morocco. Truckers wanted too much baksheesh to pull him out. So, having a generous supply of food and water, he opted to wait for a more palatable option. After several days of fruitless waiting, it came to him in form of a splendid idea. He buried his spare tire in the sand as far away as his cable allowed and winched himself out.

I didn't think that would work here, which is why I wasn't prepared to dig in one or both of my spares except as a last resort. We, too, had plenty of food and water and could set up our roof-top house in minutes. But who wants to be stuck indefinitely?

The engine was only a few revolutions from stalling when its low drone slowly turned into a whine. We were picking up speed again. Relief! We aimed for the closest trees on the horizon and, maintaining momentum without further problems, reached dry land with acacia trees and shrubs. We were grateful to have terra firma under our feet again. About an hour later we came upon a Land Rover that was so hopelessly stuck in a ditch, that we could only help the driver by taking him to the park headquarters to summon a tow truck.

I was also reminded of an earlier occasion, when we got stuck in our Volkswagen bus in Tsavo National Park in Kenya. The best time to see lions is either in the cool of a very early morning when they go hunting for breakfast, or in the evening when it's supper time. Hence, our timing for wildlife viewing was not the best in the heat, shortly after noon. But that proved to play in our favor, even as we were about to participate as the main actors in our own wild life story.

We had inquired at park headquarters as to where we might be able to find lions and had been directed to this dirt rack. It started out at only about twelve feet wide, slightly below the surrounding landscape of low grasses and scrawny bushes. The further we drove, the narrower and rougher it got and the more it called for four-wheel drive. But since our Volkswagen bus had only rear-wheel drive, we couldn't answer that call. Fearing we would get stuck, I decided to turn around and promptly realized my fears. We had been driving on a surface of crusted sand. To move the vehicle back and forth even in the widest spot available, we had to drive onto the slightly elevated sides of the track. And then it happened. We broke through the crust, leaving our back wheels spinning in the sand.

We had nothing on board to put underneath for traction and faced two unattractive choices: We could choose caution – stay put and face the possibility of spending the rest of the day and the night in the mini-bus with little water (Never ever travel in Africa without plenty of water!) – or I could opt for valor and search for something to put under the wheels while facing the possibility of my wife becoming a widow and our children fatherless.

The area's thin bushes worked in favor of going for it. They were not the best providers of shade in the afternoon when a lion prefers to rest, rather than stalk a skinny muzungu for his meat. And, what's more, they allowed us to see further.

There was a ridge about a hundred yards away with a few scraggy trees at the bottom. With Debbie and the kids on the look-out, I moved cautiously towards that ridge, keeping my eyes pealed for any sign of movement.

I can think of all kinds of scenarios that might have brought this episode to an exciting end (exciting for the lions, that is), but then this story might have never been written, at least not by me. Instead, I am happy to relate that I found the wood we needed, put it under the tires, and off we went. It had not been much more of a nuisance than changing a flat tire at an afternoon outing in our own Rocky Mountain National Park.

*   *   *

The Ngorongoro Crater within the Ngorongoro Conservation Area is half-way between the Serengeti and Arusha near the Kenyan border. The collapse of a volcanic cone created this 100-square mile, 2,000-ft deep caldera – this planet's largest. It is home to over 20,000 large animals, including the "big five." Though the area is not fenced, most animals stay in the crater year-round since there is plentiful grazing and water.

We arrived at the crater's rim. It was raining – the kind of day on which one would rather curl up on a couch with a book of African adventure stories, a fire crackling in the fireplace and classical music wafting through the air from a fine surround-sound system, than battle the elements of the dark continent. But, one takes the bad with the good, especially if one has no choice in the matter, and so far the weather had been mostly good.

We drove to the campground and looked to the sky for any promise of blue and a soon-to-appear sun, but prospects, like the sky, were bleak – all was uniform gray. We hoped to avoid the steady drizzle while setting up our car-top tent in the open of the camping area and had taken note of a large overhang at the entrance of a tourist hotel we had passed just minutes earlier. With permission from the staff, we erected it under that overhang before returning to the campground. It rained most of the night, but we were happily ensconced in our tent; dry, warm and looking hopefully forward to a sunny safari the next day. We were not to be disappointed.

By morning the skies had cleared – it was a beautiful day with bright colors and bright countenances. After allowing our tent to dry, we stowed it away and descended in four-wheel-drive-low the rocky, steep, winding track into the grassy plain of the crater's bottom. Before we saw any wildlife we came upon a Masai moran (a young warrior) grazing his cattle. His long, braided hair, saturated with ocher, was pulled back, and his shuka, a red checkered blanket, was draped over one shoulder and reached just below his loins. He was tall and lean, like the Tutsis of Rwanda and the men of other Nilo-Hamitic tribes. His right leg was pulled up, the foot resting on his left thigh. For most of us that would be a balancing act. For him it was a way to relax.

Relax?! Would you relax if your most prized possessions were threatened by robbers? Lions are not herbivores, and cows are not dandelions. And the first game we saw were neither Impala, nor Thompson's gazelle or Wildebeest, but a pride of some seven lions lazing in the grass. One might think that if that Masai couldn't find a pasture or watering hole reserved for herbivores, he would carry a submachine gun. But no! He sported just a spear – a Masai, his cattle, and his spear – and, seemingly, had not a worry in the world.

Young Masai males were accustomed to killing lions as a rite of passage to manhood. They used the mane of the male to make a tall ceremonial hat that resembled the towering black bearskin hats worn by the Scots Guards of the Queen of England. Now, the Kenyan government is seeking to enforce a ban on hunting the king of beasts, from which only those lions are exempt that have developed a taste for livestock. It appears that the Masai and the lions have reached a truce. They have learned to live side by side, as this experience proved.

The rest of our trip went without a hitch. We arrived back home with gratefulness for God's protection and renewed awareness of the wonder, the variety, the beauty of his creation. The Masai had made the greatest impression on me. They held a particular fascination for me because, like the many tourists that come to Kenya to see wildlife and the Masai, I did not know much about them, as the following interlude proves.

We had come upon two Masai youngsters out in the middle of no-where. Thinking we were tourists – and for all intents and purposes we were – they waved us down and shouted "picha, picha!" Well, since they weren't carrying a camera to take one of us, I figured they wanted us to take one of them. I wasn't particularly interested, but, hey, why not do them that small favor. We snapped a couple of shots, I put the vehicle in gear, and, as we waved good bye, they got angry and shouted "money, money!" Now I understood "picha, picha!" Very tricky, but it didn't work with us.

We visited Bungoma in western Kenya one time. In front of a shop was a crowd of locals craning their necks over one another as they tried to get a glimpse of whoknowswhat inside. As we joined them, trying to find out what was going on in there, nobody took particular notice of us, the wazungu. But it turned out that two or three of their own countrymen inside had caused this stir – Masai, all decked out in their festival finery for a rare day on the town.

*   *   *

Shortly after John and Leslie had given us the Daihatsu, I became acquainted with a British high-school teacher and chaplain turned self-supporting professor at the Nairobi Evangelical Graduate School of Theology in Karen, a coffee-growing area outside Nairobi. (Karen was named after a former resident, the Danish Baroness Karen Blixen, who was immortalized in the film "Out of Africa.") At about 50 years of age, Peter Johnston was a soft-spoken and self-effacing British gentleman, with thick eye-glasses, good communication skills, an inquisitive mind and above it, a pate of thinning, windblown hair. He taught Koine Greek, Old and New Testament Survey, and New Testament Textual Criticism. In 1983 he had earned his Ph.D. from the University of Kent in England by collating the Gospel of Matthew from six Syriac documents. Syriac is an ancient, near-extinct language with its own script, closely related to Aramaic which, some believe, was the language of the New Testament. He also worked on Syriac evidence for the Interlinear Greek New Testament, specifically the Gospels of Luke and John.

At regular intervals Peter would pile some of his theologically-sophisticated post-graduate students into his 1950s long-wheel-base Land Rover and take them on mission trips over rutted, dusty roads into primitive Masai land. That presented them with an opportunity to remain anchored to the practical biblical base of Christian living and prevented their drifting too far into the stratospheric musings of theoretical theology. What a contrast! Ph.D. candidates mingling with a people who lived in the time-capsule of windowless, cocoon-shaped huts made of cow dung and sticks; people whose lives revolved almost exclusively around their cattle and who, for the most part, couldn't read and write and, though peaceful now, were Kenya's Karamojong of yesteryear. Not quite the contrast of the God-man walking among us to be sure, but still not normative in 21st Century mission experience.

Whenever I had the opportunity to visit Peter in his jumbled bachelor apartment, I was struck by all the books propped open on tables, countertops, and other level surfaces. I would soak up his knowledge over a cup of Earl Grey and listen to his expositions on such topics as New Testament Textual Criticism, Alexandrian and Byzantine manuscripts (MSS), Majority Text vs. regular text and the like. It was all beyond me, but I reveled in the presence of this man of higher learning and hung on his every word. I am still in touch with Peter, now in his early eighties, and he doesn't seem to have slowed much. He is currently collating the Gospel of John from five MSS in Old Ethiopic (Ge'ez) – a Semitic language like Amharic, Ethiopia's native tongue, but totally different – while still supervising several doctoral students at another theological institution, Vision International University in Tigoni, Kenya.

For the writing of this book, I asked Peter to explain the importance of these early versions as they relate to our understanding of the Bible. Here is what he wrote (those not interested in the technical details, please skip down to: Yeah, of course!)

> *I had time to write more of my comments on my completed text of St. John's Gospel in Old Ethiopic against the 28th edition of the Nestle-Aland Greek N.T. (which does not supply Old Ethiopic evidence in the "critical apparatus" which is placed below the text, and gives*

evidence (for or against) their chosen text. The first class of evidences is Greek manuscripts followed by the versions, and then the quotes of the early church fathers' commentaries. The versions of greatest importance are Latin, Syriac and Coptic. What we do not know is what type and quality were the Greek MSS which the very early translators made use of. The versions provide evidence on very early Greek MSS which have perished while, of course, the versions continued to be used and copied. Huge numbers of Latin MSS exist and bear witness to the Greek text(s) Jerome used.

One example from St. John's Gospel will help – a very obvious one. John 1:18 had two different translations. 1. …the "only begotten Son" (see KJV/NKJV) based on a majority of early Greek MSS. Latin, Syriac (some MSS), Armenian, Georgian support "Son," Coptic is confused, as if aware of both readings (NIV is still confused!). BUT, 2. the main Syriac Peshitta has "only begotten God" plus Old Ethiopic! No early version is later than the fifth or sixth century.

And in the margin he wrote, "Textual critics have to then weigh the evidence."

Yeah, of course!

(As an interesting sideline: In *A Skeptic's Quest*, Josh McDowell writes, "…I have been able to document 24,633 manuscripts of just the New Testament. The number two book in manuscript authority in all history is *The Iliad* by Homer, which has 643 manuscripts.")

Because Peter had lived and worked in salaried positions in West and East Africa most of his life, he initially found it difficult to establish a support base. Shortly after we left Africa in 1987, John A., who had been one of our main benefactors and had provided us with that Daihatsu, began to support him single-handedly for six years. He also helped Peter with the purchase of some very expensive, limited-edition tomes for his research work.

When I hear of skeptics who dismiss the Bible as unreliable, I think of Peter Johnston, one in a long line of devout men who have devoted their formidable intellects and decades of their lives to research and verify the trustworthiness of the Judeo-Christian scriptures.

10

FALLEN PEOPLE, FALLEN WORLD

...all have sinned
and fall short of
the glory of God.
Romans 3:23

The Iteso are a gentle, agricultural, and cattle-keeping people. Their homesteads in Teso are in scattered, often shrub-encircled compounds. Inside are, on average, anywhere from two to four round, grass-thatched mud huts. One of these, the smaller one with the choking smoke billowing out, is the kitchen. There are three or four slightly elevated grain-storage bins, locally known as granaries, made of mud and reeds with removable thatched roofs and a small chicken house on ten-foot stilts, with a flimsy ladder pointing the way. In a central open area of flat, hardened earth, cassava or coffee beans are dried, children play, chickens peck, and women move about busily between the huts. At the edge of many compounds is a small corral made of thick tree branches and trunks, interwoven with twigs from thorn bushes. That's where the family's cattle are kept at night.

Rounding out the setting may be several mango trees, with a few low-slung wooden chairs and a bench under their leafy canopy revealing their secondary purpose – shade. The men socialize here after working in the fields from around six until ten or eleven o'clock, when the beating sun drains every ounce of energy from even the most willing body. Any male passer-by may join the group after an elaborate greeting that includes inquiry about the well-being of individual family members and livestock. Such greetings generally end in a reciprocal singsong – high notes held for about a second and exchanged in place of words by the greeters. Then, abruptly, follow normal words in normal tones.

Passing women will kneel as a sign of respect, unmindful of their colorful dresses being pressed into the dirt. They greet from as far as twenty yards away, going through the same ritual as the men, but without looking at them. (Their avoidance of eye contact is self-effacing and should not be confused with that of men in powerful positions, whose motive is just the opposite.)

Traditionally, women and children keep to themselves and will participate only infrequently in the men's discussions. Also traditionally, they will rarely sit on chairs. Instead, they will carry on lively conversations while sitting on reed mats, where they engage in their daily chores of meal preparations that may include cleaning lentils, shelling peanuts, cutting dried cassava, or winnowing sorghum or millet. They grind grain with a two-fist-sized stone while kneeling in front of a large, flat stone that lies permanently under the overhang of the thatched roof. In West Africa it is more common to pound grain with mortar and pestle, often several women together in the cool of the early morning hours.

The lot of the African woman is decidedly harder than that of her male counterpart. To put a simple meal on the table, she must not only prepare most of its ingredients, but fetch fire wood from as far as a mile away, in some areas from even further, and cook in aluminum pots that require frequent stirring over a fire that requires frequent feeding. Between that and washing dishes, hand-washing clothes, caring for oodles of children and weeding the fields, she is kept busy from sunup to after sundown.

Girls learn at an early age to help with chores, particularly with the early morning ritual of sweeping the compound, fetching water from the well, and helping to care for younger siblings, one of whom they often carry on their backs. Boys learn to ride bicycles early, frequently older Indian or Chinese models. They may be sent to the well for larger quantities of water – two or three jerry-cans-full – or to deliver milk in the neighborhood, purchase essentials from the duka – a general stall rather than a general store – or take messages. If the parents have the money for school fees – not at all a given – the children will get an education; boys first. The men will till the soil with a hoe, or, if they have oxen or the money to hire them, with a plow. They may also ply a trade such as repairing bicycles, building, fishing, or tailoring – sometimes with ancient Singer treadle sewing machines or with newer, Chinese models.

Take away the Karamojong, and that was the picture in Teso district. But after 1980, this traditional, peaceful scenario had disappeared in eastern Teso. It had been erased by that plundering and murdering band of uncontrollable outlaws. After they had raided all the cattle, they came with women and children to carry away whatever household goods had been left behind in frantic flight.

Once, our friends Tony and Joy Otim were surprised by a group of Karamojong men breaking into their European-style house in Arapai, outside Soroti. Tony was a slender man in his late twenties. He was always impeccably dressed, wore a pair of air-force style sunglasses on sunny days – meaning most of the time – and, with a university degree in agriculture, taught at Arapai Agricultural College. When the Karamojong broke a window and climbed into his house, he, Joy, and their two daughters hid in the attic. The Karamojong departed with the usual household goods, but left his bicycle – they felt more comfortable on four hooves than on two wheels. When surprised in a cattle raid by an overwhelming government force or the Teso militia, they could drive a cow while hanging on to its side so they wouldn't be seen or, if seen, wouldn't be shot at. But they had never learned to ride a bicycle.

Iteso caught in a Karamojong raid were lucky if they were just beaten and allowed to live. Their cries of desperation saved their neighbors who fled with whatever they could carry on their heads and in their hands: rolled-up foam rubber mattresses, blankets, cooking pots, grain wrapped in a large cloth, plastic jerry cans. Older brothers and sisters, though not necessarily yet in their teens, carried their younger siblings. Babies were already strapped to their mothers' backs. Without sufficient food and no shelter, these traumatized people sought refuge by the thousands at their county and sub-county headquarters where police and the Teso militia provided security.

It was early 1981. One might wonder what the federal government was doing for the Iteso when all this was happening. The answer is simple: nothing. It was engaged in its own fight for survival. The rebels, under Yoweri Museveni, were winning crucial battles against the government forces of Obote. Museveni had started in "the bush," the guerilla-related term for countryside ("the village" is its synonym in peaceful times) fighting for the freedom of Uganda from Obote's second, tyrannical regime. However, before Museveni reached Kampala, Obote was overthrown again.

Whether in Africa or elsewhere, a man fighting for freedom may be a freedom fighter or a terrorist. Both terms are often used to describe the same people, reflecting different political, ideological, and moral perspectives. But a freedom fighter will only engage a country's defense forces to accomplish his goals and will never employ the means of terror by targeting innocent civilians. That would be contrary to his mission. If, among freedom fighters, renegades abuse their position of power by killing the innocent, then they alone are terrorists. War crimes are committed in revenge by undisciplined soldiers in every army, but, more often than not, they are aberrations. In Obote's Uganda though, the military had routinely used terrorist methods by savaging defenseless civilians, particularly in the Luwero triangle, whose population had welcomed and fed the insurgents. The skulls of hundreds of Obote's victims were displayed there on elevated platforms for up to a year after the war.

While the Karamojong were plundering, the bishop of the Church of Uganda in Teso and acting bishop of Karamoja, the Right Reverend Gershom Ilukor, sought to provide the refugees with tools to build new shelters in safer areas, hoes for tilling the soil, and seed for planting. Food was not a problem yet, because the refugees were willing to take the risk of returning to their fields to harvest their crops. They were also willing to risk the possibility of an ambush to be able to plant new crops in the affected areas.

Alfred Farris and Bishop Ilukor

Bishop Gershom was a tall and lean no-nonsense guy, and this desperate situation weighed heavily on him. The displaced had been settled into loosely-organized camps by the local government with help from the Roman Catholic Church and his own Church of Uganda. There were twenty-one camps with some 42,000 refugees. These camps were composed of mud huts – one per family – spaced tightly together. When it came to caring for the most basic needs of these displaced, neither church was up to the task. They simply did not have the resources to deal with a humanitarian crisis of that magnitude.

*　*　*

Enter Alfred and Carney Farris from Nashville, Tennessee. Both were raised in an environment of prosperity and privilege. Their wedding, some fifty years ago, brought together numerous influential people from Nashville society. Now in their seventies and still active and attractive, it is as if their youth has been preserved through their devotion to meeting the needs of others. They were members of the First Presbyterian Church of Nashville, where Alfred served first as a deacon and, later, as an elder. But despite an imposing façade, they perceived an inner void. Something was missing in their lives.

In 1970, Alfred attended a seminar on spiritual renewal in the church and came to the realization that such renewal had to start with him. He formed a Bible-study group that met in his home to consider the subject further. That small gathering became the catalyst for his and Carney's involvement in Uganda more than ten years later. Through it, they came to believe that giving priority to some of the values they had held – individualism, status, and financial success – was incompatible with the biblical position. As Alfred put it later: "Our previous lifestyle was made possible through debt, as we tried to leverage borrowed money and assets to increase our wealth." While that may be a common financial practice for many Christians, for Alfred and Carney it fell short of the standards they set for themselves as a result of their study.

Influenced by several spiritual leaders in the church, they decided to open their home and several smaller houses on their farm to whoever was interested in living and working communally in the servant spirit of Jesus the Messiah. People from all walks of life and social standing joined them.

Some learned and lasted, others didn't and left. It wasn't always easy, but it taught them to work on their rough edges as they submitted to one another and made room for each other's failings. "Iron sharpens iron, and one man sharpens another." (Proverbs 27:17)

Though none earned any income, their material needs, which they made known only to God, were always met. Once they prayed for two specific items: A cutting horse and a pick-up truck. Without divulging these needs to anyone but God, both were met within a month. The cutting horse was offered by a Texan who had sold all his other horses but didn't have the heart to sell this one; and a local woman told them they needed a pick-up truck and took them to a car dealer for a brand new one.

With numerous such encouragements, and aware of the unmitigated benefit of living simply and selflessly for the benefit of those less fortunate than themselves, Alfred and Carney decided to reorganize and align their personal affairs with the mandate of Rom. 13:8, "Owe no one anything, except to love each other" – and they got out of debt. They cashed in a life insurance policy, sold their interest in another farm, and finally sold their prize-winning home.

"When it was all over," Alfred, telling me the story, concluded, "I felt like a bird. I could fly."

That freedom was tested several years later with a sad incident, which proved their mettle. In a phone call from the post office in Soroti, Carney learned that their farm house in Tennessee had burned to the ground. Everything in it was lost. The house had been considerably underinsured. When, with tears in her eyes, she told Alfred the shocking news, he embraced her and said, "Now we can better identify with the refugees. 'The LORD gave, and the LORD has taken away; blessed be the name of the LORD.'" (Job 1:21b)

Alfred and Carney were influenced by Ron Sider's book: *Rich Christians in an Age of Hunger*, well summarized with its injunction to "live simply so that others may simply live." It fortified their resolve to find an outlet for their compassion for the poor. Apart from Jesus' own supreme example, Mother Teresa's life gave them incentive for the practical outworking of their convictions. Thus, when the opportunity presented itself, they reached out to a suffering, persecuted people. And that's where our paths would cross.

Carney and Debbie had much more in common than Alfred and I. In fact, we were and are still quite different – he, the American, college educated, formerly affluent, laid-back gentleman farmer who forsook his previous lifestyle; I, the German grade-school graduate who arrived in the United States with two suitcases, but through hard work had realized the American dream. I had also read Sider's book but, while acknowledging its noble principles, found myself more in tune with David Chilton's rebuttal, pointedly responsive with its title, *Productive Christians in an Age of Guilt Manipulators.*

In summary – there can be unity in diversity of thought. As I learned from another former missionary: in essentials – unity; in non-essentials – liberty; in all things – love. Some put more emphasis on Jesus' words to the rich young ruler who had asked what he should do to inherit eternal life. When he claimed that he had kept the commandments, Jesus replied, "One thing you still lack. Sell all that you have and distribute to the poor, and you will have treasure in heaven; and come, follow me." (Luke 18:22) Others relate more to Jesus' words in Mark 14:7, "...you always have the poor with you, and whenever you want, you can do good for them. But you will not always have me." Different situations, different instructions, but both looking out for the innocent destitute – "innocent," because the Apostle Paul exhorted that "if anyone will not work, neither shall he eat." (2.Thessalonians 3:10) In other words, according to the Scriptures, couch potatoes need not apply.

The Farrises and the Roells had arrived by different paths at the same goal – to give aid and comfort to the poor. And so, our mutual respect and our tolerance for one another's perspectives would later allow Alfred and me to work together and to see good accomplished on behalf of Him who has assured us that as little as a cup of cold water, given in His name, would not go unrewarded.

When Debbie and I first met them, they were working with the Africa Foundation (AF), a Kampala-based ministry to street children. Orphaned in Uganda's several wars, these urchins, locally known as "bayaye" (the bad ones) were roaming the streets in survival mode, creating all sorts of mischief. The AF had a caring home for them in Kampala and another one on a tea and coffee plantation near Jinja. That's where Alfred and Carney were based. They had come to Mbarara to look at the possibility of starting up another branch for the AF on a government-owned tract of land. They had heard about us – the mission community in Uganda was small in those days – and came by to see us. Fellow-wazungu, fellow-Americans, fellow-missionaries – we hit it off well immediately, and that networking would pay dividends in the not-too-distant future.

Meanwhile, acquaintances of the Farrises from the First Presbyterian Church of Nashville had founded the Uganda Committee (UC). Shunning glossy brochures and modern fund-raising techniques, this charitable organization brought awareness of the dire needs in that part of the world to its largely uninformed circle of friends with a simple letter that, without appealing for money, described the problem and the UC's desire to help. Word spread and funds came in and were used to purchase relief supplies and to pack and ship three sea-going containers to the AF.

Unfortunately for Alfred and Carney and the other expatriate co-workers at the AF, the Ugandan founder of the ministry turned out to be an unscrupulous politician whose selfish actions belied his words of Christian charity and sacrifice. He had actually studied theology in the U.S., was an ordained pastor and author of a book that could move the reader to tears. But it would seem that, in the end, he was corrupted by temptations that came with his political and spiritual status and power. "Es ist nicht alles Gold was glänzt," says a German proverb. (Not everything that glistens is gold.) Virtually all relief goods from the containers were stolen. By the summer of 1981, all expatriates decided that they could no longer be part of the organization. Before they left, even their personal vehicles, including a new Toyota pickup that had been shipped from Nashville in one of those containers, were confiscated by the leadership of the AF with threats that could not be ignored. As it turned out, that duplicitous man also happened to be the one whose guest I had been at the Apollo Hotel in Kampala on my first visit to Uganda.

All too often, regrettably, the faith-based "sweet by and by" of song is outshone and out-hustled by the tangible realities of its secular counterpart, the "nasty here and now," in a subliminal battle for minds and hearts. That was true of some of God's most trusted servants in Bible-times, and is true today, not only of formerly famous, now infamous, televangelists, but also of us lesser lights of the faith. The question, then, is not, "Did we fall into sin?" – we all do – but, "Did we get up in repentance and continue from where we had strayed?"

This is a painful subject that reemphasizes the fact that we are a fallen people in a fallen world. Even in Christian missions, a term that evokes thoughts of benevolence, love, peace, and brotherhood, relationships can sour, disappointments can break the spirit, and supposed divine leading can prove to have been a figment of the imagination. In such discouraging times, the promise in Romans 8:28 is worth remembering: "...all things work together for good to those who love God..." In some cases, such trials lead to the next flight home with unresolved bitterness; in others, they become a learning experience – the fertile soil in which faith can grow – and a steppingstone to further, fruitful service.

Our friends, the Farrises, were cut from the latter cloth. When they left the work of the AF in June of 1981, along with their daughter Evelyn and another American couple, Tim and Cathy Kreutter, they hitched a ride to Soroti on a truck that carried relief food for famine-stricken Karamoja. That vehicle belonged to a Christian organization, the African Evangelistic Enterprise (AEE). The Farrises and Kreutters were introduced to Bishop Ilukor by an acquaintance, David Wakumire, the director of an AEE orphanage in Mbale, about sixty miles south of Soroti. That evening, over a cup of tea at the Soroti Hotel, they learned from the bishop not only about the starvation in Karamoja, but about the raiding and the displacement of Iteso into camps. And he asked them if they could help with the crisis or knew of anyone who could.

At that point both couples were too worn out to make any kind of commitment. Having just waded through their own crisis, they had to pull back for the sake of their own emotional well-being and ponder their next step. They left the following morning for Nairobi and took the train from there to Mombasa on the Kenyan coast, where they agreed to split up for a month to pray and consider their options. The sounds of the breaking waves and the invigorating sea breezes would help gain a new perspective. In a Sunday morning service at a local church, Alfred and Carney were challenged with a passage from Luke 9 that concludes with "No one who puts his hand to the plow and looks back is fit for the kingdom of God." That was a message for them.

Though some of their friends back home had encouraged them to return, they, together with Evelyn and the Kreutters, returned to Uganda in an old Land Rover they had purchased on the way in Nairobi. Also in Nairobi, Alfred had managed to find a container that had arrived from Nashville and was slated for the AF. He arranged for it to be rerouted to Soroti, the first one of many that would bring much needed help. The Kreutters and Evelyn went to work with street children in Mbale under David Wakumire, the stout, light-hearted, and indeed ever-smiling orphanage director. Alfred and Carney drove on to Soroti to join the bishop's efforts in the camps.

In December, the Farrises returned to Nashville after selling the Land Rover in Nairobi. Alfred gave the proceeds to the AEE for the purchase of a small car for David, who had agreed to work in the camps, and a motorcycle for Epaphras Edaru. Epaphras was the assistant principal of Teso College and had been introduced to Alfred by David. He, too, was committed to working in the camps. Things were beginning to roll.

L. to r. Cathy and Tim Kreutter, Carney, Alfred, and Evelyn Farris

PART III

RELIEF AND DEVELOPMENT

11

SATISFYING THE AFFLICTED

*If you pour yourself out for the hungry
and satisfy the desire of the afflicted,
then shall your light rise in the darkness
and your gloom be as the noonday.*
Isaiah 58:10

The Farrises' departure for the States was not to be permanent. In March of 1982, Alfred returned with three members of the Uganda Committee (UC) to do a survey of the camps. During their three-week visit, he and the committee members agreed that the plight of the displaced Iteso deserved all the input the UC could provide. The disappointment with the Africa Foundation was replaced with a wonderful opportunity of service to a desperate people. The change required nary a shift for the Nashville organization. The displaced had similar needs to the orphans. In both cases provisions from overseas were required, but, whereas the orphans were simply met at their point of need and supported through the AF, the displaced, in addition to receiving short-term aid, were enabled to help themselves. That was an important distinction, because for the latter it preserved the dignity of a normally self-reliant people.

Having learned from the problems incurred by one-man leadership, Alfred and the UC men formed the Teso Displaced People's Project (TDPP) to serve as a conduit between Nashville and Soroti. After a remarkably short interruption, the UC would now continue to be involved in Uganda through their representatives, the Farrises, who returned to Soroti in November of 1982 to direct the work. They bought a large, used Toyota Land Cruiser in Kenya and rented a house in Soroti.

Relief and development work requires much caution to avoid ill-conceived, pie-in-the-sky projects, mismanagement, and graft. (See also chapter 14: AIDING WITHOUT ABETTING) Recognizing the importance of a local body of respected Christian community leaders to represent the interests of the displaced, Alfred asked the bishop to form a steering committee for the TDPP. Its role was to identify and prioritize the needs in the camps and to select camp committees that would help with the orderly distribution of goods and the coordination of work projects. Procuring from Kenya those supplies that were unavailable in Uganda, was also a priority.

By early November, another container was shipped from the U.S., loaded with blankets, second-hand clothing, and Bibles, and with bicycles for pastors and relief workers. Seeds were purchased; some, ironically, in Karamoja from a British mission project, others in Kenya. Alfred bought 2,500 hoes and 2,000 blankets in Nairobi and had them shipped to Soroti. A second shipment was readied and awaiting clearance by the government. Without doubt, a desperate Ugandan bishop's search and prayers had been wonderfully answered as over 40,000 suffering people were about to experience an all-out, no-holds-barred effort to relieve their suffering.

*   *   *

During their Nairobi visits, the Farrises and we reestablished contact. Through them we learned of the desperate situation in which the Iteso found themselves. Our hearts went out to them, and I felt a strong desire to become part of the TDPP's humanitarian mission. Here was an opportunity for the two-pronged involvement I was seeking: the spiritual work that is coupled with social action, which Samuel Moffet had talked about. Procuring goods, organizing their distribution, communicating the imperatives of the Word of God, thus participating in both physical and spiritual redemption – that was my aspiration.

Having begun in development in southwestern Uganda, our focus was now beginning to shift from the work in education in Kenya to relief work in eastern Uganda. Initially we remained in our home in Nairobi. We liked our little refuge on Mimosa Road, and Debbie was not anxious to return to a place that was less about the thrill of living than about the agony of survival. But she also wanted to see us engaged in work in which I could be most effective and thus fulfilled. And if that would be back in Uganda, a much needier country than Kenya at the time, then she would be at my side. I enjoyed the work in schools and felt that I was making a valuable contribution. But that involvement was part time, whereas the camps, in desperate straights, required fulltime attention. Debbie also knew that I thrive under pressure and that I am at my best when performing the type of practical work required in the camps. But, before uprooting once more, we wanted to be sure that we would mesh well with the TDPP outreach. To explore our compatibility with the organization, I discontinued my regular teaching at Nairobi's schools and began to commute every month for two weeks at a time between Nairobi and Soroti. While at home, I continued to be involved in schools as a visiting speaker.

* * *

Overland travel in East Africa at the time was arduous and dangerous for two reasons: the physical condition of many roads and the mental condition of many drivers. In the West we grow up with cars. Back home, driving is said to be a privilege, but in reality it's a forgone conclusion – everybody does it. Not so in Africa or, for that matter, anywhere in the Third World. Anyone who has braved the traffic in downtown Cairo, seen the game of chicken played on country roads in India, been a passenger on a careening bus as it overtakes another in a blind turn in Latin America, or ridden in overloaded, speeding matatus on Africa's two-lane highways, knows that safety is a luxury most of the world's countries don't offer.

When I would get back from the nine-hour drive between Soroti and Nairobi, Debbie would hear the creaking of the gate, and by the time I would come up our long driveway, she, Karsten, and Misha would come out for an affectionate welcome. Once, when I ran late, she sat on the front steps of our house, waiting, and maybe worrying just a bit. It was always nice to be welcomed with such focused anticipation.

In Nairobi, I acted as the liaison between the TDPP and the Asian shop owners. I enjoyed working with the latter. They were dependable businessmen with a welcoming smile, a warm handshake, a can-do attitude, and a hot cup of spicy chai. They were always willing to bargain. When we first established a business relationship, they sought to assure us with "you are my friend, I make you a special price," but with patient and persistent negotiation there was usually room for a better deal. Once our relationship had been established, bargaining was limited to the occasional "Is that the best you can do here?" Many were eager for our business and, if our orders exceeded their stock, would help with the procurement of the goods from their fellow-Indian business acquaintances. They would also help with the paperwork for the cross-border transport of those large orders.

Driving home from an errand in the city with the big TDPP Land Cruiser one day, I got a flat tire. I was not far from our house on a heavily-trafficked road. There wasn't any room next to the left lane, so I pulled over against the oncoming traffic onto the uneven grassy shoulder on the right that ran along a ditch. I had nothing to block the wheels, and, wanting to save time, I neglected to look for a couple of rocks. The uneven positioning of the vehicle caused it to roll off the hydraulic jack after I had removed the tire. Having now inched closer to learning that haste makes vehicles roll off jacks, I fetched some rocks and secured the Land Cruiser for my second effort. I didn't have the aid of a number of passengers who could have simply lifted the right rear end, as is the custom in Africa when there is no jack, which is the case all too often. Fortunately, I had a back-up, a mechanical high-lift jack with which I finally succeeded in mounting my spare tire.

It was dusty, dirty work, and I had removed my shirt. By the time I got home it was dusk and Debbie, concerned about my safety – Nairobi was not your safest city – was again sitting on the front steps, awaiting my arrival. Of course, she was relieved to see me coming down Mimosa Road and through the gate up the driveway. But her smiling face changed instantly into one of concern, and her voice was filled with compassion as she said, "Oh, Schatzi!" (German for "little treasure") and was about to hug sweaty, grimy me. I had exited the vehicle, briefcase in hand, with a mischievous "Well, Tweedle (my form of "honey"), at least they didn't get my briefcase." Baaad joke! Her reaction made me feel so guilty, I immediately retracted my words. Had Boots had a doghouse, I would have probably traded places with him.

*   *   *

Crossing the border between Kenya and Uganda was never predictable, always interesting, and seldom without problems. Once an inebriated border guard asked me how much of the local currency I was carrying – always a delicate subject. For us it was desirable to carry more of it than the officially permitted amount, just in case we needed it on our return when banks might be closed or we might be pressed for time. I had been a boy scout in Germany, and our motto had been "Allzeit bereit" (Always prepared). That was a good motto here, too, where most surprises were nasty. Besides, we felt morally justified as we firmly intended to return with all the money. Complicating matters was the fact that lying was out of bounds. But then, honesty has its own rewards.

The amount we had on us was above the limit, and the border guard began to give me problems, hoping, no doubt, that I would share a small portion of that money with him. But I didn't believe in paying bribes. Quickly tiring of arguing with him, I leaned over and whispered into his ear something like, "If you promise not to tell anybody that I'm over the limit, I promise not to tell anybody that you are stone drunk." That was the end of our conversation, and I was on my way.

In Africa, bribes can get people out of the most impossible situations. The Asian mother of a playmate of Karsten once ran over and killed a bicyclist. Between the victim's relatives and the police, a bribe in the thousands of dollars was demanded, and negotiations went on for a protracted period of time. Perhaps the idea that time heals all wounds came into play, as well. Eventually, a satisfactory settlement must have been reached, because she never served any jail time.

But sometimes a little commonality, a small personal touch, can create that bond that is stronger than money. On one of their border crossings, Alfred and Carney encountered a cantankerous customs official who had also imbibed on the job. Checking their passports, he discovered that their home was in Nashville and excitedly exclaimed, "Why, that's the home of the Grand Ole Opry – you go!"

* * *

I stayed with the Farrises during my frequent visits to Soroti. When they first settled there, I helped them move into one of a row of modern-looking bungalows that belonged to the East African Flying School. Situated at the outskirts of town, this area was the closest thing to suburbia Soroti had to offer and, considering the alternatives, this house was in fairly good condition. Giving the illusion of security, a fence surrounded most of the property, adorned with colorful bougainvilleas in the front – a welcoming sight.

This house sported one of the amenities that come with living in a town – running water. As in many American communities, the water was pumped into a huge, elevated holding tank, in this case two of them sitting atop Soroti Rock, a smaller, granite version of Australia's Ayers Rock. However, unlike the American system, in which the water flows directly to the faucets in the house, but very much like the system in England, Uganda's erstwhile colonial master, in Soroti it was gravity-fed into a small holding tank in the attic. That tank was equipped with a shut-off valve like that found in a toilet tank.

Some inconveniences in Third World living can be detrimental to your health if not approached with foresight and caution. In most of the developed world, one can drink running water straight from the tap without fear of repercussions. Not so in a majority of African countries. Here, part of the daily house-keeping routine is disinfecting the water by filtering it and boiling it for ten minutes. It is then allowed to cool off before getting stored in the refrigerator, generally in recycled glass bottles. In the African village, most water comes from boreholes and is safe to drink untreated, unless nearby industrial activity has polluted the groundwater – certainly not a common problem in the village, however. Investigating the source of your tap water is always a good idea, as the following incident shows.

After enjoying two or three days with Alfred and Carney in the relative comfort of their newly acquired home, he and I climbed, a little late, as it turned out, into the attic to check out the water tank. While crawling over the rafters in the grayish light that shone through ventilating louvers, we could see immediately that only half the lid covered the tank, the other half was sticking out over the edge like a lid only partly covering a pot of simmering soup. In this case, the "soup" temperature was that of an average Soroti day. And the ingredients?

Like two little boys on the verge of uncovering a menacing plot, Alfred and I crawled to the fifty-gallon holding tank. Imagine our revulsion when we saw the bodies of several bats in various stages of decomposition floating in the tank. We had been drinking boiled bat water!

*   *   *

Having met the immediate needs of the refugees in their displacement camps, we expanded our self-help program from giving emergency goods and tools for the construction of shelters and pit latrines to selling, at our wholesale cost, non-emergency goods that we purchased in Nairobi. These included replacement cooking pots in various sizes, plates and cups, plow parts, and hand tools. When the Farrises went on furlough to the States, I filled in for them for two weeks at a time and stayed in their home.

Distributing relief goods to desperate people is a major chore and can be a difficult and dangerous exercise if it is not properly organized. Even then, it can be a risky undertaking. Harry Garvin, our Baptist colleague, told us of an experience that could have resulted in serious injury.

It was a hot day in the dry season, and hundreds of people had gathered with expectation at the Katakwi County headquarters in Teso district. Dressed in rags they huddled in the protective shade of nearby trees, awaiting the distribution of emergency food. A drought had wiped out these subsistence farmers' plantings, and they had consumed the last reserves in their granaries. Many were now surviving by eating leaves from trees. Harry had informed the county chief several days earlier of his intention to distribute a pick-up load of millet to the starving. The chief set about to organize the distribution by informing the people in advance and compiling a list of the names of those in the most affected area of his county.

When Harry and his son Kenneth arrived on the prearranged day, the chief had already seated the men by their precincts in groups of twenty to fifty. Harry was no stranger here. He had already made a food-distribution for CARE, USA. Now he parked the pickup under a big mango tree whose protective shade the chief had reserved for the occasion and unloaded one sack of millet with Kenneth. The county chief called the first name on the list, Harry scooped the first portion with a gourd – and all hell broke loose.

Hundreds of people jumped to their feet and raced towards the truck as fast as their thin limbs would carry them. Dust was flying, voices screaming, bodies pushing and falling over each other. Amidst the bedlam, Harry, trying to protect the sack from getting knocked over, was knocked over himself. Other bodies were pushed on top of him. It was like a pile-up in a football game, only more ferocious, induced by survival instinct, and Harry had been the ball-carrier. Four emaciated men tried to hold the mob back and shouted that they were killing the muzungu, but they, too, became part of the mangled mess. From 150 yards away, Kenneth and a member of the local militia raced to the rescue. The militia man fired several shots into the air, which got everybody's attention. Harry managed to free one arm, with which he raised his red baseball cap, and Kenneth worked his way through the crowd and pulled up his father.

It was not always possible to avoid confusion, but, fortunately, no scenario like that had ever happened to us. It must have helped, that, in our fulltime work with the destitute, we could count on our camp committees for organization instead of relying solely on the authority figure of a county chief. The members of our committees were refugees themselves and were known and respected as elders in the camps. They were always on hand to make sure that things didn't get out of hand.

On every trip to the camps I was accompanied by Epaphras, who had become the chairman of the TDPP. Of medium height with a strong build and a keen intellect, he was a graduate of Makerere University and an eloquent communicator. As our liaison to the camp committees, we could rely on his knowledge of his own culture to help with decision-making and to communicate effectively those decisions to the displaced in our care. In his role with the TDPP he could also take his observations from the field to the committee for their input as our work developed. He doubled as our interpreter, and without him it would have been difficult to accomplish the goals his committee had set.

We visited each camp at least once a month. Following is my account of one such trip to the one nearest the border with Karamoja.

A black man and a white man in a green Toyota Land Cruiser with red Christian crosses front and back bounce over a brown strip of dirt road into the wild blue yonder, trailing a large cloud of yellow dust. The vehicle is packed with hoes, blankets and several boxes of plastic plates and cups, and hard soap. Soon the savannah opens up as trees get more isolated and the tall grass recedes.

After a drive of an hour and fifteen minutes, we reach a settlement of round thatched mud huts and three or four flat-roofed stone houses that form the closed-down trading center of this sub-county – a vestige of a more prosperous era. The large wooden accordion doors, designed to expose the entire store front when opened, are shut. A small door leads to a dingy room, where matches, candles, some bars of soap and a handful of flashlight batteries are sold.

To the east are several red-tiled buildings, euphemistically referred to as "the dispensary." One wouldn't recognize them as such. There is no medical equipment and no medicine – just marked up walls, grimy floors, leaky ceilings and a few twisted metal contraptions that resemble beds without mattresses.

A hundred yards ahead, left of the road, a group of women with plastic jerry cans and clay pots are drawing water with a hand-operated pump from a bore hole. Two pigs are half- submerged in the muddy runoff of spilled water. In one of the compounds of huts and grain storage bins, eight men are sitting on low-slung wooden chairs around a clay pot, drawing the local equivalent of Budweiser, a millet-based brew, through four-foot-long hollow branches that are doubling as straws.

At the sound of our approaching car, a mother, baby on her back and three more offspring in tow, all carrying their share of an afternoon's find of firewood in large bundles on their heads, steps off the road to let us pass. We pull into the shade of a huge mango tree. The clanging of our diesel engine gives way to peaceful silence.

Welcome to Kapelebyong, North Teso, Uganda. I am the only white man in a sixty- mile radius.

Children scamper up from all sides. Forming a circle at respectful distance, they stare at us. (Who needs ET when you have Ebu, as I am known there?) Adults follow, shooing some of the bolder youngsters away with a staccato of words and a throaty rasp that is supposed to show disapproval. Some chairs are brought and set in a semicircle near the car.

I am directed to a chair in the center. I am flanked on my right by my companion, Epaphras, and on my left by the chairman of our camp committee.

Within minutes 200-300 people have squeezed together on the ground in the protective shade. Most are barefoot. Their secondhand clothing, though patched and re-patched over the years, is tattered and torn. The protruding stomachs of some children are telltale signs of worms or, if accompanied by reddish-brown hair, of kwashiorkor, a form of malnutrition caused by a protein-deficient diet. Near the front, I spot a man whose left leg is swollen into a massive pillar from the knee down – elephantiasis.

More of the local leaders come forward to greet us. Some are relatively well dressed with tire-rubber sandals or well-worn, cracked leather shoes; some even wear watches, a reliable status symbol in the bush. They shake our hands, showing respect by holding their left hand to their right forearm. "Yoga! Yoga noi! Yalama noi!" (Hello! Hello indeed! Thank you very much!) We remain seated.

Three wizened old women approach haltingly. Starting on the right, they shake our hands kneeling, crawling on all fours from man to man. Women's Lib hasn't reached here yet. Falling back on her haunches, one of them stops in front of me. She raises both hands to shoulder height, palms facing me, as if to implore me for something I can't give or for a power I don't have, jabbering in a language I don't understand. Then she grasps my hand, squeezing it for a long time, while continuing her monologue. No one seems to notice. My mind wanders 10,000 miles away. "Yes, God, do bless America, but please don't forget Uganda."

Young women, some of them just teenagers, carry babies in their arms, or in their wombs, or both. A few are nursing. Clad in bits and pieces of army uniforms, young men round out the circle, AK-47 automatics with three loaded clips rubber-banded together at the ready – the militia. The Karamoja border is only ten miles away, and there are still cattle in the camp.

The camp chairman welcomes us in Ateso, and the people clap. Epaphras says a word of greeting, then invites me to speak. I have been here several times before and recognize many of them. I assure them that we understand their problems. All have been displaced from their isolated homes near the border by Karamojong cattle raiders. They have moved together for mutual protection, but are still exposed to occasional raids in spite of the heavily armed militia and some members of the Special Forces of the police. They are starting over.

I tell them again the purpose of our coming. Epaphras is interpreting fluently.

"We are here to help you help yourselves. This is a partnership. Without your help and cooperation we cannot help you, because we don't have any free giveaways. But we do want to help, and we do that in two ways. One, by providing you with the tools you need to carry out the projects your committee has chosen. We have left with your committee 50 hoes, 12 machetes and 12 sickles for building your

houses and the school. We have also left 12 pick-axes and 12 buckets for digging pit latrines. Two, we reward you for completed projects. If four men dig a 2' by 5' by 16' deep latrine with mud walls, a roof and a door, they get four blankets. If your house is mudded and plastered inside and out, you get one hoe, two plastic plates and one bar of soap. I understand that the chairman has a list with the names of 36 men who have built the school and 54 women who have cut the grass and roofed it. We will reward each with one blanket after we have looked at the other projects."

Then Epaphras takes over. He speaks with conviction and compassion. Now roaring with laughter, now listening intently with unfeigned interest, many recognize that we are offering more than just temporary goods that might be gone with the next attack from the east. "For God so loved the world that he gave his only Son, so that everyone who believes in him may not perish but may have eternal life." (John 3:16). *The world included the destitute inhabitants of this patch of destroyed real estate.*

After inspecting the projects and passing out rewards, we enter the home of Lucy, one of the committee members. Her household has been busy preparing supper for us. The sun is setting, casting a red glow across wispy clouds in the African sky. In the fading light inside Lucy's spacious hut a teenage girl moves around with a tin can of water and a plastic tub. Kneeling in front of each guest she pours water over his hands and catches it in the tub below. The soap is in the tub. After lathering it is put back, and the rinsing process is repeated until the hands are withdrawn. She moves on.

Lucy, standing before us, leads in a prayer of thanksgiving. The chicken is tasty but tough, and I am glad I have my Swiss army knife with its plastic toothpick with me. The broth makes the rice delicious. It is amazing what magic the African housewife in her village can work over a three-stone "stove" and without any cookbooks, cupboards, measuring spoons and cups, or grocery stores around the corner. We eat with our right hand. For dessert, Lucy serves tea with milk and peanuts.

It is dusk as we say our last good-byes. I slip behind the wheel of our green machine and in silence relax as much as the road will allow. Epaphras relaxes by chattering away, or is he just trying to keep me awake? He talks about African thought and culture, about the colonial past, about African politics and politicians from Amin to Nkrumah of Ghana and Tshombe of the Congo. There is much to learn, and Epaphras is an excellent teacher.

At Achowa are several camps, not yet well organized. In his compound we chat with the pastor of the Church of Uganda while water is heated for a bucket shower. We are offered food, but gratefully decline with a word of explanation.

At 10 p.m. Epaphras spreads his sleeping bag on a mat on the dirt floor of the church. I spread mine on the card board of an emptied box on a concrete platform not far from him. We pray. Thoughts of Debbie (and our water bed) and the kids, some four-hundred miles away, cross my mind before a tropical downpour lulls us to sleep.

Unbeknownst to us, less than a mile away, Karamojong, armed with guns and spears, abduct a family from their isolated hut, to be led to cattle. Since most have already been taken, the raiders are unsuccessful. The woman is raped and the whole family beaten, but they are allowed to live.

We learn of the night's incident during a short meeting at the sub-county headquarters. We take the violated family to Amuria which, at county level, does have medical services available. We spend most of the rest of the day in a newly discovered camp of some 260 people before returning to Soroti.

My regular two-week stint in Soroti was up, and, like a kid anticipating Christmas presents, I was excitedly looking forward to being reunited with my family. The red electrician's tape that formed the Christian crosses on the Toyota Land Cruiser was peeling from the glass. The crosses were there primarily to enhance our chances for survival as members of a humanitarian organization in a violent country. However, since we were not operating under the auspices of the Red Cross, we had chosen to extend the bottom of the vertical bar. These crosses declared that we represented an emergency-relief group with Christian emphasis – they acknowledged that we gave credit for our being there to the One who had died that we might live and love in His name. Without Him we would probably be back home, working in a regular job – perhaps chasing after a pot of gold.

But, beyond a body and a mind, man has also a spiritual dimension, and our purpose was to address that. As the French mathematician and philosopher Blaise Pascal observed, man's heart has a God-shaped vacuum. And we were there not only to fill empty stomachs, but spiritual voids as well, wherever and whenever we could. As I started on my way back to Kenya and to my loved ones, the dog ears on that most significant of all Christian symbols seemed to mirror the contrasts of good and bad, joy and sadness I had seen and sensed on this last journey.

The Farrises' three-bedroom house in Soroti had been so empty and silent. Just the month before, Debbie and the kids had accompanied me for the first time, along with three friends from our church in Colorado. Tom and Marcia Moore and Joe Hart had been sent to encourage us and to get acquainted with our new work. It had been good to introduce them to it and leave them with impressions to take back for input from home.

Still fresh on my mind was an incident on their visit that, in any other setting, would have been inconsequential. Driving north toward Soroti for our joint adventure, I remember a rainbow, the most vivid and beautiful I had ever seen. But that's not the reason it is indelibly etched into my memory. Debbie, the first to see it, screamed in her excitement at the top of her voice. In an environment in which danger was ever present – and screams suggested danger and tended to make your blood curdle – my adrenaline was pumping in a flash, and it seemed that my hair was standing on end as I screamed: "What?! What?!"

I am reminded of a time when we rented a house at the edge of a forest in Estes Park. We had gone to bed, lights out, and were about to fall asleep when Debbie thought she heard someone walking on the porch that wrapped the house on three sides. Holding our breath, we lay still to listen. Suddenly my normally cool, calm, and collected wife, just inches away, unleashed her voice in a high-pitched scream. I went flying out of bed. My hair felt as if it was standing up, Don King-like, and screaming in a voice that was hoarse from exertion, I ran through the house, ready to do battle with whomever or whatever. Out on the porch, that deer or elk must have wondered what was going on in there!

Back in Soroti with our friends, between visits to the camps and a game park three hours northwest, the house had resounded with laughter and reverberated with music and aerobic dancing. It had been a grand visit. But on this trip I had only memories, coupled with an increased sense of loneliness.

One memory was of Debbie and Marcia jogging in front of the Land Cruiser as we were going from one game park entrance to another. At the crest of a hill, about two-hundred yards ahead, I saw a black-maned lion crossing the road. I tapped the horn, Debbie turned around, and I pointed and mouthed the words, "There is a lion up there." With her elbow Debbie nudged Marcia and, while they continued to jog, passed on the information. Without so much as looking for the lion, Marcia turned, stepped out of the way of the vehicle and got back in, joined by Debbie, who wasn't interested in confronting the lion all by herself.

Events and non-events were competing for the up-and-down gradations on my emotional barometer. There was the unqualified success of our self-help program in Amuria County, which stood in sharp contrast to our failure to evoke similar cooperation from the displaced in Usuk County and from two camps in a third one. In the Amuria camps, the huts were built to the highest sanitary standard achievable in simple construction with mud, poles, and grass. All cracks in the walls inside and out were sealed with a final layer of mud to deprive insects and spiders of places to hide. The floors were smeared with cow dung. This may sound revolting, but it is an effective, strong, crack-resistant, and dust-free seal that is harmless and near odorless when it has dried. An earthen apron was built around the whole structure, "ebalasa kere," to prevent deterioration of the lower wall from water running off the overhanging grass roof during the rainy season.

In this part of the world, the largest and probably most effective pill in preventive medicine is the pit latrine. Here, in Amuria, twenty to thirty were added each week – some with great effort, as they had to be hacked through several feet of granite. Health authorities at the sub-county level had informed us of a notable decrease in sickness and death and related this trend directly to the increase in sanitary facilities.

Our work with the displaced had come to the attention of the federal government, too. Several visits earlier, I was returning to Soroti with a vehicle loaded with people, including some who where sitting on the roof rack. It so happened that the chief of police of Amuria County stopped us as we approached the town of Amuria. He was a burly man with a booming voice and fully aware of his position of authority. He stopped us. He objected to the people on top, and I told him that the laws he was trying to enforce were established by the British at the time when Uganda was still a protectorate, but that times had changed. Then, public transport was available, but now people had to foot (that's African English) fifteen miles and more to get to town.

Admittedly, I was rather blunt. Yes, I could be diplomatic, like the time I needed a favor done by an airline at Frankfurt airport without being charged for it. The pretty clerk behind the counter looked Arabic and the name on her tag appeared to be Egyptian. "You must be from the land of the Pharaohs," I said with a smile. She was — and between my flattery and her surprise, my request was granted. But to this gruff and conceited law-man I responded in a straightforward manner — a very German thing.

The chief's reason for the reprimand was out of step with the country's methods of coping with adverse circumstances in those days. Uganda was rebuilding its infrastructure, and much was done that was unconventional by prevailing safety standards elsewhere. Many everyday practices here would have been considered dangerous in any country that regulated its citizens' safety through equivalents to our helmet laws for motorcyclists. And I would do within reason whatever I could to help diminish these people's difficulties.

The officer was not impressed. He reminded me of Idi Amin as he, like the menacing boxer Amin had been, stuck out his chest and lowered his chin and glowered at me for my challenge of his authority. To look like the "Field Marshall" he lacked only the medals and the cap with the gold-wreathed visor. But I refused to back down.

Accustomed to unquestioned and subservient obedience and fully aware of more than a dozen sets of eyes and ears following our conversation, he ordered one of his men to take me to the police station. For an African that would have been a fearful prospect. But I had nothing to fear and, in fact, found it amusing. It was unheard of that a muzungu involved in relief work would be arrested. I knew he could not detain someone who was there solely for the benefit of serving the people in his care without a serious charge. Separating me from my passengers on the strength of his authority was merely a face-saving move.

Remarkably, in an area where no more than a dozen vehicles passed all day, at that very moment the Mitsubishi Pajero of the Deputy Minister of Housing and Urban Development, Ben Etonu, stopped on the opposite side of the road. Well dressed in a gray safari suit and exuding all the authority vested in his office, he came over, a big smile creasing his face. He did not seem to notice my "double-decker" passengers, and I was not surprised. He pumped my hand vigorously as he thanked me for our efforts and asked us to continue with the full support of the authorities.

Given the irony of the situation, I felt at once humbled and exonerated. For all intents and purposes under arrest by now, I could barely suppress my sense of vindication as I thanked him for his generous compliments. He then told me that if there was ever anything we needed not to hesitate to call on him. That was a carte blanche I couldn't pass up.

"Well, Sir," I replied, "I appreciate that offer. You could help me by keeping the police off my back."

Not unlike the Hutu general in "Hotel Rwanda," who castigated a hotel worker insubordinate to the manager, Mr. Etonu turned to the now stultified, embarrassed enforcer of the law. If, as an African, the officer could have blushed earlier, his face would now have paled, as he was reprimanded in no uncertain terms. The tension in the hot afternoon air dissolved, like a shimmering mirage that recedes at forward movement in the desert, into the freedom to pursue my work without restriction. If my passengers had felt free to clap they would have, and there was much laughter as we traveled on and they retold one another the story of what had happened. It was nice, I must admit, to have my own personal cheering section.

We arrived in Soroti with our two-tiered load of grateful almost-pedestrians. From then on, whenever the police chief would see me, he would wave with a big smile as though we had been buddies for a long time. There was a rapport between us now, brought about by a shared experience and an intervention on behalf of people in our charge. I wonder how Dale Carnegie would have looked upon this example of how to win friends and influence people.

*   *   *

Our joy at our success in Amuria County was partly offset by the unresponsiveness to our offer of practical help in Usuk County. Between packing and unpacking the car, changing flat tires, and digging ourselves out of mud holes when even four-wheel drive left our Land Cruiser a useless hunk of metal and us sitting ducks, Epaphras and I felt as if we were doing more work in each Usuk County camp than 400 men headed by ten committee members with molasses in their veins.

We were also at a loss as to how to change the situation. We were certain that, once the program would take hold, its benefits for the people, going far beyond the material incentives we offered, would make it self-perpetuating. The question was how to make this horse drink after we had led it to the water.

Then we had an idea: On a prearranged day, call it G-Day for "Get up and Go," we whisked six chairmen and five committee members from six Usuk County camps to three of our Amuria County camps. To accomplish this undertaking during daylight was nearly impossible. On the other hand, after dark, the risk of a Karamojong ambush was many times greater. Therefore, when we did get up and go, we moved with German precision in this sleepy African countryside and flew over its dirt roads as though we were on a debilitated Autobahn. In each Amuria camp we were warmly welcomed and taken on a tour by the committee chairman. He proudly showed off the improved living conditions and pit latrines throughout the camp. A number of refugees testified to the success of our work with them and displayed some of the rewards they had earned by carrying out their self-help projects.

After the tour, we were invited into the chairman's home for a brief exchange of ideas and a final challenge to our Usuk County guests over chai and freshly roasted peanuts. Before the day was over, they had been powerfully challenged, a fact to which they testified in numerous speeches. But time was pressing, and we regretted that we had to urge them to keep their remarks short. Epaphras and I were encouraged when our unofficial safari rally ended in Soroti thirteen hours and two-hundred-seventy miles later.

But there was one more contrast I shall never forget. We were on the last leg of our return trip with only three more chairmen and two committee members to be dropped off at their camps. In one of the most violent tropical storms I have ever witnessed, we were slipping and sliding in four-wheel drive over a soft dirt road that had turned into a riverbed. Trying to maintain our momentum without slamming into the ditch made steering more like steer wrestling. In the descending darkness, the buckets of water that poured down from above were met, it seemed, by barrels of water and mud that splashed up and over our seven-foot-high vehicle from below.

Then, suddenly, the rain stopped. Black clouds, etched against the deepening blue of the evening sky, were still menacing. But, as we came out of a gradual curve, there, right at the end of a long stretch of the narrow road, was the orange ball of the setting sun. With rain drops reflecting its last rays on trees and on the tall grass that whipped against the sides of our passing vehicle, everything glistened in a splendor that spoke of life, beauty, and the love of a caring Creator. I thought of a German song, "Auf Regen folgt Sonne" (Rain is followed by sunshine), but then started us into an Ateso song of praise, "Ejokuna edeke, ejokuna eka edeke" (God is so good, God is so good to me).

But that was all part of the past. Now I was looking forward to my reunion with my family in about nine hours, provided the border crossing would be smooth and there would be no surprises on the rest of the journey. Debbie would tell me of the fortnight's events, Karsten would show me his newest Lego contraption and Misha would tell me of her latest accomplishments in the swimming pool. They would both challenge me to a wrestling match, and we would roll on the floor like puppies at play. Part of the game was to shout "Kaugummi, Kaugummi" (German for chewing gum) while trying to nibble on each other's ears. There would be letters to read and answer, reports to write and maybe a speaking engagement to fill. There would be big and little involvements with people and other ministries, a date with Debbie to one of Nairobi's many fine restaurants and, before we knew it, the green machine with new red Christian crosses would be on the road again, heading west.

But that was all part of the future. Presently it was heading east, encapsulating me in my own modern world as I sped past a way of life that has changed little in centuries. At the sound of a vehicle, the farmers in their fields and the pedestrians by the road turned their heads. They saw a muzungu with a wire wrapped over his head and two small disks over his ears. His mouth was moving. *He must be talking to someone I don't see*, some must have thought. Maybe so. One of the reasons I was there was to help them see Him.

The voice of Keith Green started into another song; "Holy, holy, holy, Lord God Almighty! Early in the morning my song shall rise to thee." And so it did, that early morning in September 1983.

12

BACK TO UGANDA

*Prosperity is not without many fears and distastes;
and adversity is not without comforts and hopes.*
Francis Bacon

In July of 1984, the LaPointe family – Bill, Betty, and their four children – came for an extended visit. They were members of our church, and our missions committee had encouraged them in their desire to uproot for six months for an African adventure in short-term missions. They had also been neighbors, only four houses down the street from us when we had lived in Boulder.

Bill and Betty were an adaptable, capable, and independent couple. I appreciated Bill's companionship in work and play. And play he could, as well as work. He was athletic, a former number one in hand ball doubles and number three in hand ball singles in Colorado. I had been introduced to squash in Nairobi, officially known as squash racquets and started in England in the 1850s, and had played enough to hold my own as a recreational player. For Bill it was a new game and, while I held him off for a while, he caught up soon and then overtook me in Soroti's colonial-era court.

Bill was as straight as an arrow, positive to a fault, and always eager to tackle anything the day might bring. He simply did not seem to be able to express a negative thought.

I watched him play squash against Harry Garvin once. Harry and Doris had worked for some twenty-five years among the Iteso with the International Mission Board of the Southern Baptist Convention. Harry had a heart bigger than life itself. He loved God, and he loved the people he served. He spoke their language fluently and had established congregations throughout Teso. Debbie and I became regulars at the Sunday-morning gatherings in his and Doris' home.

When it came to squash, Harry was also very competitive. Short and powerfully built, he was an excellent player, having started when the British colonial government was still running Uganda. When I first played against Harry, he asked me if I wanted him to go all out or if he should go easy on me. When I expressed surprise at the question, Harry explained, "Well, you know, we missionaries are generally a tough and independent lot. And sometimes pride gets in our way." Oh yes, I knew! And a good share of the time, Harry had no problem keeping me humbled.

Bill and Harry slugged it out one day in a tough, close match. I was watching from above the back wall of the semi-open court as the ball, the bodies, and the sweat were flying, mixed with grunts, words of disappointment that didn't need to be beeped out, and laughter at some incredible shots. At one point Harry had moved Bill out of position and delivered a hard, low shot along the right wall. As Bill moved laterally across the back of the court, he yanked his racket from the backhand to the forehand for the return shot. The combination of his right leg in forward motion and his right arm whipping the head of his racket from behind, twisted his torso, injuring his back. He lay on the floor for several minutes and could barely crawl out of that court, but dismissed the injury as temporary and not that serious. Harry must have included short-term missionaries when he had talked about a "tough and independent lot."

Betty was athletic herself, holding her state's high school one-mile track record for several years. Like Bill, she exuded a good deal of self-confi-dence backed by a cool head and a practical streak. As a fellow home-school teacher, she was a support and encouragement to Debbie as they forged through this new endeavor together.

Their children, Abby, Zak, Adam, and Aaron were well-behaved and became close study and play companions to Karsten and Misha.

We had planned to move to Soroti from our home of two years in Nairobi after returning from the States, and the LaPointes' coming coincided fortuitously with that move. They could not have chosen a more convenient time. They booked into the Mennonite Guesthouse, which, only 200 yards from our home, was at the beginning of Mimosa Road. Then Bill and I went to Uganda for two weeks, and his family moved in with mine.

We traveled there to find permanent accommodations for us and, if they proved too small for our two families, temporary ones for his. In the latter attempt we were successful as we secured the house of friends, Ted and Hilary Mason. Ted worked as a layman with the Anglican Church in Soroti and would later become not only my squash partner but my companion in several, let's just call them "challenging," experiences. The Masons were returning to England for a six-month home leave. Having found a home for the La Pointes, we had accomplished half of our objectives.

As we started on our way back, we were anxious to see our loved ones. We noticed a bird flying alongside us as we traveled south. It was carrying a branch in its beak. As it was racing us on the west-side of our Nairobi-bound car, it seemed to be as determined at building a nest as we were at finding one. I thought of Jesus' words, "Foxes have holes and birds of the air have nests, but the Son of Man has nowhere to lay his head." (Matt.8:20) We still had, if barely.

Every trip confirmed to me that to continue indefinitely my monthly commute of 700 miles on African "highways" was, apropos, for the birds. Those roads were extremely dangerous, especially after dark. Our friend, Tim Kreutter, had lost his mother when, blinded by oncoming traffic, their Land Rover slammed into a broken-down truck that blocked their lane. There had been no warning; the truck had been unmarked and unlit.

Additionally, we needed to be together as a family. My priorities had always been God first, family second, work third. Yet for the latter I had to be in Soroti, and that called for a move. We had already given our landlord notice. Bill and I had made this trip with the first boxes of our belongings, driving the TDPP Toyota Land Cruiser and our Daihatsu. Now we were returning with some prospects, some promises, but still no premises.

Three days after getting back to Nairobi, Bill and I returned to Soroti in one car to put feet to our prayers. Rentals were hard to come by. Available properties were often badly run down and, by western standards, uninhabitable without renovation. We found a single-story, three-bedroom, two-bathroom house with a large entry, parquet-floored living and dining room and a kitchen with a pantry – no wonder the cockroaches liked it. It was on a third-of-an-acre corner lot with a broken-down barbed-wire fence, a heavy double-drive iron gate, a paved road in front and a dirt road along one side. The neighbors next door were John Ateker Ejalu, a Member of Parliament, and his wife, Janet, their four sons, and two big dogs.

The proximity of a government official promised improved security for this house, and their dogs could join Boots in a chorus of barking, should circumstances warrant it.

The East African Flying School (EAFS) had leased the house for the previous five years and was interested in renewing the lease. However, the tenants had not endeared themselves to the owner. There was an electric range in the kitchen, and, like many items that had been imported into Uganda from overseas without sufficient spare parts and experienced maintenance personnel in the country, it had reached the local level. It was not only out of commission – it was filthy and banged-up and should have graced a junkyard.

That was not much of a bother to the EAFS employees. They had just left it sitting there and worked around the problem by preparing meals on an open wood and charcoal burner on the kitchen floor. (Had they been airplane mechanics, I would have been reluctant to fly their airline!) Since the door to the kitchen and the hand-through to the dining room had been left open – probably since they didn't shut properly – the walls and ceilings were sooty throughout the house. The walls were also grimy from the hands that had stabilized bodies over the years that had passed since the interior had last been painted – which had probably been at the time the house was built.

In Soroti's hot climate, one would expect such a run-down place to be a haven for cockroaches, and, sure enough, it exuded that distinctive cockroach smell. In short, the house had seen better days and would need extensive cleaning and painting before I would want Debbie to lay eyes on it. Leaving the comforts of Nairobi would be challenging enough. I wanted to do everything I could to make her new environment as welcoming as possible.

That was precisely the attitude the owner was looking for. He knew that wazungu had higher living standards, more money to effect the changes desired, and the cultural sensitivity to appreciate the difference between cooking in a kitchen and cooking in a campground.

A U.N. family from Australia was interested in the house as well, but the husband was too laid back to compete for it successfully, and we became the new renters. I signed a contract with the landlord's lawyer, a western-educated man, who seemed to be as interested in our satisfaction with the arrangement as in that of his client. We negotiated several months free rent in return for our renovation of the place. This included repairing the fence with barbed wire, which, along with the paint, would have to be imported from Kenya.

I remember the lawyer emphasizing a specific point at the bottom of the contract. It assured us of "quiet enjoyment of the premises." In the western world that might suggest a rendition of "Für Elise" wafting through the open window from the neighbor's house on a dreamy Sunday afternoon. But in Soroti, "quiet enjoyment" was to become a rarity, and one couldn't just hire a lawyer and take the offenders to court – not without a gun battle, anyway. And that would ruin any dreamy Sunday afternoon.

Our Soroti "premises"

Bill and I set about to transform the place. We started by spraying roach killer around all the woodwork. The next morning we swept the critters up – about a gallon of them. I am reminded of an outhouse in a compound in West Africa. Debbie and I had been invited by a Senegalese man to stay at his place, one of many rooms off a courtyard with a communal toilet. As usual, I had pioneered the way to the comfort station and found that it was not all that that description cranked it up to be. I warned Debbie. I just told her to keep in mind that cockroaches neither jump nor bite. She remembers the experience well and has recounted it off and on over the years in different settings, making me more aware just how much that warning had meant to her. It helps me to further understand that even little events can create life's fond-after-the-fact memories.

We hired three young men to wash down the walls and ceilings with soap and bleach. We left one four-by-eight-inch rectangle at a corner in the hall. I taped it off carefully at about chest height, so that the scrubbing of the walls around wouldn't damage the "art work" that had taken years to create. I wanted to preserve it in the current condition for a case of "show and tell." It would also make the painted areas look all the better, since in its contrast a matter is magnified.

Then we painted with the best available latex paint we could buy. Like the milk in those days, it came watered-down, but at least we didn't have to boil and filter it. It took two coats and seven gallons just for the walls, and we still didn't get total coverage. Nonetheless, at the end of that exercise we had, what an English friend called, "the nicest house in Soroti."

Before Bill and I returned to Nairobi, we poured "Doom" powder around the woodwork to kill any cockroaches that had survived the first assault. We would sweep up another gallon upon our return. Later I discovered a way to rid our home of those pests for good – I killed them at their base. I lifted the lid to the holding tank of the sewer in our yard and fumigated them there. They were so crowded in there that it was not surprising they had used our house as overflow accommodation.

If "U-Haul" is "Adventure in Moving", then what was our haul? Two four-wheel-drive vehicles with nary any sitting room and four-foot-high loads on top, a refrigerator sitting on boards outside the back of one of them, followed by a car with anywhere from four to six children, the number depending on who wanted to ride with whom from one break to the next, and a seventy-pound dog. We blended right in with local haulers. Debbie and Betty alternated driving our Fiat behind Bill, who drove the Daihatsu behind me in the "green machine." From six in the morning to nine-thirty that night we moved with only brief stops in between. But the trip went relatively smoothly. Crossing both sides of the border was surprisingly easy. I think the officials had come to know me by then. Additionally, although we traveled in the rainy season with almost daily downpours, we were grateful that it didn't rain once during the whole journey.

* * *

"Adventure in Moving"

One of Debbie's concerns was for honest, dependable house help. Part of our Third World experience encompassed a myriad of daily chores practically unknown in our advanced western societies. There was the ongoing battle against dust whipped up by vehicles and wind from the unpaved road on the side of our house. Since we had to keep the windows open in the stifling heat, the dust came in and, if the electricity was not cut, was distributed by whirring fans. It descended on everything.

With no washer and dryer, clothes and linens had to be washed by hand and hung out for drying. Most air-dried clothes needed to be ironed. Food was bought in the market, washed, and disinfected if eaten raw. Prepackaged goods were only available in Kenya, so that most everything had to be made from scratch. We baked our own bread and, when raw cow's milk was available, churned our own butter. Water had to be filtered, boiled, and stored in bottles in the fridge. When the town's water failed to come into the tank in the house, we had to haul it from a hand-operated communal borehole before the tank was empty. This could take as much as an hour. The dishwasher was not mechanical but flesh and blood – our trusty houseboy, Dennis.

I have heard of Westerners who arrive in the Third World with a know-it-all attitude and look askance at the idea of employing someone to do their "dirty work." They mean well, certainly, but behind their idealism is a naiveté that could be labeled "newcomer syndrome." I never had any qualms about giving locals an opportunity to do a service for us in exchange for remuneration. It is a simple business proposition. Nobody is forced, and both parties benefit. Besides, even at a median-income level, locals themselves, with rare exceptions, hire full-time help for mundane chores.

There are several practical problems associated with refusing to employ house help. First, newcomers who do everything themselves don't tend to last long, at least as "help-less" individuals. Common sense kicks in sooner or later. Not only might they ruin their health, but they wouldn't find the energy or the time to perform the task that brought them to their new home in the first place. Secondly, they deprive locals of the opportunity to earn an honest living. In our case, we not only paid above the going rate, we fed our house help and would pass down clothing to them and their families. For that we were much appreciated and often looked up to as parents by those who derived financial stability from us.

Word spreads quickly in Africa, and on the first day in our new home a young man jingled the chain on our gate. He was looking for work. Julius Omutu was sharp, single, and in his early twenties. He knew me from visits to his village area, about nine miles from Soroti. He did not have any experience working for Europeans, but his bright countenance, his good command of English, and his outgoing and friendly way convinced us that he was the right person for the job. He was with us for only about two months. His clean exterior concealed a troubled interior, and, after we caught him in some shady dealings and lies, we had to let him go. Several years later, while still in his prime, he died of heterosexually-contracted AIDS.

Dennis Epiu came recommended and proved his mettle with us for the rest of our time in Uganda. He was about the same age as Julius, quiet, attentive to our every need, with serious demeanor and few words, though his English was good.

The Farrises eventually rented a house on the other side of the Ejalus, two houses down from us on the dirt road. Their houseboy, Moses Orieki, worked for us part-time as a gardener, car washer, and gatekeeper, and, when we ran out of water, he hauled it with his bike in jerry cans from the borehole. Like Dennis he was in his early twenties. He exhibited a positive attitude, was always deferential, and one would have been hard-pressed to discourage his smile.

Part of his job was to clean up behind our dog, Boots. Other than our cars, we couldn't leave anything in our fenced yard overnight, because it would be gone the next morning. (No, I'm not talking about that!) That included the poop shovel. Once, after Moses had performed that chore, he brought the shovel into the house unwashed. After Debbie had made him aware of that faux pas, Dennis looked at her and asked something like, "Did I do silly stuff like that when I first came?" I'm not sure what Debbie answered, but that incident showed in a small way the difference between city and village life.

We were grateful that we had dependable help in Dennis. We could leave every three weeks for our "visos" – visits from Saturday morning to Sunday afternoon with Karsten and, later, Misha at the boarding school in Kenya and know that our dog and our place were in good hands. Since we did not have servant's quarters, Dennis rented a room nearby, but slept in our house whenever we were absent.

Near the time of this writing we learned that Dennis has died. We are not sure of the cause. But death in Africa comes more prematurely than almost anywhere else in the world. Several African countries are at or near the bottom of the world's longevity list. To be sure, AIDS is a major contributor to that unfortunate distinction, but violence, poor sanitary conditions, lack of proper health care, and starvation are not far behind. I can think of a dozen friends and acquaintances that have died from violence or AIDS. Epaphras Edaru, my close companion in our work with the refugees, would become, several years later, one of those who met a violent death.

* * *

Without doubt, the greatest adjustment Debbie and I ever had to make was putting our children into boarding school. Though part of life for many expatriates, it was certainly not our first choice. Initially we decided to educate them at home but, with many other distractions, we had no idea of the obstacles we would face. We were not prepared to deal with the emotional strain home-schooling put on our family, especially on Debbie. Even now, here in the U.S., with all the resources and home-school support groups at one's disposal, it can be a challenge, though an eminently worthwhile one. In Uganda, after the first year, lots of prayer, and some outside counsel, we looked into other options.

St. Andrew's School, Turi, was a British-run boarding school in the Kenyan highlands west of Nakuru, a good five-hour drive from Soroti. Situated at an altitude of some 8,000 feet in beautiful, wooded surroundings with large, manicured lawns, it had a cool climate and could have easily passed for a place somewhere in the U.K. St. Andrew's had an international atmosphere, with children of expatriates from all corners of the globe, as well as some of well-known Kenyan and Ugandan politicians and well-heeled businessmen. It had high academic credentials, and its uniformed students were held to strict behavioral standards.

While all that was small consolation for the price of separation from our seven-and-a-half-year-old, we knew that we had to make that sacrifice for his sake. There he was challenged intellectually, socially, and physically, and we quickly saw that the benefits outweighed the heartache of separation. There was also a spiritual emphasis with Sunday chapel services, a voluntary Scripture Union assembly, and Christian teachers. His love for sports gave him plenty of opportunity to develop close friendships. As a second-grader, Karsten became one of three boys to represent the K-8 school in squash tournaments and proved to be St. Andrews' best ping-pong player.

But parting was always painful. I remember specifically one day after we took him back from his first five-day break with us in Soroti. The children got five days off every six weeks. We had picked him up with plans of camping several days at Lake Baringo and taking in a game park. But it had been Karsten's call, and he wanted to go home to play with Boots and ride his bicycle. Now we had returned him to his school. As we said good-bye, he started to weep, clung to us, and would not let go. When we finally tore ourselves away, he ran behind the car crying desperately, and we, too, cried as we sped away. It was gut-wrenching. I still cringe today at the memory. At the time we consoled ourselves in the knowledge that he would forget

Karsten and Misha at St. Andrew's

our parting sooner in the company of his friends than we would with the empty seat in our car, the empty spot in our hearts and the picture of our frantic little boy embedded in our minds.

The decision to send Misha to Turi a year later would create a bittersweet experience. We would sorely miss her joyful disposition and mourn the new void her departure left in our hearts and in our home, even as we would be glad that they had each other. Karsten would always make sure to look after his little sister, and she would stop by his dormitory every evening to receive a good-night kiss.

13

WINDS OF CHANGE

*Life can only be understood backwards,
but it must be lived forwards.*
Sören Kierkegaard

The TDPP was transforming life in the refugee camps. With our cost-free inputs we had enabled all families to build their mud huts and the heads of households to dig communal pit latrines. We had provided the camps with thousands of blankets and with access, at minimal cost, to several tons of seed, thousands of hoes, cooking pots, sufficient spare parts to repair some 2000 ox ploughs for those who still had animals, fishing nets for refugees near lakes, and many of the essential items one would normally find in a typical African trading center or market, apart from food stuffs, which the refugees still planted and harvested in their fields.

One day I received a letter from a longstanding friend and leading elder in our church, Marvin Dunaway, in which he reminded me of the importance of meeting also the deeper spiritual needs of the local population. I needed that reminder. Marv was a family physician and as such, his life's work was caring for the physical needs of those who entrusted themselves to him. That kept him busy not only during the day but, when he was on call, on many a night, as well. Knowing about busyness and where the most important verities of life reside, he pointed me back to them. We did proclaim the Good News to many receptive hearts and minds in the camps, but there was no time to teach in depth, to make disciples as Jesus had instructed His disciples. One can get so caught up in the dire physical needs of the destitute that there is little time for much else. The Farrises had enough African co-workers now to carry on the work, but I was not aware of anyone training local church leaders. Since my leaving would not create a major void, I was free to move in that direction.

With over two-thirds of the population professing to be Christians, Uganda is by popular definition a Christian nation. Why, then, was the place in such a mess? Why had Christianity not permeated the country enough to give it political and social stability? Why had Christianity not overcome the two greatest scourges of the African continent – tribalism and corruption? (AIDS was not yet an issue at the time.)

One likely answer to those questions is found in the history of Uganda. Following a report by the Anglo-American journalist and explorer Henry Morton Stanley in 1875, the first British Protestant and French Roman Catholic missionaries arrived at the source of the Nile within two years of each other. Christianity, in other words, arrived in the form of two rival tribes, and they began to vie for converts with all the material, intellectual, and spiritual means at their disposal.

When we first reached Uganda, I learned of cases where the arrival at a church compound of a sea-going container with relief goods from well-meaning Christians in America or Canada was used to bribe the faithful to leave one denomination for another, because "we have a shirt for you also." Yet the responsibility of the Christian community is not to steal "sheep," symbolic of Christ's followers, from other churches, but to steal "goats," who are wandering about without any knowledge of redemption, lest they be separated from the sheep on judgment day (Matthew 25:32-33).

The first missionaries arrived on the shores of Lake Victoria with a message of hope and with good intentions but, instead, ended up bringing about division and strife, even as they claimed to be spokesmen for God. This is not to say that they didn't have the population's best interests at heart. I don't doubt for a moment that most, if not all of them, brought their own message of salvation with conviction and dedication. But the rivalry became so heated, that in 1892 armed intertribal conflict broke out. Protestant and Catholic members of the Baganda, Uganda's largest, most dominant tribe, fought each other. The Protestants won, if it can be called that, when Captain Frederick Lugard machine-gunned the fray their way, and the Catholic mission was burned to the ground. There is no greater dichotomy than seeking to bring people to Jesus Christ through means so diametrically contrary to His life and teachings. Power grabbing, greed, and arrogance stem from selfishness. Jesus' life was marked by service, sacrifice, and humility.

A cursory look at the country today reveals that these early "men of the cloth" had a good measure of success. Even in present-day Uganda, churches are full every Sunday, and people respond in droves to midweek religious gatherings. Gospel preaching in weekly village markets by men with megaphones and plenty of zeal attracts attentive audiences, with individuals kneeling unashamedly in the open to make first-time or fifth-time commitments to Christ. There's a lot of religion here, and religion feels good.

And that's precisely where the problem lies – the vicissitude of feelings in place of the certitude of conviction and accompanying commitment. Among Uganda's dozens of denominations many leaders, even those with training from Bible schools in Kenya, but especially at the village level, were more concerned with emotional appeals than addressing the down-to-earth realities faced by the common man. It seemed as though theology was taught without emphasis on the practical outworking of that theology in the nitty-gritty of daily life. In theological terms, the problem in the Christian community – comprised of those who were active church members of whatever denomination – was more one of omission than commission, namely friendly, smiling people caring mostly about themselves.

As a result, those outside the Christian faith were attracted to Christ not so much by what they saw in His followers, such as sacrificial love and concern for the welfare of others, but by stirring, vociferous speeches and emotional appeals. This resulted in Christians with shallow lives – Christians who lived out their faith only as long as it was convenient. While, admittedly, the temptation to surrender one's principles to convenience is universal, one to which I, too, have succumbed at times and have to guard against constantly, there was plenty of opportunity to work alongside the leaders of several denominations with practical suggestions for Scripture application in every-day situations and to say, "Hey, let's walk this road together."

Mahatma Gandhi is said to have rejected Christ because of the shortcomings he saw in "Christians." Gandhi was one of the greatest humanitarians ever to walk the earth. But he, too, was fallible, and for his sins, too, Christ paid the ultimate price. It is not wise to seek to hide behind an object smaller than oneself, and hiding behind those lesser than he was Gandhi's most egregious mistake. There are many today who, like he, reject the Messiah because of the failings of man-made institutions and their shenanigans. Specious televangelists, self-appointed prophets of doom, and other talking-heads with fancy hairdos and three-piece suits may be an improvement over the Crusaders and the Inquisitors, but they still serve to emphasize the tragedy of a morally challenged church that has rites, rituals, and stirring oratory but, all too often, little or no life. Nevertheless, whoever points a finger at others has three pointing back at himself. Christ's call is not to follow people and institutions. His call is to deny ourselves, take up our cross daily, and follow Him.

History is replete with people and movements that have shown the way to God from the day of the resurrection to the present. Even in the darkest of times, God had a remnant, not unlike those 7000 in Elijah's day who, imperfect as they were, hadn't bowed their knees to the heathen god, Baal. Among them: Saul of Tarsus, who persecuted the early Christians and later became Christ's most vocal advocate; Augustine of Hippo, who lived a life of debauchery until his conversion, after which he became a major influence on the Christian movement; Martin Luther, the Augustinian monk, who pointed a wayward church back from selling indulgences to salvation by grace through faith; Mother Teresa and her Sisters of Charity, who in the name of Christ reached out to the downtrodden in societies worldwide and continue to do so since her death; Billy Graham, who preached to some 210 million people in 175 countries, offering life and hope in the name of Christ. None of them is/was perfect – all have/had their faults and failings. When Christ brilliantly saved the woman caught in adultery from sure death by stoning as permitted in the laws of Moses by asking those without sin to throw the first stone, they all had to turn away. The One who could have broken the deadlock and thrown that first stone was He Himself; but He loved and forgave her.

Becoming a follower of Jesus Christ is not like joining a club by signing on a dotted line. It is a turning away from a self-centered life to one in submission to Him and His teachings as found in the Christian scriptures. This results in a transformation of the mind, affecting our motives, our goals, and our conduct. Because of human nature which, though redeemed, is still susceptible to temptation, our transformation needs to be nurtured in the company of the like-minded through mutual encouragement in Scripture exposition, prayer, repentance, worship, and fellowship. Whatever additional expressions of faith may be unique to one denomination or another, groups that follow those minimal practices are part of "the Church," the world-wide Body of Christ.

And so Marv Dunaway reminded me of the need not just to reach out to the uninitiated, but to make followers of the greatest leader ever. Jesus had admonished His students to make disciples. That calls for mentoring – teaching, spending time with them – not to *show* the way, but to *lead* the way. That's what He did – on-the-job training by example. There were many committed pastors and laymen in Uganda who could preach with fervor, but few of them knew how to make disciples, what in business might be called "training mid-level managers." As a result, there was plenty of emoting and shouting, but there wasn't much depth.

* * *

I was invited to speak at a village church the Sunday after the arrival of Marv's letter. My theme was discipleship. At the end of the service, the leaders invited me back for more teaching. I accepted on one condition: that they choose from among themselves twelve leading men and women to attend that meeting and no more. I told them that if Jesus settled for twelve, why should we settle for more? That was a new concept.

The next day I drove the thirteen miles north to our meeting at Ochuloi. Almost there, I veered off the dirt road onto a footpath that didn't look as if it had ever seen an automobile before. Through the stillness of a hot, lazy Monday afternoon I bounced along on parched earth and dry grass. For miles around, the only sound came from chirping birds and the clanging of my Daihatsu's diesel engine. But soon I could make out faintly the voices of men, women, and children singing. There was drumming and clapping, and it grew louder as I got closer to the meeting point where I was expecting twelve adults. Within minutes, the need for practical discipleship was reinforced to me. It seemed the whole village had turned out. There was lots of excitement as my vehicle came into sight, with children scampering all over the place, women ululating, and men obviously proud of the good turn-out.

We hadn't even started our meeting, and I was still shaking hands with this exuberant throng of people surrounding me at the car, when this chaotic scene motivated me to chuck my prepared lesson. Had we not just yesterday agreed that the class would have no more than twelve students? Here was a mob - welcoming and enthusiastic, but a mob nevertheless. The situation provided my teaching points:

- Noise is rarely a substitute for anything.
- More is not always better.
- Activity is no substitute for productivity.
- Agreements are made to be kept.

It was almost painful to watch these well-meaning friends quiet the enthusiasm and send most of the revelers home. This muzungu had just stuck a needle into their festive balloon, and now the party was over before it had ever started. It took them about half an hour to trim the number of attendees down to twelve church leaders and to create an environment of distraction-free learning. We met in the semi-dark of the rectangular mud hut of the denominational leader, who was then in Nairobi for theological training.

It was oppressively hot outside, but the hut was pleasantly cool. Ugandans, like indigenous people everywhere, adapt to their environment with products they fashion from readily available materials. Both the grass roof and mud walls were about six inches thick. Between the walls and the overhanging roof was an eight-inch opening all around, broken up only every foot or so by thin vertical supports of the roof structure. That opening, the open door, and four two-by-one-foot glassless windows with open wooden shutters allowed a breeze to waft through the room. In the corner was a clay pot covered with a plastic dinner plate that held an enameled metal cup – more village technology: The water it contained was cool because the pot was porous and allowed the water to evaporate. It was borehole water, drawn from a depth of 180 feet, and did not require boiling, even for a more sensitive muzungu stomach. There was a large table with three chairs on one side, and simple benches lined the walls.

My foundational lesson was from Luke 2:52, "And Jesus increased in wisdom and stature, and in favor with God and men." I used this verse to emphasize the importance of a well-rounded Christian life. We need to grow:

- Intellectually – God has given us a mind to use;
- Physically (or, in the context of African poverty, materially) – It is ungodly for a pastor to go out to talk about God while, back home, empty granaries leave his family hungry;
- Spiritually – The Scriptures enjoin us to make disciples and to look out for the welfare of others.

- Socially – We Westerners can learn from Africans about that. I had nothing to contribute.

Subsequent lessons dealt with other subjects, such as:

- Liberality – not hanging on to what is yours for all you're worth.
- Dependability – the ability to be depended on.
- Punctuality - 15 minutes early is preferable to 5 minutes late.
- Accountability – the ability to not count in your favor.
- Perseverance – hanging on instead of letting go.
- Initiative – is self-explanatory. It's spelled with four "I"s. It's up to YOU!
- Excellence – striving for the best – doing it right the first time.

All in the group were in their twenties and all but one spoke English. David Elweu was a former witch doctor. How wonderful it was to have him with us. Someone translated for him quietly. Soon a young teacher named Jackson Mugerwa stood out among that group as the above attributes began to crystallize in his life. Jackson was about 23 years old (that's how he put it – "about," as he wasn't sure himself.) and, in addition to being fluent in five tribal languages, spoke English well. He didn't miss a meeting in six months and was nearly always on time, though he came from several miles away and had to remove his clothes to wade through a swamp to join us.

What I brought to these eager learners was totally new to them, and word of our meetings spread quickly. Within a month I had invitations from several areas and various denominations to start instructing their leaders. They were eager to be challenged with down-to-earth biblical concepts they had never heard before, nor, for that matter, associated with the basics of a God-honoring life. Eventually our work would grow to twenty-four classes and cover most of the Teso district.

It has been said that there are three types of people – those who make things happen, those who watch things happen, and those who don't know what's happening. Jackson fell into the first category. He became my regular partner as he caught on to the value of working selflessly with church leaders irrespective of their denominations, and he made that his priority.

One evening as we returned from a meeting in Usuk County, an area bordering on Karamoja and particularly poor even by Ugandan standards, he suggested to me that he stay an extra three days after our next visit to spend more time teaching. When I mentioned to him that he would only be able to teach in the afternoons since they would be cultivating their fields in the mornings, he suggested that he could plant with them.

But there was more. Jackson had a plan. He informed me that he would bring his own food and, from his own supply of sweet potato vines and cassava stems, plant a field together with all the men of the class. He was telling me indirectly that he would teach all day long – by deed first, then by word.

Now, this generosity may not sound all that unusual to the average Westerner. But in a country where nearly everybody was just trying to survive, often at the expense of others, and the word of the day had been "looted" every day for several years, this was a big deal. Marxism and socialism don't work because they don't take into account the selfishness of fallen human nature. In Uganda, the prevailing motto was "everybody for himself" – and here was a man who demonstrated the change that's brought about when the vision of discipleship becomes real.

One time Jackson went by bicycle into the same area with one of our men. That night, after dark, Karamojong cattle raiders attacked. There was shooting and shouting and running all over the place. Because of that proximity to Karamoja, nobody spent the night there if he didn't live there; nobody except Jackson and his companion. But the latter never returned after that. Jackson, though, remained undeterred.

I was invited once to fill in for a lecturer from America who had to cancel his commitment to a Church of Uganda conference in Tororo. I accepted on the condition that I could share the lectern with someone I would bring with me. From all over eastern and northern Uganda came Church of Uganda priests with their black suits and starched white collars. By contrast, Jackson Mugerwa didn't even have a proper suit and tie, and I had to help him get appropriate clothing for the occasion. Most of the clergymen were older than Jackson – some could have been his father – but when he spoke with clear exposition, targeted illustrations, and a passion that betrayed his unswerving conviction in what he communicated, he captured their attention. After each of his sessions he was surrounded by the priests in their formal garb as they wanted to hear more. In a country

With Charles Orieba, preparing to go to the village

where cameras were still uncommon and people went to photo-studios for their family pictures, he had his picture taken several times. The clear communication of truth relevant to lives surrendered to the Almighty is attractive.

I had rigged up my Daihatsu to carry five bicycles. I had also made small, portable blackboards. I would carry five men with their bicycles from our first class in Ochuloi into an area where we had established several classes. Once there, they would disperse through the countryside to teach about the transforming power of discipleship as well as reading, since most of the villagers were illiterate. The local people, though poor, would show their appreciation by feeding us. Their hospitality made them full participants in our efforts to help them, for it legitimized our work and opened them up for further blessings from the One who said, "Give, and it will be given you..." (Luke 6:38).

One day, as a number of us were returning from a fulfilling day deep in the village, one of our men came up with a new idea. Clearing his throat, a serious look on his face, and speaking with unaccustomed formality he said: "Now, Brother Eb, now that we are moving up and down, going here and there, don't you think we should organize?" I had expected the subject of organization to be raised inevitably and was surprised it hadn't been brought up sooner. This man was suggesting that we form an organization, which would involve writing a constitution, electing officers, registering with the government, designing a letterhead (probably for fund-raising purposes), and holding regular board meetings.

Several years after that question had been posed, a recent graduate from a Nairobi Bible school, an acquaintance and widely respected spiritual leader, came to me, a folder in hand. After exchanging common pleasantries, we sat down with a cup of tea and cookies, and he divulged his plan. He would start a new denomination, open a Bible school, build a conference center, establish a vocational training school and rehabilitate the local radio station for gospel preaching. He had already drafted the constitution to be presented to the government for registration. He had also printed stationery, with his name and exalted title. Rather than putting his newly-acquired learning, his initiative, and vision to good use with an existing ministry and pooling with it the overseas financial contributions that alone could fund such projects, he preferred to go it alone.

"So, what do you think, Eb?"

Now, you must remember that I am 100% German, and we Krauts speak our minds. I looked at him, smiled, and said, "Well, Brother, there is only one thing you have forgotten."

"What's that?"

"You haven't planned to pave the roads on which your evangelists will travel."

And now here, on our way back from Usuk County at the end of a productive day together, my fellow-disciple, companion, and soul-brother asked me about forming an organization. I answered his question with a question.

"What would that accomplish that we aren't accomplishing already?"

Since he didn't have a ready answer, I helped him by recalling that Dr. Donald Grey Barnhouse, a famous American preacher, once said that we have X-number of denominations and each one of them was born in pride. I added that forming an organization would rightfully raise suspicion of our motives. It would diminish our effectiveness, as we would likely be more interested in building our own little kingdom, than benefit the churches and, ultimately, the Kingdom we were serving. In other words, forming an organization would be self-defeating in that it would feed our pride and destroy the very purpose for which it would be formed. Many ministries had been started with noble intentions but then were sidetracked by secondary issues and eventually collapsed under the weight of bureaucracy and dispute. I said, concluding, that we want to be slow and steady and persevere in selflessness and humility and only that way would we continue long after some top-heavy organizations have collapsed.

I am reminded of a quote once given in a speech by Dr. Vernon Grounds, the former head of the Denver Theological Seminary: "There's many a man with a gallant flair who's galloping off to the fray. But the man who counts is the man who's there when the smoke is cleared away."

Without flair or fanfare we went about our business of teaching the leaders of Soroti's numerous denominations. If our work proved its mettle, we would indeed be the ones who count, who would still be there long after the smoke is cleared away.

14

AIDING WITHOUT ABETTING

*The more that is given the less people will work for themselves,
and the less they work the more their poverty will increase.*
Leo Tolstoy

In July of 1984, I wrote the following to friends and family:

Greetings from America the Beautiful. We are on a three-month furlough that includes visits to Holland and Germany. The words of the Declaration of Independence pinpoint to us returnees what is beautiful about America and, for that matter, Western Europe – men free to discover life and happiness.

But freedom without restraint leads to problems. The fruit of the Holy Spirit is self-control, and to the extent that we lack it, we lack another part of that fruit – joy and peace. (Gal. 5:22) It would appear that many of us in America have taken too much liberty with our lives, and our happiness has suffered.

But to anyone with Third World experience it is self-evident that, what is largely taken for granted as an inalienable right here, is a rare experience amidst the planet's community of five billion – political, intellectual, and spiritual freedom and resultant prosperity. Our prosperity translates into self-sufficiency in five areas: Food, clothing, shelter, healthcare, and education. Obviously, many are "less equal" than others: not created so, to be sure, but man-made and, often, self-made so.

To the elite in our society, prosperity may mean Chateau Briand, Gucci shoes, a mansion in Malibu, the best medical facilities in the world, and the Ivy League. To many it means a square meal, comfortable shoes, a four-bedroom – two-bath house, Blue Cross and Blue

Shield, and a good college education. Are we too comfortable, too pre-occupied with self?

It seems to me that the question is not "What have we done with our opportunity?" but "What have we left undone?" Opportunity carries with it responsibility, which translates into accountability. Most of the Third World is suffering from hunger and disease, victimized by political oppression, corruption, and economic mismanagement. Meanwhile most of the industrialized – or is it now computerized? – world asks, "Am I my brother's keeper?" One side is fiddling while the other is burning. The words of Jesus remind us: "...one's life does not consist in the abundance of his possessions." (Luke 12:15) Mother Teresa proved that. So did Howard Hughes. True happiness comes from surrender of man and means to Him who came that we might have life and have it more abundantly.

But no matter our spiritual persuasion, even nature teaches us: The Dead Sea is dead because it has only an intake; no outlet. The very waters of Israel's Jordan River, that bring life to the fertile Jordan valley, flow into a stagnant sea and contribute to the mineral build-up in water so potent that life cannot exist in it. Are we stagnating in our prosperity? "Let each of you look not only to his own interests, but also to the interests of others." (Philippians 2:4)

To be sure, we didn't have any Guccis in our closet. But we did have some extra dollars to help on a small scale those in our Ugandan circle of friends who lived from one harvest to the next.

Helping faithful men to provide better for their families was right in line with our objectives, and so I started a revolving-loan fund (RLF). $50 would buy a bicycle, which would enable a man to ride to the lake, buy fish and charcoal, smoke it there and bring the preserved fish back for sale in his village. $50 would also enable a man to hire oxen to plow land left uncultivated for lack of money. Cowpeas could be harvested within three months of planting. That was good. It enabled our limited fund to revolve in a timely manner. Cassava would take two to three years – that would put people on too long a waiting list. I loaned the money without interest and would be paid back within six months. Thus the fund revolved. Since the exchange rate did not keep up with runaway inflation, I had to maintain the value of the fund. But the material help to the borrower and his family, and the learning opportunity that came with responsibility were well worth the cost.

The two biggest projects I funded, both for overseers of their denominations, were $150 each. One was a fishing project for David Eguru who lived near Lake Kyoga. With his loan he built a narrow, twenty-four-foot-long boat, bought a dragnet, and paid the wages for two people for a month of fishing on the lake. The other was a burnt-brick project for Job Eliru, who would later become the chairman of the TDPP. That loan paid the wages of eight men to build two five-foot high, thirty-foot by twelve-foot open-sided grass shelters for shade-

Two brick ovens, one not yet mudded

drying bricks. It paid also for simple equipment, for the labor of mixing clay and water by stomping it with bare feet, forming the brick, felling trees for firewood and, finally, for building the oven and firing it. The oven was built with the raw brick and covered with mud, so that it became the product itself as it burned. With another $50 loan Job planted fast growing Australian Eucalyptus trees to replace the firewood he had used to fire the brick. Stewardship of the environment is part of discipleship also.

One day, Joel Ekiru, one of our disciples, visited me. Joel was in his early twenties and a recent university graduate. He had a wide face with pronounced cheekbones and could easily have passed for the younger brother of the Hutu general in the film "Hotel Rwanda." Joel could listen with such intensity that a frown formed on his face but then, usually ended up flashing a big smile while responding. Since the death of his father several years earlier, he had taken on the responsibilities of the head of the family and was struggling to pay the school fees for several of his younger siblings.

We were talking in our living room over a cup of chai one day, when I had an idea. I had to drive to Tororo the following morning, about 85 miles south, so I asked Joel what they grow in Tororo that is ready for harvest and not grown in Soroti.

"Onions," he replied without hesitation.

I asked him: "How would you like to go with me to Tororo tomorrow and buy onions?"

A slightly embarrassed look came over his face. "I would like to," he replied, "but I don't have any money."

"Never mind that. I've got the money."

The next morning Debbie provided us with boxes, sacks, and shopping bags; anything that could hold the onions. About ten miles from Tororo we turned onto a small dirt road and within a mile came upon fields of onions. Joel was right. There were the green shoots and in the ground the bulbs, ready for harvesting. We found the owner near one of the fields. Joel negotiated a price per kilo with him for all the onions in the field – a little back and forth bargaining – and an agreement was reached. I left to take care of business in Tororo, while he joined the owner and two of his sons to harvest the onions.

When I got back, they were in the process of weighing them with a mechanical crane scale hung from a tree: 135 pounds for 35,000 Ugandan shillings, about $17 at the time. I paid, we loaded up and returned home, excited that this part of the endeavor had met with good success.

I was really impressed with Joel. Everything had turned out the way he had predicted – onions ready for harvesting at the precise place he had told me. And, indeed, there was immediate demand for them in Soroti. Upon our arrival he put samples into a bag and went out finding buyers. By evening he had commitments for nearly all of them from two restaurants and two or three Arab grocery stores in Soroti. He delivered them the next morning and sold the rest at a discounted retail price to expatriates. He doubled his money and paid me back. That, too, was discipleship. Consideration of others, cooperation, initiative (what my African friends called "starting force"), diligence, and an enterprising spirit, all fused prayerfully to yield encouraging results. Indeed, everybody benefited; the farmer with an easy sale, Joel with free transport and the briefest of loans, I with the satisfaction of having made a difference that hadn't even required any sacrifice.

There was also one long-term project. Timothy Okalani was a furniture maker in his early thirties. He had lost most of his tools in a burglary of his work shop. As a result, he had to lay off his two helpers and could barely support himself and his family with what tools he had left and some borrowed ones. Over a period of a year and a half, I purchased in Nairobi handsaws, planes, clamps and whatever else he needed to revive his ailing business. Whenever he had paid off one tool, I brought him another, until he had a fully-equipped shop once more and could employ two workers once again. Alfred and Carney Farris hired Timothy to make their furniture after they purchased a house several years later.

With this RLF we enabled those living hand to mouth to plant larger fields and fill their granaries, start up small, simple businesses, and create jobs. Of thirty-one projects, only one was a failure, and I had to reclaim a bicycle. At one of our classes in South Teso a farmer made this observation, "Other missionaries have brought us the fish you have talked about. You have shown us how we can help ourselves and one another. You have brought us the hooks." I could not have asked for a bigger compliment.

Poverty was widespread, and I considered only family men who were trusted disciples, since that vastly increased the chances for success of the ventures as well as for the repayment of the loan. The development assistance worked because the project idea came from the recipient and was governed by simple guidelines. I assessed the level of need and the merit of the applicant for a loan. In the evaluation of need I had to be cautious. My perception might differ from local perception. Seneca said: "It is not the man who has too little, but the man who craves more, that is poor." Therefore, refusing to imitate Madison Avenue, I sought to meet need, rather than create a perception of it.

Once I had identified a worthy prospect, I made sure that project projections were realistic. The Book of Proverbs says that "the eyes of a fool are on the ends of the earth" (17:24). Initial enthusiasm does not assure long-term endurance. There was no substitute for success in the long-run. After a loan was made, I closely supervised the faithful use of the funds for their intended purpose, which had been outlined in a simple, one-page contract.

I provided plenty of coaching and encouragement, and sometimes exhortation became necessary. I made clear from the outset that, in the unlikely event of a delay in the repayment of the loan, it was imperative to alert me early, so that I could reschedule and not lose confidence in the borrower. That was an important aspect in learning at least three character traits of discipleship – accountability, initiative, and communication.

For the sake of total disclosure, I have to add that, with all the tangible success I had with my small RLF, there was also disappointment. As already indicated, I have always believed in reciprocity – one good turn deserves another. We are blessed that we might be a blessing. Beyond elevating the standard of living of some few individuals, I had hoped that, once they would be reaping the benefits from their loans, they, in turn, would help other trustworthy people in need. And I encouraged loan recipients to do just that. Unfortunately, I learned of only one second-generation loan. The expectations of the extended family in Africa exert on any prospering family member, a description with a low threshold, instant pressure to share. That results in the African equivalent to our revolving-door welfare system: it creates dependency and disincentive.

Our revolving fund was an example of microfinance. In the January 14, 2006 issue of WORLD magazine, founder Joel Belz wrote about a front-page story of the December 19 issue of the *Wall Street Journal*:

> *If, whenever you ponder the immense problems of the African continent, you don't think about the role of microenterprise and microfinance, it could be that you're just not thinking small enough.*
>
> *The very enormity of Africa's challenges might tempt you to reason that only enormous programs with equally enormous budgets can faze them. AIDS and poverty and tribalism and famine and endemic corruption in government are not likely to be brushed aside with light-weight efforts.*

Belz then goes on to juxtapose a failed scheme in Swaziland by the evangelical author of *The Prayer of Jabez*, Bruce Wilkinson, to that of nineteen-year-old Peter Brinkhoff, who started a microfinance project with Hope International in the Democratic Republic of the Congo.

Wilkinson's project envisioned the building of 50,000 cottages for a million AIDS orphans and intended to charge Americans $500 a week to live with and mentor the children in those homes. To cater to our low tolerance for hardship, I suppose, a theme park and golf-course was planned

– all that and more calling for an investment of over 50 million dollars, which, as Belz wrote, "was going to take a lot of Jabez-type praying."

Brinkerhoff's project, on the other hand, had "a simple strategy of feeding a modest stream of capital into the local economy, from the grassroots up, and then watching it have its effect." He trained a team of loan officers to supervise the projects and monitor the loans. In nine months the scheme funded 800 projects with about $50,000 dollars. The repayment rate for principal and interest was 95%.

Large schemes tend to be inefficient. They may work nonetheless, but only as long as there is on-going funding, management, and monitoring. But let the donating agency stop the flow of money and organizational support, and the project is likely to die and become another example of a project grandiose in conception, poor in planning, and inadequate in execution.

Outside of Soroti was a bushy area strewn with the carcasses of green German Deutz tractors. I don't know the history of these, but I'll venture a guess: A well-meaning organization introduced them into the local economy to help the farmers increase their productivity. But the recipients used them not only for plowing, but also as taxis to shuttle people around. Of course, some of the proceeds of the increased production were used for fuel and oil, since those machines wanted to eat also. But most of the balance was pocketed and maintenance was neglected. When one broke down, it was sidelined and cannibalized for spare parts for the other tractors. Eventually they all suffered a premature demise and ended up in that junkyard.

That project lacked, without doubt, firsthand knowledge of local realities and the institutional commitment to long-term training and monitoring with financial accountability. It was another example of what I wrote while still in Uganda: "Between the West's coaching and Africa's poaching there may soon be more white elephants than gray ones."

* * *

In the summer of 2005, several cities hosted Irish rock star Bob Geldorf's brainchild "Live8" concerts, whose aim was to get donor nations to cancel billions of dollars in debt relief. Since this is my pet peeve, I will add a few more thoughts on this subject.

Writing about the transitory nature of fads (specifically of rock stars' temporary engagement in the plight of the world's poor) I wrote in a letter to my church from Kenya in June, 1986:

The hippies were followed by the yippies, who were followed by the yuppies. Then came – let's call them the happies – Hunger Alleviating Pop Personalities. I trust that long after the hype is forgotten, the hope of the world's poor is still recognized to be just that. Meanwhile let us realize that 'Live Aid' for the dying and 'Sport Aid' for the weak is but a band-aid for the cancer of hunger and poverty. It's good. It's also not enough.

Perhaps their ultimate value is not measurable in dollars raised, but in their raising, at least temporarily, the level of consciousness in our smug societies to the grinding poverty in which most of us who "... are the world" (remember the Coke ad?) are languishing. But let us not think that "Hands Across America" will break poverty's grip across the world. More money is not the answer. Look at Zaire (now the Democratic Republic of the Congo): One of the world's richest nations in natural resources, it is also one of the poorest in per capita income. Its president, Mobutu Sese Seko, with a personal fortune estimated at $4 billion, is only about half as rich as Ferdinand Marcos, the past president of another aid recipient – the Philippines.

One problem, I think, is such lack of political will that it borders on political ill will. Take Ethiopia: While Mick Jagger and Tina Turner were gyrating-in millions of dollars for Ethiopia's starving, the Marxist government was dancing to a different drummer – millions of dollars and no sense were spent celebrating the 10th anniversary of the removal of Emperor Haile Selassi from power by the Dirgue. To help offset the rash bash, ships bringing American grain for their starving population were charged for the privilege of unloading the free, compassion-borne food. How do you say "chutzpah" in Amharic?

Shortage of grain is certainly not an issue, as some opponents to certain fast-food chains and grain-fed beef would have us believe. According to the March 31, 1986 issue of Newsweek, Asia, North America, and Western Europe are awash in grain. The U.S. Department of Agriculture has predicted a world grain surplus of 300 million tons by the end of 1986. A quarter of India's population lives day to day with famine, while the country's granaries are packed to capacity and pyramids of sacks stand in the open air – a 32-million-ton surplus.

Despite rampant government abuse of power, the bad consciences of Africa's former colonial masters outweigh reason. And Western handouts continue to perpetuate dependency and, indirectly, poverty itself.

And that brings us back to the Irish rocker. According to editor Mindy Belz in the June 25, 2005 issue of WORLD magazine, Tony Blair named Geldorf "to an international commission on Africa, which concluded that donor nations must eliminate more than $40 billion of debt owed by 18 of the world's poorest nations, including 14 from Africa, by writing off the debt and increasing multilateral aid." Belz continues:

Western nations have been down the debt-forgiveness road, writing off $33 billion in debt for 41 poor countries from 1989 to 1997. Yet those same countries incurred new borrowing totaling $41 billion, according to a World Bank report drafted by New York University economist William Easterly. 'African governments could not repay zero-interest World Bank loans that required no repayment until 10 years after the loan was made and then had a 40-year repayment period,' wrote Mr. Easterly in an editorial appearing this month in The Independent, a London daily.

Nevertheless, "Live8, ONE, Make Poverty History, and the Long Walk To Justice, are all part of the latest gizmo-laden, concert-driven, wristband-toting, venue-hopping extravaganza powered by aging rockers and their fans in search of – and perhaps sincerely committed to – a cause," writes Belz.

I have no doubt about the sincerity of the celebrities. I just wish that, to avoid graft at all levels, more attention were given to the details of distribution and operation – to where the money meets the need, because that's where the rubber meets the road.

15

THE GRASS SUFFERS AGAIN

When two elephants fight, the grass suffers.
Kikuyu proverb

It was not long after we had moved to Soroti that Yoweri Museveni's rebel movement advanced on Kampala. The Obote II government had been ousted and Tito Okello, the Acholi general, was in power and fighting for his and his government's survival.

But in the late fall of 1985, hope for a peaceful solution to the conflict dawned on the horizon like the morning sun after a cold dark night. "Peace at last" shouted the headline on the cover of the National Review, a Kenya news magazine. Over a period of four months, the two main groups of Uganda's warring factions, Okello's Uganda National Liberation Army (UNLA) and Museveni's National Resistance Army (NRA), had hammered out a comprehensive peace agreement under the chairmanship of Kenya's president, Daniel arap Moi.

The elation proved precipitous. Setting their hands to the lofty lawyer lingo of a legal document was easier than overcoming the scourge of tribalism and giving up the hate and violence they had developed in years of fighting. Uganda had become a self-devouring monster as people had perished by the tens of thousands. Even today's villains were tomorrow's victims. The only end in sight seemed to be that which comes out of the barrel of a gun. The peace accord, though signed, remained a dream.

Kampala fell to the NRA in the third week of January 1986. UNLA soldiers, mostly Acholis, but also members of other northern tribes, were fleeing through Soroti on the way to their tribal homelands. They still had their guns; they were still dangerous. Along the marauding soldiers' route north, all the officials of the defeated government - the district commissioner, the county and sub-county chiefs, and the police – had deserted their posts and fled into their villages in the countryside, leaving a power vacuum.

The defeated army was retreating from Kampala with anything that had wheels. They fled in cars – from rickety jalopies to government limousines – on buses and trucks, on tractors, motorcycles, and bicycles, all commandeered at gunpoint. Only two soldiers would fit on a bicycle, but 200 would squeeze inside and on top of a bus, hang out of windows and, with sufficient handholds, sit on hoods and stand on bumpers; a wild gang of fighters uncontrolled by any authority. They would carry with them the most incongruous assortment of loot – cassette-radios, foam rubber mattresses, whiskey, you name it.

By the time they reached Soroti, some 180 miles northeast of Kampala, many, especially those on foot, bicycles, and motorcycles, had lightened their loads by shedding their loot along the way. Some were left only with their guns and up to six magazines of bullets rubber-banded to the one clipped into the gun. Guns were better than credit cards – no rejections, no limits, and no reckoning in the form of bills. If a vehicle ran out of fuel or broke down, it would be left by the side of the road, or in the middle. Who cared? Vehicles with blown tires continued running on rims – up to sixty miles of grooves in the pavement remained as evidence.

Yoweri Museveni, an Ankole tribesman, and just seven other soldiers had launched a five-year guerilla campaign in 1981 to oust the Obote II regime. By 1985, his handful of loyalists, with the support of the Bantu tribes of southern and western Uganda, had swelled into a disciplined and formidable force. The NRA proved strong enough to execute a violent coup d'état that Okello's new government couldn't stop.

Mao Tse-tung once said that political power grows out of the barrel of a gun. Perhaps nowhere else is this more evident than in Africa and particularly in the Uganda of the 1970s and 1980s. To Museveni's credit, he did something unheard of in African politics: In November, 1994, he sent a plane to Nairobi to return his former enemy, General Tito Okello, from exile, allowing him to live out his years in his home in Acholi.

Soldiers from the Iteso tribe, with whom Debbie and I worked, were also among the fugitives. When they reached Soroti, they were home. Some hid their military background and kept their guns for nefarious reasons. A few identified themselves with their guns and were eager to help secure the town against their former comrades-in-arms.

The following is my diary account of the most volatile days. I had sent it with an introduction to our church and to our supporters back home. Later I added comments in brackets for explanation – the parentheses are part of the original diary.

Many of you prayed for us during what, after Debbie and Misha were air-lifted out of Uganda by the UN, became the most dangerous days of my life. The fact of my being able to write to you is evidence of God hearing your prayers. On several occasions I walked the edge, though never losing a sense of control. You may ask why I, as a missionary, got involved with Ugandan soldiers. I saw the need to fill, for the sake of peace and security, a vacuum left by the authorities. I don't know how much property was saved or how many lives, if any. I do know that my involvement was appreciated by the people who were enslaved by fear. I was free of fear and therefore enabled to establish connections and leverage that allowed me to work on containment of savagery.

Here are notes from my diary from Jan. 25 - Feb. 8 when I arrived at the Kenya border with the Kreutter family. Jan. 25 was written 'live'.

Jan. 25 *I have just brought my typewriter down from the attic again to bring you up to date. The quote from Jesus in John 14:27 is appropriate: "Peace I leave with you; my peace I give to you. I do not give to you as the world gives. Do not let not your hearts be troubled, and do not let them be afraid." If you did not know our situation you wouldn't think anything was unusual. Things in the house are calm. If you did know, you would rather have us back in America. I feel a bit like a war correspondent just now. We woke up this morning to gunshots just a few blocks away. Just now gunfire is starting up again. It's no further than a few blocks away. Now an artillery shell exploded. I could hear it whistling overhead. (It's good when you can hear the explosion!) There's a war, and now it's in Soroti. This morning it was only individual shots. Now it's rapid fire. Soldiers have fled the fray in Kampala and are commandeering vehicles to get home to Acholi. To rule by intimidation they are shooting into the air. Nobody has been killed yet. Debbie and I moved our most important belongings into the attic last night. This morning we added more. Excuse me while I play a game of UNO with Misha.*

In spite of constant troop movement by our house, mostly with looted goods from local stores, none attempted to get our cars. Tim [Kreutter], a U.S. co-worker in the ministry to the displaced, walked over with his houseboy. We discussed the situation. In the afternoon I returned his visit, walking through town center. Not many soldiers around. People are huddled in small groups. They are fearing the night. [At night, shooting increased, much of it into the air. We could tell the trajectory of the bullets as they zipped over houses, because about every fourth one was a tracer bullet.] I found Tim with the remaining two UNICEF men who were contemplating leaving through Karamoja. But presently the danger is just driving out of town. Those two have radio contact with the police who advised them to sleep in the bushes opposite their house. Kreutters, Newmans – a new couple with the World Bank – and we will stay put. There's another addition to our little white community, John [Mattison], a mechanic whom I met in Kampala in 1980. Masons are on the [Kenyan] coast. If we decide to make a break for it, we will go in convoy. It will take a bit of doing for me to get mobile again. I have disabled both cars.

Jan. 26 *Much looting and shooting during night. House across street looted by 20-30 people hauling jerry cans of paraffin, all locals, but with help from army. [It is likely that the army forced these civilians to carry the loot for them.] Find Tim at Toni's (Toni and Rudolph with UNICEF) discussing possibility of going out through Karamoja. Toni and Rudolph want to stay. Back through town. Many shops looted, one burning, restaurant bombed out. Back to Tim's at pm. Shooting 100 yards away; cut down alley, across sports grounds. Tim at Newmans. At 2 p.m. 8 soldiers heavily armed arrived at Kreutter's. Tim met them at gate. Have driven from Mbale (60 miles) on rim. Request Land Cruiser spare; respectful, courteous. Leave 3 wheels of wrong size. [Debbie, Misha, and I] Move in with John at Masons', racing with Daihatsu. Sleep in car top tent. Can't stop Boots from barking. Get down to put him into back of car. Confronted by 4 soldiers. "Father, we are hungry, tired. Give us bicycles, give us anything." "Why are you here? Should be guarding town from looters!" They disappear. Minutes later shoot locks off Bishop's store. Get rice, powdered milk for selling next day. [As I was talking with those soldiers I got stung on my neck by a wasp from a nest above us. I did a little dance and swatted at it and let out a nice Christian exclamation, hoping it would appear as though I hadn't* *a concern in the world. Debbie, in the tent just feet away, could hear everything, of course, and was praying up a storm. One of the soldiers commiserated with me, "Yes, Father, I got stung also. See here?" It was too dark to see anything, but it gave me a rapport with him – we had something in common. You just don't kill someone who has "suffered" the same fate you have.]*

Jan. 27 *Walk to town early. Shirro (Arab mechanic + trader 2 blocks from our house) robbed twice during night; glass on cars smashed; lost everything but life. I'm grateful for angels. More shops looted. Fewer people, soldiers around. Kreutters move in with Newmans. I go see Teso commander at Liberty Bar – new "Command Post". Drinking beer – they say its "breakfast." Some haven't eaten in 3-4 days. District Commissioner and Bishop keep distance. Police have fled. I try to work out security for town w/them. Get Tim and Toni. Toni offers UNICEF Land Rover pickup for patrol. I go home. Hear UNICEF plane. Circles low. Tell Debbie to get ready. Run to Toni's. On way alert Newmans. Plane now circling 20 minutes. Near Toni's I get picked up by Tim w/patrol. Get Toni, go to airport. Plane just landed. With patrol to Newmans- they'll stay. P/up Debbie and Misha. Airport. Toni and Rudolph wanted to stay to help organize security, but ordered to go by UNICEF. Pilot has difficulty starting 2nd engine. They're off and so are tons from my shoulders. With commander I work out stationing of troops around town to protect civilians – for food. I station myself in patrol P.U. behind cab with soldiers on both sides, guns on roof of cab. More soldiers behind us. Guns, grenades, 1 M.G., rocket propelled grenades, the works. Motley crew, caps on every way but correct. Francis on my left wears black, long-haired, curly woman's wig. We catch a soldier looting hostel. Others have run; mattresses, etc., dropped over 50 yard area. Take to nearby Muslim center. Ali, UNICEF driver, African father – Swedish mother, tough, smart, very helpful. We patrol until 2:30 a.m. No looting, no shooting until we catch guy stealing beans from warehouse. FEDEMU soldier (guerilla movement aligned w/Museveni) shoots into air at 1 a.m., my guys almost kill him; short fuses! Whew!!*

Jan. 28 *At 6:30 Ali picks me up; more patrolling. Towns people grateful. But soldiers stationed at Muslim compound, UNICEF houses, have looted those places and disappeared. Tim suggests we repair power. Get UEB repairmen (Uganda Electricity Board), add more* *soldiers,1 on bumper, 2 on hood, 2 in cab, 3 w/me behind cab, about 10 behind us, moving fortress. Tim joins, go to Kumi (some 25 miles towards Kampala). On way disarm several soldiers on foot, bicycles, 180 miles from Kampala. Mango grove confrontation. "Sisi na sisi!" (Us and us – we're together) [We could not disarm those guys as they had taken cover behind trees and refused to surrender their guns which they had leveled against us. We had to avoid a firefight. Rather than shouting back and forth, I felt more personal contact was needed. I left my position in the vehicle and with arms raised walked up to them and asked them not to bother people in town, hence their reply "Sisi na sisi." They understood, and we hoped we had a gentlemen's agreement. That's all we felt we could safely do.] At Kumi electr. men restore power. Soldiers start into town. Tim + I go ahead to calm people. At shuttered shop women looking through cracks see us – start rejoicing. We're signs of peace and security. [Here I was referring to Tim and myself. Most whites in Uganda at that time were missionaries and aid workers. As such, we enjoyed the trust of the people. Women feared soldiers in those days for obvious reasons. I still get a bit teary-eyed when I think back to that situation with those frightened women and the difference our white faces made.] Buy bananas and sweet potatoes for hungry troops. [In those days soldiers didn't buy ANYTHING.] Return to Soroti. On way start water pumps at Awoja. Agip tanker with troops on top passes. They're waving. [We] Reach Soroti, pass Agip station and tanker. Troops had hijacked it in Mbale. We get called by driver for help. Troops want him to drive to Gulu (Acholi) [district]. Fears for his life. Careen back. On turn into station Ali almost rolls Land Rover. One soldier falls off, gun, grenades and all. One of the others grabs [his own] grenade. They're about twenty, as are we. (But we roared in and have aggressive momentum.) [I suppose Tim's and my presence made a difference, too.] Tense moment. Guns ready. Much shouting. We promise other transport. They get off. Start walking. Now we have 1700 liters diesel to help retreating troops move to Lango + Acholi. (Trucks, buses passed Soroti running low on fuel. Kept many soldiers in town. Now we could supply.) My right knee swollen from walking, standing in P.U. By evening stiff. John anoints my knee with oil, prays. No immediate effect. Bed at 8:30.*

Jan. 29 At 3 a.m. can't sleep. Knee perfect. Praise God. Take Daihatsu out first time. Look for Ali at wrong place. Drive into town to start patrolling. Can't get soldiers. To town center, Muslim compound, shut off engine, look for soldiers. [Our own!] Full moon. Silence - not even any dogs around. Want to move on, but faithful Lady Di (Daihatsu) first time ever, won't start. What timing! Get tools out, clean battery cables and sing "What a friend we have in Jesus". [I sang with full voice for a witness to our Asian and Arab Muslim friends who had sought refuge in the Muslim association compound and found that it also had a reassuring effect on me.] Get started. Find Ali. Suggests we help FEDEMU [Federal Democratic Movement, an anti-Nilo-Hamite insurgency group] commander make contact with his men in Mbale (60 miles toward Kampala), to help secure town against fleeing troops. Agree to go w/2 vehicles. I go ahead to FEDEMU. Their guys ready to go. Wait for Ali. Suddenly shooting all over place. I jump into car + drive behind row of mud houses. Run w/FEDEMU up a hill. They answer fire. Danger of getting encircled. We go down hill + deep into village. About 5 trucks, 1 Land Rover of Acholis have returned. I get guide part of way into town. [Before I left, the FEDEMU commander ordered an old woman to go into town to reconnoiter. She knelt, crossed herself and walked off.] People in village, but paved road deserted. Gary Cooper-High Noon, Lord instead of six-shooters. Walk to within 30 yards of car before finding soldiers. [These three soldiers had taken a bright-red Land Rover from the fire department, and had stopped in the middle of the road to look at all the gauges and valves when I startled them. I told them with firm voice that I want them to help me get my car back. Just then I heard it getting started up behind the home where I had hidden it. They took me there.] Ali w/soldiers with car. [My Daihatsu, not Ali's UNICEF Land Rover] Lock, ignition busted, car hot-wired. First hot confrontation. Can't drive my own car, but at least get to sit in front, soldiers behind – important victory. At Central Park I demand to see Major Odora. (I had had dealings w/him when he commanded Soroti troops.) [I had actually had the opportunity to show the Jesus Film to him and his troops.] Talk to commanding officer, vacuous, vicious looking. Ali calls me "commander" in front of them. I call him "my driver." Car released to me immediately. Praise God! Find Odora. [Odora had ordered my vehicle to be released to me when I was found. I found him at the Liberty Bar, having "breakfast." I took a drink out of his bottle to cement our tenuous relationship. When your life depends on that relationship, every little *bit helps.] Talk to him about security for town. Can't win w/o support of people. Help Kreutters move in with John and me. Plane arrives. I pick up Newmans. Take short-cut to airport, appears like I'm avoiding new roadblock. How stupid of me. Soldiers screaming, waving guns. I scream back. Want me to leave car and march us to park. Refuse and take André [Newman, Angus' wife], but Angus and Ali marched at gun point. To Odora, back to park. Ali's been hit with flat side of panga (machete) across back. Long cut but not deep. [Angus was left untouched, which goes to show the respect we whites enjoyed and the disdain Africans had for some of their own.] Take Newmans, pilot, UNICEF + Red Cross men to airport. [I don't remember how the pilot got into Soroti according to my diary. Mistake?] Angus finally allowed by pilot of 4-seater to sit in baggage comp. Message to Debbie = a.o.k. Tim joins me in drive to park. Soldier with gangrenous arm, hundreds of flies. Tim applies tourniquet. "How could you do it?" "I didn't look!" "How could you take the smell?" "I didn't breathe!" Odora gave me escort. ("I want a man who speaks good English and is sharp.") Angelo! Courteous ("Angelo!" Click of heels- "Sir!") Sharp. He disarmed drunk officer waving pistol at his men w/o any fuss. Kept him w/me for 1 day. [I used a similar situation to establish respect with the soldiers at the park. Another drunk officer was pointing his pistol at the windshield of a parked, looted Mercedes with one of his men at the wheel. I walked over, put my arm around his shoulders, and turning, walked a few yards away with him. It showed that I cared and that I was in control – sort of – and it helped to instill respect.]*

Jan. 30 *Museveni sworn in. Power off again, water follows. Troops in town change daily. Keep up acquaintance. I'm only civilian driving his own car. Make daily visits to Frieda Adiamo [Inspector of Teso area schools], Sunny (American woman w/ Catholic Church) and Peter Jones, British R.C. priest. Play scrabble daily w/Sunny. Before Newman's left, Teso soldier tried to hijack them w/their Land Cruiser to Usuk. Tim talked him out of it. Tim and I again weigh odds re. leaving for Kenya via Karamoja.*

Jan. 31 *Visit Frieda on foot and learn from Dennis (our houseboy who lives near our house) soldiers have broken into our house. I run to next roadblock and get ride w/soldiers. Gate forced open. Kitchen window busted. Fiat trunk open, spare outside. Nobody in house. Ride Karsten's bicycle to Masons. Come with John, African friends to load* *up fridge, stove, other valuables. Ready to load when 4 soldiers come shouting. Biggest confrontation. They came with 2 wheels, had already fixed battery. They don't want to back off. I don't either. Very tense. Dennis runs through house and jumps out kitchen window. ("It got too hot there.") [He later told me that he had understood enough Acholi to know that one soldiers had suggested killing me.] Finally they back off. Then tell me they only wanted to take wounded soldiers. I get John to fix tires. I insist on driving. We look for fuel. One by one they drop off. (They just wanted to flee.) I go to Masons to get African doctor who wanted to get Chloroquine. Bishop and others gather around me and pray for my immediate return w/car. Touching. I drive off not looking back. [Real men don't show their tears!!!] Learn later that John thought he'd never see me again. At park no one interested in my going. Guy with bullet in head had wandered off. Twenty minutes later I'm back. John had moved everything safely with the others. We put Daihatsu into container in workshop. I drive Fiat with looted battery and tires.*

Feb. 1 *Impressed by Psalm 44. Victory comes from God. I'm still only civilian driving. Turn over of soldiers demands continued establishing of authority with new commanders. Every morning like going into lions' den. But I feel its time to go into hiding. After dark Tim sets off a fire cracker. Takes Francis (the guy with the wig, had made his way back in civilian clothes after fleeing, then carried his gun in a mat) 2 minutes to answer from 200 yards away.*

Feb. 2 *Tim taught from Isaiah 12:2. Fear masters people. But God hasn't given us spirit of fear. (2.Tim 1:7) Chess, Boggle, Scrabble. People come, tell us Land Cruiser taken out of garage after all-night attempt to break into Garvin's house. (Harry Garvin, missionary in Soroti 25 years, on furlough.) Kreutters stayed in their house. Tim and I get there just in time to stop more looting by locals. All doors in house broken down. We saw vehicle on way over at park, but it's too late to do anything. [That was one confrontation I did not think we could win in front of all those soldiers, and once started I would be hesitant to back off and put myself in greater danger. The vehicle wasn't worth risking our lives.] We secure house as best possible. I empty Fiat tank at Masons. John + I walk to Sunny – Scrabble. Mbale taken by NRA.*

Feb. 3 *People moving around freely. All soldiers gone. Get Daihatsu out of container, take Boots [our dog] to house, get Dennis from* *village (where he had fled, as almost all Soroti inhabitants.) At house learn of new arrival of troops. Boots back to Masons, alert Sunny, Peter. Word is that Land Cruiser was left on Lira Rd. Drive with Tim to Mile 7. Dangerous, but we can outrun any army vehicle. [That report turned out to be wrong.] [C]Kathy sick. I cook. Daihatsu back into container. Before dusk 4 trucks, 1 Land Rover leaving towards Lira. [These were military vehicles. Their departure was good news.] Where's the NRA?*

Feb. 4 *Only one thing worth reviewing of this day. Otherwise I only complained about the Teso militia being cowards in not wresting control from the Acholis. While I was gone a soldier robbed Africans near our house. He threatened to shoot them if they gave not more. Tim walked out. Soldier told him to get back into house. Tim kept coming. Soldier knelt down, cocked his gun and aimed at Tim. Tim just stood there looking at him for about 30 seconds. Guts against guns. Then the soldier got up, said "o.k." and walked off.*

Feb. 5 *Newmans' house has been looted. I walk w/Dennis to our house and move things in attic further away from the opening. Also repair window with wood. Go to meet Tim at Garvin's. Their house has been blown up. Everything gone. [Tim and I had blocked doors by moving furniture door to door or to wall. Apparently the soldiers had failed to shoot the lock off the chain that tied together the protective steel grids that covered the front door, so they shot rocket-propelled grenades through the wall, setting the place on fire.] At Mason's Tim tells me 7 soldiers came looking for my Daihatsu. Said they'd come back later. I'm waiting. Alibhai who maintains radio contact w/Kampala told me he got message for Debbie out. [Alibhai worked for the East African Flying School in Soroti. He had a radio hidden under his bed. He's the one who talked to the pilot when the plane had circled earlier.] Hope it reaches Nairobi. Will Garvins ever return? This is a sick society. Iteso looted their house. [The local people whom they had served.] I'm struggling with the thought of remaining (or returning). But Jesus came for the sick, not the healthy. Tim and Simon back to Garvin's to rescue cast iron skillet. Found people looting servants' quarters. 3 PAG [Pentecostal Assemblies of God, Canadian branch] brothers stay to secure the place.*

Feb. 6 *The 3 arrive early to tell us that looters came with guns, so they fled. Tim goes to give what's left to brothers for storing. Meanwhile we pack to leave. [Kreutters and I decided that it was getting too dangerous to stay any longer. With the return of the Acholis we expected that there would be a battle for Soroti. We had our families to consider.] John stays. "They can blow my bloody head off; I'm single." Like Mission Impossible. Quiet rolling out Daihatsu [out of 20-foot container], packing inside workshop, rolling in Fiat. Seconds count. Dennis getting info of troop movement at road. John prays for us, I for him and brothers left behind. Dennis rides bicycle ahead. We take 20 minutes through bush to cover 5 miles of main road. We're out. Detour to avoid 30 Karamojong soldiers going home. Near Iriri (just inside Karamoja) run into 75 - 100 Karamojong warriors on a cattle raid. Wild looking; wave us to stop, then on, but we stop, shake hands. No arguing with them or instant death. [As we approached them, Tim and I hung our white arms out of the window, trying to take every advantage possible. They were known for killing whites as well; once even several Roman Catholic nuns driving to their mission. We stopped because they were coming at intervals, about ten abreast. We wanted those not yet in sight to know that we had been cleared by the leading group. The Karamojong are known to ambush vehicles. Killing means nothing to them, so I drove at high speed on those dirt roads to minimize the time any, not on a "warpath" already, might have to get their guns when hearing an engine. I learned years later that Cathy, Tim's wife, who was with their two small children, Eric and Jessica, on the mattress in the back, had been jostled around so much that she had cried much of the way. I suppose the stress of the last two weeks hadn't helped.] Spend night with German doctor near Kenya border. Flat tire upon arrival. [But we had two spares.] Good night's sleep; first twenty-four hours w/o shooting in almost two weeks.*

Feb. 7 *I have no entry here. I called Debbie from Kitale. She would be taking friends out to dinner that night. I didn't expect to make it because of an as yet unidentified noise on the vehicle. But we arrived at 8:30 at the restaurant, a bit dusty, a bit tired, and quite a bit hungry. Mike [Nunn] kindly took the Kreutters to a guesthouse. After Debbie's exclamation of surprise in the elegant restaurant, people looked at us and knew, I bet, why she had screamed. Some must have thought we had just returned from a wild life safari. Well, we had, I* *guess. Only now it didn't matter how wild it had been. What mattered was that we had returned. "Yea, though I walk through the valley of the shadow of death, I will fear no evil; for You are with me; Your rod and Your staff, they comfort me."*

As I copied my diary on these pages, it occurred to me that this verse in Psalm 23 is easily misunderstood. It is not a spiritual life insurance. It doesn't promise protection from harm. This Psalm simply promises God's presence in the face of evil. Many a missionary has entered "the valley of the shadow of death" without emerging on the other side. Death holds no fear when there is an awareness of the presence of God. Our experience, as well as that of many other missionaries, like of those five missionaries who were killed by the Waodani Indians in the jungles of Ecuador fifty years ago and relived in the film *End of the Spear*, testifies to that, as does *Fox's Book of Martyrs*.

* * *

There is an unexpected conclusion to Debbie's and Misha's dramatic departure from Soroti. As the plane approached Nairobi's Wilson Airport with my world's most precious cargo, the pilot radioed the manifest to the U.N. Headquarters. Just then our good friend Kate Lawless, wife of UNICEF employee Paul Beni, was in the office that received the pilot's communication. (They were the Australian couple who competed against us for the Soroti house.) They and their three children had already been evacuated. Kate overheard the pilot referring to "a woman and her young daughter." Knowing that Karsten was in boarding school, that was all the information she needed. *That could only be Debbie and Misha*, she thought and jumped into action. She called our friends from our earliest Nairobi days, Mike and Helen Nunn, who worked in Kenya with the Church Missionary Society, a British organization. Then, while Helen readied their guestroom, Kate raced to the airport.

"Kate! What are *you* doing here?" Debbie was startled.

"I came to pick you up."

I still get touched when I think of people going out of their way like that for us.

16

IN HARM'S WAY

*Yea, though I walk through the valley of the shadow of death,
I will fear no evil; For You are with me;
Your rod and Your staff, they comfort me.*
Psalm 23:4

The Bantu, living in Uganda's central, western, and southern regions, comprise two-thirds of the country's population, the other third going to Nilo-Hamitic northern and eastern tribes. The newly-installed Museveni government began to settle in and assert control over all the Bantu-inhabited territories. However, the Iteso, Acholi, Langi, and other Nilo-Hamitic people groups were not easily appeased, and more trying times lay ahead. Acceptance or rejection of the Museveni government was largely a tribal issue. Apart from the three-and-a-half year rule of the Baganda king, Edward Mutesa II, to whom the British had handed over the colony, only three Bantu had reigned for a total of eighteen months.

By contrast, three Nilo-Hamites (Obote, Amin and Okello) had been Uganda's heads of state for seventeen years. Most northerners had favored Obote over Museveni, a Muntu – in particular the Acholis, who had lost the war, the Langis, who had lost their president and the Iteso, who had always taken to Obote. The northerners were reluctant to accept a southerner again. Apart from the violence, it was a bit like the belief and perhaps desire in America's more populous northern states that no southerner could/would ever become president. In America the mold was broken with the assassination of JFK and the subsequent installation of LBJ.

These northern tribes also believed, not without reason, that they were shortchanged in the distribution of foreign aid and services that the world began to pour into the country, and that added fuel to the fire. Since Museveni's army had conquered the north last, lingering instability could well have accounted for inequity in the distribution. Tribal militias, comprised largely of ex-soldiers, began to rebel. They launched hit-and-run attacks against Museveni's troops, the NRA. Predictably, the result was new unrest with an attendant crackdown on the population.

Museveni instituted two important changes to minimize tribal divisions. He increased the number of districts by subdividing them from an original seventeen to a current seventy and renaming them after their capitals and major towns. Before, districts were identified by the names of their main tribe – Buganda - Baganda, East and West Ankole - Banyankole, Teso - Iteso, Acholi - Acholi, etc. Now they are named after their capitals: Kampala - Buganda, Mbarara - East Ankole, Soroti - Teso, Gulu – Acholi. The same goes for the smaller districts. At first I regretted that change – being sentimentally inclined towards tradition, I suppose – but then began to appreciate, if nothing else, its symbolic contribution to the unity of the country.

*   *   *

After Museveni came to power, Iteso and Kumam rebels began killing off the Bantu in their midst, even though many had lived among them all their lives; neighbor killing neighbor, just because some 200 miles away a man from the latter tribal group had taken the reins of government. As a result, the Bantu fled south into their traditional tribal areas. Jackson Mugerwa was a Muntu of the Bakenyi tribe. Debbie and I helped him and his wife Demmy move with their meager possessions to Nakyesa, a coffee-growing village about thirty miles from Jinja, or about a one-hour bus ride from Kampala. They were given a piece of land by a well-to-do landowner and leader of his clan, Mzee Sirasi.

Mzee is a respectful Swahili term for an older man. It could not have been more appropriate for this quiet and humble gentleman with dignified bearing. Mzee owned a lock-and-key shop near the main taxi park in Kampala – probably the most appropriate business of all for one of the most insecure cities in the world at the time. He spent weekends in his home in Kayunga, a small town halfway between Nakyesa and Jinja. He had already given land to numerous Bakenyi who had fled Teso, and set aside land for an elementary school to educate their children. After teaching some one

Newlyweds Jackson and Demmy

School under a tree

hundred pupils under a shade tree for about a year, Jackson built a school with financial help from our church and became its first principal.

Jackson's compound with Dr. Marv Dunaway

Following his arrival at Nakyesa, Jackson erected three mud huts; one to serve as a living room/guestroom, one as a bedroom, and a smaller one as a kitchen. Behind them he built a three-by-five foot roofless stick-and-banana-leaf enclosure with a stone floor – the shower. He also dug a twelve-foot deep pit latrine on top of a dormant anthill, around which he built a five-foot square hut with five-foot high mud walls, a thatched roof, and a tiny, flimsy, corrugated-iron-sheet door. He planted cassava, sweet potatoes, beans, and pineapples in the red, fertile soil around the compound, leaving an approximately ten-foot wide walkway that connected his compound with the gravel road.

Justin Etobu was about twenty years old when Jackson Mugerwa began training him in discipleship in Teso district. At 5'8", Justin was stocky and muscular and tended to be serious, though he would readily smile and, in fact, could get quite animated in a circle of friends. He was of the Kumam tribe, which lived peacefully among the more numerous Iteso. Intermarriage was common. Most Kumam are fluent in both languages, and Justin was conversant in English as well. He was a simple young man from the village, raised in a mud hut and not accustomed to wearing shoes, let alone riding his own bicycle. Like Jackson and many of my acquaintances, he had never seen ice or tasted butter or jam. Even those who grew them, like Charles Orieba, one of our co-workers, considered raw carrots and tomatoes rabbit food. They had to be cooked. Justin had never looked at a building higher than three stories. Kampala was a city he had only heard of.

With Jackson gone, Justin Etobu walked eight miles once a week from his home in the village to our house in Soroti for a ninety-minute face-to-face meeting. After a meal or some refreshments he would start "footing" back. Later developments would prove that his sacrifice and investment of time were not in vain. But trials still lay ahead.

The night before one of our get-togethers, Iteso and Kumam rebels ambushed a government road-block on the northbound road that linked Kampala with the Sudan. Several NRA soldiers were killed in the firefight. Unfortunately, that was the same road Justin took to get to our house. He would recall later that he had wondered why it was so deserted; no one dared pass that roadblock that day. The surviving soldiers and their new reinforcements were seething with anger and suspicious of any young man who dared to come anywhere near them. It was blood for blood, and if it wasn't innocent, then so much the better.

Justin arrived at that hornets' nest, still oblivious to what had transpired the night before. He was not prepared for what followed. His identity card was confiscated, he was led into the bush, beaten, and forced to undress. He was shoved into a hole in the ground, about six feet deep and large enough to hold some thirty men. Others had died in places like that on similar occasions.

One of the partners in our work, a young pastor named John Onaba, had been killed within a mile of that location even, I was told, as he prayed for his NRA murderers. With his untimely death, John had followed his father, who had been shot several years earlier in front of his house in the village during a robbery. John's death was hard on all of us. He had been a reliable partner in our work, a man dedicated to God and to the service of others.

John had also distinguished himself as our fastest bicycle rider. I remember an occasion when that distinction came in particularly handy. Every year before the beginning of the rainy season the Iteso burn grass to clear land for farming and to encourage fresh growth for their cattle. During that period all of Teso can be in a haze. We were teaching in Usuk County, and, to meet at the prearranged time for our rendezvous to return to Soroti, John and another of our men were riding their bikes when they came upon a wall of fire, eight to twelve feet high, feeding on bushes that lined the road. They were undeterred and raced through the heat. By the time they had passed the flames, their hair was singed, and John's nylon Bible cover had partially melted. They had laughed about it, and we with them. But now John was gone, and it looked as if Justin might join him for a happy reunion in a more tranquil place.

Justin had been taken to that hole with another man who was now moaning and circling with nervous energy, fearing the worst. Every once in a while he would stop and, looking for support, peer into Justin's eyes and cry that they would be killed. But Justin, full of faith, held steady and refused to accept that.

Soon the commander returned from an errand in town. He must have surmised what his men at the roadblock had been up to, because, without first checking on them, he investigated the hole.

"What are you doing there," he shouted. "You get out, pick your clothes and you go!"

A Ugandan version of Daniel in the lions' den? Perhaps. Without doubt, God restrained that man. Considering that some of his soldiers had been killed just the night before, it was uncommon at the time not to exact revenge. Showing restraint was not considered a virtue, especially in the lower ranks. After facing the distinct possibility of death, that ending was fortunately anti-climactic. Justin arrived at our house, visibly shaken but uninjured. It was, understandably, the last time he would make that trek.

Within four years he would attend a small Bible School in Kampala and start a humble church. On one of my visits I saw him and his wife Ruth feeding some fifty children from poor families in the neighborhood. They did that once a month from their own meager income, and I determined that I would try to organize help.

Back in the States, I alerted my church to the opportunity of participating in this worthwhile cause, and nearly all families got involved. A total of around sixty children were "adopted" for feeding at $10 a month per child. In keeping with the admonition in the Bible that the laborer is worth his hire, I told Justin to keep ten percent of that money to remunerate himself and Ruth for their labor of love.

For us, helping them help those children was a small sacrifice. In Uganda, it made a big difference and laid the foundation for further, more significant outreach: When food became plentiful again, we switched to paying school fees as Justin enrolled the children in various primary schools around the city. Giving them a basic education that most of their parents could never have afforded cost us no more than the equivalent of one Starbucks coffee a week per child.

Today, Justin is pastor of a congregation with three hundred members and runs an elementary school. Liberality? Check! Initiative? Check! Diligence? Check! Perseverance? Check! And the checks from America have enabled dozens of children to finish grade school, and a number of them have been supported even into and through high school.

But there is no man named Justin Etobu with Ruth as his wife. I have changed their names to keep their identities secret. Despite the wonderful promise of a bright future in continued godly, benevolent work, Justin got sidetracked. As I look back, I can see that it was long in coming. Accountability, one of the foundational character qualities I had taught him back in the village, had gone missing. As more money flowed into the children's work, some of it went to its intended purpose, but increasingly more went into his pocket. His 10% remuneration did not satisfy him. He not only enriched himself at the expense of many of the poorest children, but sent his own to the best and priciest schools.

But Justin isn't the only one who bears responsibility. We have to shoulder much of the blame ourselves. Our trust, based on past experience, caused us to place too much temptation before him without the constraints of proper oversight. When questions arose, we gave him the benefit of the doubt even as the corrupting influence of money took over, fed generously by our naiveté. We Christians must understand that, not only in affluent countries like America, but especially in the poor nations of the Third World, leaders of the flock can become as debased by greed as the Nigerian letter-writing crooks.

Within the last twelve months, Justin, the "poor" pastor and our school-fees administrator, has been gallivanting around the world – America, Sudan, South Korea, Trinidad and Tobago – finding ever new gullible Christians who will dig deep into their pockets for the "humble" African with his purported call from God, a three-piece suit, and dignified-sounding "Christianese." May God keep us from destroying people and relationships with our "almighty dollar."

*　*　*

The rebel activity against the government added another danger to villagers already hard-pressed by the raiders, night-time robbers, and the NRA. Government soldiers suspected any male villager who had not suffered at the hands of the rebels of being complicit with them. By the same token, the rebels were suspicious of anyone who was not harassed by the NRA. When either group arrived at a village, they often demanded to be fed, thereby putting their involuntary hosts in even greater danger. It was a life-threatening case of Catch-22, in German illustratively described as "Teufelskreis" – devils' circle – meaning if it's heads, you win; if it's tails, you lose.

Whenever there was an "operation" – the word of choice for an armed attack by the rebels or a counter attack by the NRA – everybody within at least a one-mile radius had to flee as all the males of the area would be suspect, and everybody would be punished by either the rebels or the government soldiers. For the lucky ones, that punishment would be a vicious beating.

I passed through the dirt-poor village of Ngariam once with Ted Mason, the Anglican layman in whose house Debbie and I had stayed during the northward retreat of Okello's defeated army. Ngariam was in a lightly wooded area, about twenty-five miles from Soroti on the main dirt road to Karamoja. Adding to its destitution was a refugee camp, and Ngariam was one of the places in which we were helping with our refugee relief program. On this day we weren't prepared for what we were about to encounter.

As wazungu, we were normally not bothered by the NRA. We were neutral aid workers and not considered a threat to any administration. But this time we surprised Museveni's soldiers right after they had conducted an "operation" in Ngariam, and they weren't happy about it. They had suspected the village of being a rebel stronghold and had taken, what they considered appropriate measures knowing, nonetheless, that those measures wouldn't stand up to international scrutiny.

Ted Mason preparing a lesson

We had already sensed that something was wrong as we approached the village. Normally we would have seen some movement – a farmer in his field; a woman with a haul of firewood on her head; a young bicyclist on his way to or from the well – but nothing. We hadn't seen anyone for the last few miles. As Ngariam came into view we knew why. The whole place had been burned to the ground. The round walls of the small mud-huts had partially collapsed and were black with soot. Smoke from the still smoldering embers of caved-in roof structures was rising into the heavy, motionless air of the hot afternoon. The atmosphere was laden with the odor of fiery destruction. We did not see any sign of life, not even a chicken. It was eerily quiet.

About halfway past the village, we came upon NRA troops and were stopped, but it was too late – we had already seen the devastation. The arbitrary killing or displacement of a whole village and its destruction by government soldiers on nothing but a hunch – how could they be so sure, anyway? – was something I had never seen. We were taken to the commander who sat on a stool in a clearing in the bush, surrounded by some of his underlings. He was a slightly-built man with brown skin, a haughty stare, and a dismissive attitude. He exuded an air of authority that refused to be influenced at the presence of foreigners. Judging by his appearance and rank – he had a pistol in a brown holster, a sure sign that he was an officer – he was a Munyankole, i.e. from Museveni's tribe. The others were a mix of northerners who had joined the NRA. Some were Anyanyas, Sudanese with charcoal-black skin and tribal markings across their foreheads and known particularly for their indiscriminate brutality.

The soldiers had captured an older woman, whom they forced to cook for them. We hoped that most villagers had been able to flee, but it was doubtful. Any young man who had not escaped faced a fearful end. The NRA had learned nefarious practices from the Karamojong. Sometimes they would tie the homeowner to the center pole that supported the roof of his hut and burn the place down around him.

"Osibereje, Ssebo," I said, greeting him in Runyankole.

He looked at Ted and me with an odd detachment, as though he was already trying to calculate the political fall-out that could result from our discovery of the atrocity. The tension in the air was palpable. He was not a happy trooper, and I don't remember him returning my greeting. Museveni's army was known for its discipline and restraint. But what we saw here confirmed rumors I had heard, but which I had been reluctant to believe. It was easy to dismiss them as tribally motivated when they were perpetuated by Africans. I had hoped against hope that Uganda would finally enjoy stability and equity amidst its tribal diversity. Debbie and I had been encouraged in that hope by Erica Sabiiti and his wife Geraldine at their home in Mbarara. Long retired, he had been the first black African Archbishop of the Church of the Province of Uganda, Rwanda, Burundi and Boga-Zaire. Sabiiti was a refined and godly man who knew Museveni well and was convinced that he was the right man to bring the country together.

I accept that not all governments can be held responsible for pernicious conduct by elements of its armed forces, such as the murder of unarmed men, women, and children. For example, in my opinion, neither the US government nor even the military was to blame for the 1968 My Lai massacre in Vietnam; a revengeful, mindless act of violence by a few renegade soldiers, as aberrant as it was abhorrent. I wanted to believe that the destruction of Ngariam was neither ordered nor sanctioned by the Museveni government, but just an isolated example of soldiers run amok.

"So, you know that language," he said, a bit surprised at hearing his mother tongue spoken by a muzungu over three-hundred miles from his tribal home.

"Well, I just know some words. I lived in Mbarara for a year."

It was quiet in this bushy area now. Small flying insects were dancing in the hot afternoon sun and buzzing around our faces. The smoke-saturated air was oppressive and added to the sense of the horror that had taken place. The soldiers slouched around as if in a stupor – they had done their evil deed. To us, the delay didn't matter – we were in no rush. It was just as well. The commander kept us there for about twenty minutes, questioning us about our activity in the area.

"Don't you know that you have entered an operational zone?"

"How could we have known that? There was no warning sign and no roadblock to divert us."

It was not a good idea to answer a question with a question in our situation, but his haughty attitude bothered me. *Operational zone, eh?* I suppose it was his defense mechanism, an indirect way of saying, "We are just doing our official duty, and you might as well accept that."

He left us under guard, perhaps to check out our vehicle, which was parked, unlocked, out of our view. He probably wanted to see if we were equipped with a two-way radio, or if there was any evidence of our being two of those journalists 'who like to stick their noses into other people's business.' Ted suggested that we avoid agitating him. *That's probably a good idea*, I thought. I was already agitated, but the soldiers were the ones with the guns. The commander returned and plied us with more face-saving queries and finally let us go.

I have wondered ever since what happened to that woman. War had downgraded the value of life in Uganda, and I wouldn't want to speculate on her fate.

17

SUNNY BUT DARK

There is no wealth but life.
John Ruskin

Actually, life was cheap in those days but, as mentioned earlier, we wazungu were relatively safe from the dangers that threatened our African friends. Had that not been the case, we would not have gotten off so easily at Ngariam. Nor, for that matter, would I be writing my memoirs. Other than the Karamojong and some rebels, we had little to fear. On the whole, thugs tended to avoid us. Government soldiers might be a nuisance at roadblocks, wanting to go through our belongings unless paid off with at least a token bribe. But the greatest danger to us was getting caught in the crossfire between warring factions.

There were times when embassies in Kampala would strongly advise their nationals via shortwave radio to leave a particular area or to get out of the country entirely, and some NGOs would *order* their employees to do so by the same means. The radio was our most reliable source of information not only about world events, but also about war and peace within the country. As such it was a lifeline for those of us who lived outside the capital, Kampala. Even among the local population, listening to the BBC, VOA, or Radio Deutsche Welle for the latest news was an early-morning or sun-set routine practiced in every home that possessed a battery-powered shortwave radio.

During the Itesos' most desperate struggle for survival, I had the opportunity to communicate their situation to a world-wide audience through the BBC. When we had lived in Nairobi, we had attended Children's Church, a little Anglican assembly of mostly expatriates with small children. The Africa reporter for the BBC, Mike Woolridge, was a member and upon one of our rare visits to Nairobi during those tumultuous days, interviewed me after a Sunday service about the situation in Uganda in his car in the church parking lot.

Two weeks later, Bishop Ilukor exclaimed with a mixture of surprise and excitement: "I heard you on the BBC."

He was pleased that word had reached the outside world about his people's struggle. From Uganda to Nairobi to the U.K. and back with love and information not readily available within the country.

*   *   *

In September, 1985, the BBC broadcast a directive, issued by both the American and German embassies (I was still a German citizen and registered with the embassy). We were asked to evacuate Soroti.

In our evaluation of that communication we were aware of the fact that governments depended on their embassies to look after their citizens, and, understandably, embassies would rather err on the side of caution. But we knew the situation upcountry better than the officials in the capital and chose to stay put.

Ironically, on the morning of Friday the thirteenth, a couple stopped by our house with unexpected news. After I told Mike that we were starting a squash ladder, he told me that they were leaving the country – orders from UNICEF, Kampala: "Prepare to evacuate your dependents." He had planned to get married that morning to make his friend and their child *truly* dependents. He sped off to alert the wife of another UNICEF employee, Debbie's friend Kate. Kate got her three children ready and left a bit teary-eyed at this second evacuation in six weeks.

*   *   *

We were generally safe from thugs who used their guns – the life insurance and bank account substitute they had refused to turn in when they left the military – to enrich themselves at the expense of their African neighbors. But exceptions confirm the rule, and our small white community was to experience that firsthand.

Sunny was a single American in her mid-fifties. At around 5'4" she was heavy-set and had a deep, almost masculine voice. She had been a deputy sheriff back home in the Northwest, and while her name described her positive disposition well, she was a no-nonsense, straight-talking, tough cookie. She worked on the outskirts of Soroti with the Roman Catholic diocese at Madera. With her job as overseer of a construction project in the expansive compound came the power to hire and fire workers – not always a desirable responsibility, as she would soon find out with a vengeance.

Given the dire economic circumstances of Uganda in the 1980s, theft on such large-scale projects was common. For unskilled laborers great quantities of supplies, often not tightly controlled, provided an opportunity to augment their meager income significantly. There was always a ready market for cement, lumber, steel – you name it. Whenever a thief was caught and dismissed, there was no shortage of replacements waiting in the wings. Thus, hiring and firing was not unusual.

One fateful night, Kevin, a young Australian priest on a working visit to Soroti from a mission in Kumi, some twenty-five miles south, was putting up at Sunny's place. Her house was surrounded by bushes and trees and somewhat isolated from the other residences. Still, there was no reason for concern. A single woman with the Catholic mission, working in the service of the people – what would she have to fear?

Both she and her guest had gone to bed. All was quiet. Suddenly, at around 11 p.m., a deafening bang ripped through the stillness of the night as a bullet blasted through the window of her bedroom and lodged in the plastered wall just above her head. The assailant had obviously scoped out her house during daytime and knew the location of her bedroom and bed. But because he couldn't make her out in the dark, the shot was high, missing her by inches.

At first they didn't know the source of the explosion. Kevin, in the room next door, shouted something about a transformer blowing, but it didn't take Sunny long to figure out the frightening truth. There was a distinct sulfur smell.

"That smell is from gunpowder, and that was a shot."

They jumped up, turned on the front porch light and crouched low in the darkened house. You could slice the tension in the air with a knife. It was eerie alright, but, as they strained their ears listening for any noises outside, they could make out nothing but the barking of dogs in the distance. With no telephone to call for help, there wasn't much they could do but wait out the night.

Sunny suspected that a grudge was behind the gunman's nighttime visit. Only recently she had fired one of her workers for theft. Revenge killings are common in African culture, though in Uganda they are more often committed through poisoning. Hippopotamus bile is slipped into a four-foot-long hollow branch that is used as a straw to drink the local millet beer known as "ajono" in the company of four to eight, all sitting around a large earthen pot. That gathering is the Iteso's almost nightly all-male party – just a bunch of men talking, drinking, and whiling the evening away. The brother of an African friend was killed at such a meeting. He had momentarily left his chair. By the time he came back, the bile had already been poured into the straw. The next sip was to be his last.

Since Sunny didn't frequent drinking parties, the embittered man had to find an alternative method. With many ex-soldiers unemployed and guns aplenty, shooting was the preferred choice. And he hired an assassin.

Perhaps the gunman thought he had completed his mission and had left. After hiding and listening for about an hour, the seconds slowly converting into minutes with no further sign of danger and with no thoughts of sleeping, they sat down on the floor in the living room and began to play Scrabble by the shaft of light that drifted in from the front porch.

Little did they realize that their attacker had been biding his time for a second opportunity. He had stalked them around the house, carefully creeping from window to window in hopes of getting a clear shot at the smaller one of the two moving silhouettes inside. Now, with them settled down, his patience was rewarded. Thanks to the beam of light from the front porch, he had a surefire target, or so he thought. They were sitting ducks as they tried to concentrate on their game, oblivious to the set of eyes that had followed them. Aiming at Sunny from the pitch-blackness outside the house into the semi-darkness inside, the gunman eased back on the trigger. The shot exploded through screen and glass. The name on the bullet was Sunny, but the trajectory spelled Kevin. He was knocked over with a violent jerk. His scream pierced the night as his blood was splattered on the surrounding area. He was still alive and conscious but in bad shape. The bullet had entered through his upper right arm into his torso and exited on the other side. Every vital organ had been hit or affected but the heart.

Neither Kevin nor Sunny realized how seriously he had been injured. The initial shock, the panic, the adrenaline-rush doubtless dulled the senses, but before long he was in excruciating pain and begged her to take him to the hospital. Since they had to assume now that the gunman was more tenacious than accurate, he could still be hiding outside to finish the job, in which case it was likely that neither of them would make it to the hospital. Sunny was not prepared to take that chance. She bandaged the wounds as best she could, and they waited out the hours for the first light of dawn. It felt like an eternity, but Kevin was hanging on. She then helped him into the car and, as fast as the road conditions allowed, drove him to the hospital about two miles away.

Soroti's medical facility is fairly large – several one-story buildings spread out over a few acres and surrounded by a chain link fence. It is always a busy place, inside as well as out, as relatives of the sick or injured camp out under the trees. There they cook for themselves and their sick loved ones on open wood and charcoal fires while waiting for them to recover. Some patients are brought in ambulances or plain cars, but more often on bicycles or motorcycles, sometimes even in wheelbarrows.

The hospital's size did not imply preparedness for complicated procedures. It could handle Caesarean sections, minor burns, and broken bones, but there were no qualified surgeons to deal with Kevin's severe trauma. Even if there had been, they would not have had the sophisticated equipment required to operate on him. As it was, they could only stabilize him for an emergency transfer to a hospital staffed and equipped to deal with his serious injuries. None existed in Uganda – Nairobi was the nearest possibility. But, from all I could tell, the Soroti hospital had done a terrific job that morning preparing Kevin for the arduous journey ahead.

Representatives of the Catholic mission contacted the East African Flying School, but bureaucracy trumped even this life-and-death emergency. The school's director was in Kampala, and repeated attempts were made to contact him. Without his permission, no pilot was willing to take to the air, let alone fly out of the country. Death had become so much a part of Ugandan life that it simply didn't rate the urgency it did in more peaceful times. By the same token, the possibility of a muzungu dying when death might have been avoided added to the pressure on the staff. But the scales were not to be tipped in Kevin's favor.

Meanwhile, both expatriate and local priests and lay people had come up from Kumi to join those from Soroti on the hospital grounds. They stood in small groups and conversed in hushed tones. When Ted Mason and I arrived, there was still uncertainty about how Kevin would be transferred.

Tall and lanky, Ted was an Englishman who, with his wife Hilary and their three young boys, had been assigned to the Soroti diocese of the Anglican Church by the Church of England. He was also my squash partner, and like me, a competitive and decisive individual. Neither of us had much patience with indecision. You examine your options, preferably in consultation with trusted individuals, choose one, and go with it.

With no definitive word from the Flying School, arrangements were made to take Kevin by road to the Kenyan border town of Busia, about 110 miles and a minimum of four roadblocks away. It had the closest Kenyan airport. The Malaba border crossing was closer, but there was no airstrip. The Flying Doctors, a Christian service organization stationed at Wilson Airport in Nairobi, would pick him up. A Soroti pick up would have been ideal, of course, but obtaining a permit on short notice to fly into Ugandan airspace would have risked another wild goose chase, if not worse.

My friend, Van Smith, then a helicopter pilot with the Swiss "Heli-Mission" and based in Kitale, Kenya, once flew into Soroti airspace with the goal of picking up the Deputy Secretary General of the UN for a survey flight of famine-stricken Karamoja. A high-ranking military officer had issued his clearance and, just to be sure, confirmation was promised to Van by none other than General Tito Okello, then Uganda's President. As Van was coming into Soroti airport, anti-aircraft gunners opened up on him. A former Marine and tunnel rat in Vietnam, Van was used to dangerous situations. With his adrenalin kicking into high gear, he torqued the chopper out of there so hard, he had to emergency-land within a few miles in the bush to check the engine and transmission and to look for bullet holes. Upon disassembling the engine in Nairobi, he discovered that he had melted the first section of his power turbine.

That experience ended well in more ways than one when he recovered the $4500 repair cost by flying for the filming of "Flame Trees of Thika."

Here now was another life-and-death situation, and flying was out of the question. The fathers wanted to take Kevin to the border by pickup truck, but I persuaded them that the combination of a hard suspension and a potholed road would exacerbate his condition and might even kill him. However, the hospital had put him on a drip and a car ceiling would not be high enough to allow gravity to transfer the life-sustaining fluid.

Enter a most unlikely solution and a most willing African doctor. He agreed with my assessment and, without hesitation, offered to sit on the roof rack of the Toyota station wagon and hold the drip. That was an amazing proposal and made any further deliberations unnecessary.

Nowadays the word hero is overused and its meaning thereby diminished. When everybody is a hero, nobody is a hero. According to Funk & Wagnalls a hero is "a man distinguished for exceptional courage, fortitude, or bold enterprise." Unfortunately, I don't remember the name of that physician. But as far as I am concerned, he was a hero in "his courage, fortitude, and bold enterprise." He stepped up to the plate when he committed to climbing onto the roof of that car and, of his own free will, went far beyond the call of duty.

Sunny, meanwhile, had gone back to her house to shower and hastily pack a suitcase. Would she ever return to Uganda? She was obviously under a lot of stress, and when she arrived back her eyes were puffy from crying. *Had I only...*, she probably castigated herself – but hindsight is always 20/20.

Kevin's condition called for a good plan and decisive action, and our Catholic colleagues were better at deliberating and deferring to one another than at enacting a coherent strategy. With Ted and me showing more decisiveness, they seemed to look to us to run with the ball. And so, with their blessing and prayers, we ended up acting on the decision we had jointly made with them. Ted and I agreed that I would go ahead with Sunny and prepare the roadblocks and both sides of the border for a race of hope against hope – a journey that could brook no delays if it was to be successful. That would take some persuasion, but I was confident it could be done – God willing.

Meanwhile, Ted would follow as fast as the road conditions and Kevin's injuries allowed. The doctor would help in determining that, as would Kevin's groans throughout the ordeal. It would be good to have the doctor along, even if on top of the car holding onto to the roof rack with one hand, while holding the life-sustaining fluid with the other; what a gift – what a sacrifice!

My mind was racing ahead of the car as I contemplated what to say at the roadblocks.

"They've shot a muzungu..."

No, that won't work. The soldiers may assume that the culprit had been one of their own men and will want to investigate further, perhaps even sabotage our efforts.

"Bayaye (bad people) *have shot one of our missionaries. He is badly wounded. He is in a car behind me to be taken to Nairobi...*"

That won't work either. Not Nairobi. They might ask for his papers and think, "What's wrong with our own hospitals?"

"... *to a hospital for surgery. You can easily recognize the car from a distance. A doctor is sitting on the roof, holding a drip. When you see the car approaching, would you please stand on the road and wave them through? Please don't make them ...*"

or better, put them in charge "...don't allow them to stop."

I was driving Sunny's Peugeot 504 fast, real fast. Doubtless, my adrenalin had something to do with that. But I also wanted to be sure to have enough time to secure cooperation at each roadblock and at both borders. The border guards might need extra time to get permission from their superiors for a seamless crossing.

I had only once crossed a border without getting my papers checked. That was with Debbie on the other side of the continent, going from Senegal into Gambia, and there had been no checkpoint. Debbie and our children once entered the United States at Kennedy Airport unchecked in an unusual, get-through or get-sent-back-to-Europe circumstance. But more about that later. This was obviously a different situation, one that called for drastic measures.

I tried to engage Sunny in conversation to keep her distracted. It was obvious that she was still in anguish, but she began to regain her composure. At one point a chicken decided to cross the road right in front of the car. I didn't see anything but a white blur. It flew up just prior to impact and, whack!, it hit the left headlight assembly, or, more accurately, the headlight assembly hit it. As I looked into the rearview mirror, I saw a ball of white feathers descend like a fireworks display on the Fourth of July. Venturing at light-heartedness, I remarked to Sunny, "I bet that chicken has never been hit that hard before." She chuckled as she replied, "No, and I bet it will never be hit that hard again, either."

At all roadblocks we were promised cooperation by the soldiers. Then we reached the border. On the Uganda side pandemonium reigned as usual. Hawkers with stacks of towels on their heads and cheap digital "Swiss" watches made in Taiwan, sunglasses, necklaces, and other trinkets displayed on three-foot-square boards hanging from their necks, vied for our attention with money changers and beggars as we wound our way through the crowds. Pedestrians under burdens of luggage, stalks of still-green bananas, stacks of hand-made baskets, and other goods, were scurrying in all directions, and mangy mixed-breed dogs dodged in and out between the food stands as they scrounged for anything edible. A cacophony of revving engines, grinding gears, and honking horns from smoke-spewing cars, trucks, and motorcycles was accompanied by African traditional music blaring out of cassette-selling holes-in-the-wall. Everybody was going about his business of eking out a living, oblivious of Kevin and the distinct possibility of his dying. How should they know? And, if they did, why should they care? Most were working hard at their own survival.

Amidst ringing telephones, thuds of stamps, and animated questioning and answering, a bunch of pushy truckers crowded the counters, vying for attention with fistfuls of papers and a barrage of attention-getting remarks hurled at anyone in uniform who would listen. But for my white face, I would not have been able to compete in good time. I tried to focus the attention of the apparent top-dog among the border guards on the urgency of the situation.

As I left a few minutes later I could only hope that he had really listened and would remember that he had just assured me that they would let the car pass right through. And then, as if to prove that he had indeed heard me, he allowed Sunny and me to cross no-man's land to the Kenyan check-point without having to show our passports. Through a window he gave a shout to the keeper of the gate, and we were through and headed to the Kenyan border post. Here, under the somber expression and watchful eyes of President Daniel arap Moi's picture on the wall, I found the same understanding and promise of cooperation.

Meanwhile Ted reached the first roadblock and was waved right through. Emboldened by that cooperation, he blasted right through the second some fifteen or twenty minutes later. Unfortunately, he had been forced to stop between the two roadblocks to get Kevin positioned more comfortably with the doctor's help. By the time they closed in on the second roadblock, there had been a changing of the guard, and, as in Van's experience in Soroti several years earlier, the new soldiers had not been made aware of the agreement. As the car whizzed by, there was shouting and several of them, understandably in high dudgeon and screaming with an excess of adrenaline, scrambled onto the road. Ted could see them in the rearview mirror. As some knelt down and aimed their guns, he stomped on the brakes. Kevin's body was wracked with pain that even a generous dose of morphine could not keep in check.

Running a roadblock in Uganda was fraught with danger. Soldiers could shoot with impunity at any vehicle that didn't stop. The consequences of stopping late could be frightful as well. Ted knew instantly that this could be nasty. He exited the vehicle and, with hands up, walked back toward the angry soldiers with their weapons leveled at him, fully expecting hell itself to descend on him. But this Anglican missionary feared neither hell nor a bunch of Ugandan soldiers whose inviolability he had violated and whose pride he had offended.

There was a lot of shouting. Although Ted had explained the arrangement I had made with the previous guards and the seriousness of the patient's condition, they demanded to take him in his car to their commander somewhere off the main road. Finally, Ted, stretching his frame to its full 6'4" height, pointed his finger into the leader's face and shouted, "Alright, we'll go then. But if this man dies, *his* blood will be on *your* hands!"

That threat was sufficient. They were allowed to proceed, but Ted made a point of slowing down at the next two roadblocks, which waved him through without further incident.

Ugandan emigration proved to be as prepared and cooperative as promised. Not so immigration at the Kenyan border crossing. Reminiscent of our experience at Malaba some six years earlier when the gate was locked with no readily available key, more precious minutes were lost, while the guards hunted for the one that would unlock the gate. Another chain falling away from the lock would have come in handy just then.

The airstrip was within a mile of the border, and the Flying Doctors' plane had already been sitting there for close to an hour. Transferring Kevin into the plane took more precious time while, by then, he began to drift in and out of consciousness.

It was June 25, 1986. Ted's and my mission was completed. We had done what we could. On our drive back to Soroti with our doctor friend, we committed Kevin into God's hands. In Ecclesiastes 9:12 the Bible says that man knows not his time. As the plane descended towards the runway at Wilson Airport, Kevin, whose last name I had never learned, left this life at 31 years of age. Sunny returned to the United States and, to the best of my knowledge, never came back to Uganda.

18

CONTEMPLATING CONTRASTS

If there be light, then there is darkness;
if cold, then heat; if height, depth also;
if solid, then fluid; hardness and softness;
roughness and smoothness; calm and tempest;
prosperity and adversity; life and death.

Pythagoras

In September, 1986, our two-month home leave came to an end. For the most part, it had been a wonderful, relaxing time. We had been free as birds since our supporting church made no demands on us, and friends provided us with a home and a car. We valued the opportunity to get reacquainted with them and reacclimatized to our own culture – an experience that induced in me reverse culture shock.

It was largely triggered by the incessant bombardment with advertising. We Americans are at the forefront of innovation and technology and don't wait for people to beat a path to our doors for those better mousetraps, as Ralph Waldo Emerson is said to have suggested. Through unrelenting advertising we go to theirs and push with color, gloss, slogans, jingles, and hyperbole. We tell them that our mousetrap is better even with only token improvement and new packaging; that they need more than one; that their neighbors bought a fancier model, and so should they; that the new spring colors are in stock and now is the time to match the mousetrap to their carpet; that a sale is on and mousetraps are now available at a huge discount, etc. – an all-out, no-holds-barred, loud and garish effort to sell them *on* the products and thus, indirectly, the products themselves.

Wherever I looked – on buildings, on buses, on placards and posters, on park benches, on TVs, on computer monitors, in newspapers and magazines, on receipts, on banners in parking lots or pulled by airplanes, and on billboards carried by people – somebody was trying to sell me something. It seemed at times that the effort at marketing a product was inversely proportional to the need for it – the louder the advertising, the less likely there was a clear need.

The incredible pace of this country was another factor that took getting used to again. Competition and consumer demand seem to keep America moving as if there were no tomorrow – a dizzying busyness after a Third World pace. People were rushing everywhere to keep the economic machine rolling; on foot, on bikes, on escalators, in elevators, in cars and on commuter trains and planes and with over six million trucks hauling everything they need, or don't need, from cradle to grave – well, almost everything. The most important "things" we need are neither temporal nor for sale and, therefore, cannot be seen, let alone hauled.

The barrage of advertising and the bewildering tempo created in me sensory overload. The result was confusion and insecurity – culture shock. I had faced AK-47s in Uganda with nary a thought of the danger. Here I was in a comfortable environment, surrounded by opulence and information that was to make me, the potential customer, feel important and desired, and I felt as insecure as if I had grown up in the African jungle. Well, almost. I wasn't too far off here.

Those of us living here don't seem to notice this deluge of advertising – we are accustomed to it. Many are being manipulated and made to feel needs they don't really have. Everything is "new and improved" – so you've got to have it. By contrast, in most of Africa the pressure is for little more than to provide food, clothing, and shelter for the family and to afford the children a basic education. (Africans produce many children – they are a couples' security in old age.) America is awash in food. Our problem is keeping our weight down, not keeping our families fed. While our houses are turning into mansions, African houses are, largely, still grass-roofed, mud-walled, and cow dung-carpeted. An American two-car garage would be luxury for most on the black continent. Significantly, given security and peace, the Ugandan villagers we got to know were no less happy than their relatively wealthy counterparts in the west. If anything... well, let's just say that I never met any psychologists, marriage counselors, therapists of any stripe, mental health professionals, or time-management specialists. Out there, people mingled with their neighbors, tilled the soil, smelled the flowers, and watched the sun set.

The following is an excerpt from a letter I wrote on September 8, 1986 during our visit to family and friends:

I am on People's Express flight 926 from Denver to Newark. In just a few hours I'll be reunited with Debbie and the kids, who preceded me by three days to Washington D.C. Lee Iacocca is leaning back in his chair and smiling at me, while I am reminiscing before returning to his autobiography.

A few impressions of change in America since our last visit a year ago: Even more breakfast cereals, fewer joggers – more bikers (in Colorado), "motivated" sellers (of houses), baggy clothes, crew cuts and other cuts, video players and microwave ovens in every home unless opted against, and, it appears, an even faster (is it possible?) pace.

Still the same: Smiling service, smooth roads, courteous drivers, reliable telephones, and choices, options, selections, varieties, and alternatives – take your pick. One faces so many decisions just to have lunch at a fast-food restaurant, it appears that differentiating between the nuances of the culinary art is serious business.

"I'll have a Quarter Pounder with cheese and a small salad." (The salad salves my conscience and mollifies health-conscious Debbie.)

"What would you like on your burger?"

"Everything but onions."

"Would you like fries with that?"

"Yes, please."

"And what would you like to drink?"

"I'll have a Coke."

"New, Classic, Diet, Cherry, Diet Cherry or Caffeine-free Coke, and small, medium or large?" (Wow! That's seven choices, or even eighteen. That's too much for me.)

"Actually, I'll just have water. No ice."

"And what kind of dressing will it be today? We have..."

When much of Africa is accustomed to an option of rice with beans, the number of choices found in America's fast-food places smacks of McTrivial Pursuit."

I wrote this somewhere over Iowa. It had been and, for a few more days, would be a great visit – too short, really. There were more people to be seen and more Quarter Pounders to be devoured, and I had enjoyed only four ice cream flavors with twenty-seven to go.

Meanwhile, in Soroti survival still required effort. I remember Ted Mason, having just returned from furlough, remarking to me one day, "Isn't it funny? When you have been through all this chaos here, you go home and see the same old man walking the same dog around the same corner as on your previous visit."

Recurring power outages and water shortages were our lot here. There was plenty of change, but it was mostly negative. Now, instead of fleeing from towns to villages ahead of rampaging soldiers of a deposed regime, traumatized villagers were fleeing from villages to towns to escape several thousand heavily armed cattle raiders.

One of our faithful understudies, Gideon Okello, was getting ready to be married. Back in the States that could be a simple affair, or it could be as elaborate as the couple chose and her parents' wallets allowed. Not so in Africa, where you follow a set of tribal customs as old as the hills.

Gideon had worked hard to raise the money for the bride price. He had harvested and dried seventeen overstuffed sacks of cassava that were locked in a warehouse the size of a small one-car garage in his village of Wila – a dusty little place about thirty miles west of Soroti with dilapidated semi-permanent houses (houses made with burnt or unburnt bricks and corrugated iron-sheet roofing). Its population had been between 100 and 150 souls. Now it was deserted.

And Gideon's hard-earned bride price was in danger from the raiders. He had to try to save it if it wasn't too late already, and he wouldn't know that until he got there. Because of the danger on the roads outside of town, transport prices were exorbitant. No driver was willing to take the risk of running into an ambush unless he was generously remunerated. Many truckers and merchants had died taking their chances on waylaid roads to keep their vehicles rolling and their shelves stocked.

Ambushes were common – along the Karamoja border by the raiders and, in other parts of Teso, by rebels fighting government forces. One time, Alfred Farris was driving to a Catholic mission in Mbale that had the recording equipment for dubbing films. With him was a team of Ugandans involved in the translation of the *Jesus Film* by Campus Crusade for Christ into the Ateso language. (By 2006, this film had been dubbed into 926 languages, with 232 more in progress. It has been viewed world-wide by more people than any other.) Fourteen of them had squeezed into the green machine, the Toyota Land Cruiser that I had used in my commutes between Kenya and Uganda.

Suddenly, all hell broke loose. There was shooting from the bushes by the side of the road, and, as bullets slammed into the vehicle, people screamed and crouched as low as they could. Moses Ogiel, the twenty-one year-old whom I had taught driving just a few months before, slumped over – dead. John Eluru, beloved husband of Dinah and father of eleven children, the always enthusiastic and much-respected deputy principal of a teacher-training college in Soroti and, in this project, the voice of Jesus Christ, was mortally wounded. A young girl was hit in the leg. As Alfred floored the gas pedal, the trajectory of another bullet, moving at 2100 feet a second, intersected the path of the Land Cruiser that moved at a ninety-degree angle to it and at an estimated sixty miles an hour. That bullet grazed Alfred's chin.

In anguish of body and soul as he was clinging to life, John kept uttering the prayer of the Man on the cross, "Father, forgive them." Beyond a turn far down the road, Alfred stopped to check on his companions and to hastily change a tire that had also been hit. He then sped to the hospital in Mbale after a five-mile detour via a German mission. But that proved to be a vain effort and lost time – their doctors had left the country.

Behind Alfred's vehicle had been a taxi transporting a group of Soroti merchants. They were able to turn around and head back unscathed. They informed Bishop Ilukor of the ambush and told him that everybody in the vehicle had been killed. The Bishop wasted no time and boldly rushed down that same road to Mbale Hospital. (It was fortuitous that a Ugandan bishop's life in those early days was not governed by the Ugandan equivalent of our Occupational Safety and Health Administration.) He consoled the injured, prayed with them, and returned to Soroti with Moses' body.

Alfred spent some time scouring drugstores in the city for morphine. When he finally located a source, it was given to him by the sympathetic, big-hearted druggist whom he had told of the ambush. (Tragedy brings people together as it reminds them that life's true verities don't lie in riches or status. Our hero physician would confirm that later when he climbed onto the roof of a car to hold the drip for a dying man.) Alfred drove back to Soroti later, hoping that the rebels had moved on and convinced that John would survive. It was not to be. John died later that night. He was the only one who had finished dubbing his part of the film and had urged Alfred to finish the project. He was ready to meet his Lord and to hear the voice of Him for whom he is still speaking today in venues all over the land of the Iteso. "Well done, good and faithful servant."

When Gideon came to me for help, how could I turn him down? His problem was my problem, and if he was willing to go, so was I. Debbie had mixed feelings. She didn't want to become a widow; nor did I want her to – ahem! She also didn't want Gideon to have to remain a bachelor and, again, neither did I. One has to be willing to take calculated chances. We had come to Uganda after examining our options and weighing the risks. I have been accused of having a death wish. But by God's grace, coupled with a sense of knowing the limits and my limitations, I am still here and able to write.

When faced with the decision whether or not I should help Gideon – and I wouldn't have gone without her blessing – Debbie left it up to me. She trusted my judgment, and she trusted God, and she agreed to our going.

"Just be careful."

"Okay, Tweedle! We'll be careful."

Right!!! What does "be careful" mean when ill-willed gunmen might be hiding in the bushes? How does one exercise caution then? I wasn't quite sure. That was like driving here in our Rocky Mountains and heeding the sign by a towering vertical wall of rock that warns you of falling rocks. What are you supposed to do? Close your sunroof?

A prayer, a hug, a kiss, and we were off with the big Land Cruiser. We would count on the few remaining villagers we met on the way to inform us about any sightings of Karamojong raiders. There was still some activity in compounds along the dirt roads, but the further behind we left Soroti, the sparser the population. The dry season had painted the scenery a beige-colored hue. There were large black patches of burned grass – not enough, though, to give an unobstructed view of the area. There was still plenty of tall grass in which to hide, and isolated trees and bushes broke up the monotony. *Thanks! I'd rather have the monotony!*

Beyond the half-way point to Wila the homesteads were abandoned. The only reminders of past human activity were deserted paths, neglected fields, and the uninhabited compounds. The air was still, and the ghostly atmosphere was only pierced by the fearfully-loud clanging of our Diesel engine. We trusted that that would not change.

On the outskirts of Wila we passed the cashew-nut trees that lined the narrow dirt road, then crossed the earth-carpeted center square which was surrounded by the gray forms of fewer than a dozen semi-permanent houses – including that of Valentino Adyebo.

Valentino had been an industrious rice farmer and the leader of Wila's little discipleship group. He was about fifty years old and, at five-foot-seven, had a muscular build. He had a receding hairline, strong cheekbones and communicated animatedly with a hoarse voice. He didn't speak English, but he and I shared a bond that didn't require words to be expressed. We had met regularly in his home for our meetings and always enjoyed his and his wife's generous hospitality that included chicken and rice in a wonderfully flavored broth – I can still taste it today. But Valentino wasn't around anymore: He had been killed by rebels right there in that little square several months earlier – shot in the back as he walked toward his house.

But there was no time to reminisce and get emotional. We reached a storage shed made of old, rusty corrugated iron sheets. We hoped it still contained Gideon's ticket to marital bliss and were elated to find that the lock was still in place. What relief! We shut off the engine and listened. It was quiet. Even the birds seemed to have been warned of the coming raiders. The only sound was that of pounding hearts. Or was it just one heart? Must have been Gideon's!

Doesn't everybody get excited when he/she is about to get married?

But time for listening was over, and we loaded up the Land Cruiser on the double. What didn't fit inside we tied up on the roof rack. The sacks were heavy, but our adrenalin glands were pumping, not just because of the danger we were facing, but also because we were beginning to sense that our coming had not been in vain.

We started back, every mile bolstering our certainty that our undertaking would end with success. As people came back into view our anxiety level lowered. Mission accomplished, we reached Soroti with our precious cargo and felt like soldiers in the pioneer days returning to the safety of their fort. It is deeply satisfying when you can wrest good and hope from the machinations of evil men. Yes, wedding bells would be ringing!

Wila's villagers, as others in the Karamojong's path, were less fortunate. They lost whatever they couldn't carry or herd. They sold their cherished cattle to middlemen who sold them to farmers in safe areas in the south and west or, failing that, marketed them for slaughter. A way of life was disappearing.

*   *   *

Since our work in the villages had come to an abrupt standstill, our home became the hub for frequent meetings. We had up to six men visit three times a week, sometimes staying overnight. For them it was a step into the muzungu world of luxury: sitting on a soft couch or chair while listening to stereo music – I remember Jackson Mugerwa's favorite song was by John Denver, "Country road, take me home to the place I belong" – drinking ice-cold juices or coffee with milk and heaping spoons of sugar, eating such exotic foods as banana bread, peanut butter and jam sandwiches, and tuna-noodle casserole, while rabbit food – tomato and cucumber salad or coleslaw – barely attracted a courtesy-bite. We could certainly understand. We had munched on only a few flying ants, although Misha enjoyed them en masse on an open-face sandwich – a novel idea, even for Africans.

First-time visitors would tread lightly on our wooden floor as if walking on a sheet of ice, sit on the edge of chairs as if they might collapse under their weight and talk in quiet voices as if telling secrets. At the table they would watch us as we picked up our knives and forks, then follow our example, just as I had watched when I first was guest in their homes and learned African table manners. But I found Africans to be very adaptable, and it would generally take only a few visits for them to adjust to our way of life.

*   *   *

In 1985 Campus Crusade for Christ organized its four-day EXPLO '85 extravaganza, a simultaneous, multi-lingual, closed-circuit television conference. Using 18 communication satellites and 20,000 technicians, it linked 300,000 delegates in 98 venues on five continents. Speakers were simultaneously translated into 30 languages. It was a modern marvel, the largest of its kind in history. We saw audiences in different venues concurrently singing the same song, each in their language – "Amazing grace, how sweet the sound, that saved a wretch like me." As cameras were filming and projecting, we in Uganda, would sing on Thursday at 6 p.m. with Americans in L.A. on Thursday at 8 a.m., with the British in London on Thursday at 4 p.m., and with Koreans in Seoul on Friday at 1 a.m. What joy, as we waved through cameras and projectors to one another across the world, a mass of brothers and sisters of many denominations, tribes, colors, languages, nations, all united in one purpose: to glorify the God and Father of our Lord Jesus Christ. The modern world had come to Uganda with cutting-edge technology and dazzled all of us.

For this special occasion I took a carload of my co-workers to Kampala. A number of them had never been to the big city – tall buildings, wide streets, heavy traffic and traffic lights that, if they worked, were often ignored– and it was all new to them. They observed it with turning heads and mono-syllabic expressions of astonishment, like "eh, eh!" They had also never attended such a big meeting or been in an auditorium of similar size. Their biggest churches were small in comparison. Organizers had decided against Kampala's soccer and parade stadium because of the dangers of moving in the city at night. Instead, the gathering was held, jam-packed, at the auditorium of Makerere University, which also housed many delegates in its dormitories.

Astounding as the numbers were, the significance of this international meeting lay not in its size, its technical pizazz, or organizational complexity, but in the love and unity of this multi-faceted body of Christ's followers. What mattered here were not our denominational backgrounds – Anglican and Baptist, Roman Catholic and Presbyterian, Orthodox and what have you – but our knowledge of Jesus the Messiah as our redeemer and ruler.

While my friends slept in one of the dormitories, I curled up in the roof rack of the Daihatsu. It was cooler than in the stuffy dorms, and I wanted to make sure that my vehicle was safe. Imagine how startled a prospective thief would have been at a growling voice emanating from a white-sheeted ghost hovering above in the middle of the night!

I am reminded of an experience at the beginning of my first trip around the world. I slept right next to a highway between two graves in a North Dakota cemetery. I had chosen that spot, for the same reason I would later choose a cemetery in Bernkastel-Kues, Germany, after arriving in Luxemburg from the States on Icelandic Airlines – no one would bother me during the night. Awakened by traffic in the morning, I sat up to look around and noticed that my down sleeping bag was white with frost. The appearance of a white-sheeted ghost rising from the grave could have given the passing motorists quite the scare and the water cooler topic for the day.

The Bernkastel "Friedhof" (courtyard of peace) was old, with moss growing on some of the tombstones. Some might have feared the ghosts of the departed in superstition, but I found it to be an idyllic setting. "Disrespectful," others might have called it, when I jogged in my birthday suit to a faucet where mourners fetch water for the flowers on the graves of their loved ones. I took a bucket shower as a full moon was rising over a mountain and illuminated the ancient castle (hence Bernkastel) in a soft glow.

But that was back when I was still footloose and fancy-free. I had made the change from a globetrotting backpacker to a family man and missionary in a country where danger was ever present, not from imaginary ghosts, but from renegade soldiers, marauding rebels, and cattle- rustling tribesmen. Several of my friends had been murdered. We lived to tell about some of them –Valentino Adyebo, Epaphras Edaru, John Eluru, Moses Ogiel, John Onaba – and about the ravages the "Pearl of Africa" had endured during the 1970s and 1980s at the hands of Idi Amin and Milton Obote.

Life in Uganda was not easy for us, and it was a nightmare for our Ugandan friends. We tried to meet both spiritual and material needs. To the extent that we succeeded, it was a rewarding experience for our whole family. Our children, Karsten and Misha, have traveled in over forty countries, but Uganda has remained their favorite. Debbie, my faithful companion in sickness and in health, wrote to me on my sixty-sixth birthday: "To the love of my life: Thank you for asking me to go with you on a honeymoon around the world. It has truly been an adventure these thirty-one years."

As I reflect now on the Africa-period of our lives, I can gratefully affirm again that I truly married a trooper. She hung in there with me and supported me through the worst of times as well as the best. Her flexibility

Karsten and Misha on a later visit

allowed her to be at home in affluent environments and sophistication, as well as in the village and simplicity. In danger she trusted God's sovereignty; in difficulty she trusted my judgment, sometimes enlightened by her intuition; little luxuries along the way she held loosely; inconveniences she endured gladly if it was for the benefit of those we had come to serve. Little did I know how much she would contribute to my life when, just three dates after meeting each other in that small church service in a mountain home outside Boulder, we agreed to spend the rest of our lives together.

I got teary-eyed more than once as I wrote this book and, in the process, proved the axiom that men get more emotional as they get older. Fortunately, the aging-process is accompanied by a commensurate willingness to admit to those tears without fear of embarrassment. But there was more to it than that. My memories are vivid, and, other than where indicated, nothing, not even smells or sensations are invented to make this book more interesting – it contains no padding. I lost close friends but, no more deserving than they, had survived. I had been privileged to be born in the west, thereby becoming the beneficiary of its opportunities and resultant affluence. This enabled me to give out of my abundance, rather than, born into destitution, receive in my poverty. Rightly the Apostle Paul asks, "…for who sees anything different in you? What do you have that you did not receive?" (1. Corinthians 4:7a) In Uganda I did not think much about those questions. I accepted things as they were and went with that. Now, reflection proves overwhelming at times, as years of intense experiences are relived graphically in compacted form through months of writing.

*   *   *

During our work with the E.O. in Mbarara, I wrote short essays about life from a biblical perspective. That was nearly three years before we would experience danger and turmoil in our refugee work in Teso. There I would have the opportunity to get involved with the "grass" on a personal, at times gut-wrenching level. In Mbarara, some of my musings were more theoretical than experiential. Sometimes theory is not confirmed by reality, and it is generally easier to talk than to walk, especially when your life still begs the maturing process that accompanies endurance in trials and hardships. But below is an example of just such an essay, a continuation of my contemplation of contrasts that, gratefully, became bedrock reality, not only during our Africa experience, but also after we returned to our American home. In short, it's a universally applicable truth.

My father-in-law once said something to the effect that, while we were giving of ourselves for the betterment of the destitute, our peers in America were working to enjoy the good life and accumulate assets for retirement. But I wish to make this irrevocably clear: We have missed out on nothing. On the contrary – in our work in Africa we not only enjoyed a satisfaction that money cannot buy, but, after our return, our house-painting business was so prosperous, that we could continue to be involved in Africa. I have been able to return eight times, four of those accompanied by Debbie.

It was also our distinct pleasure to bring to our home in Colorado the man who had given so much of himself to others and continues to do so to this day – Jackson Mugerwa. From riding a bicycle to flying on an airliner, from an upcountry bus station to Denver International Airport, from a duka in the village to a modern shopping mall, from a mud hut to an American home – what an experience that was for him! Still, after a month he was ready to return, not just because he missed his lovely wife, Demmy, and their five children, but because of a selfless work that had expanded even into Rwanda for the glory of God and the benefit of the people.

Here then is my exposition on:

Jackson in America

The Principle of Reverse Results

Science talks about the law of cause and effect. So does the Bible: "...*whatever one sows, that will he also reap.*" *(Galatians 6:7b)*

Man's most universal aspirations are to enjoy peace, honor, and prosperity under the overriding instinct of self-preservation. We are constantly prodded by our "common sense" that would tell us that to have peace we must be satisfied with our rectitude, to have honor we must propel ourselves to the top, and to have prosperity we must keep all we have and take all we can get.

But through the Apostle Paul we are admonished not to be conformed to this world, but to be transformed by the renewing of our minds (Romans 12:2). He also reminds us that "*the wisdom of this world is folly with God*" (1. Corinthinas 3:19). The Old Testament sheds further light on these passages with Isaiah 55:8: "*For my thoughts are not your thoughts, neither are your ways my ways, declares the Lord.*" God's way to the top is down – so to be honored you humble *yourself; peace comes from confession of your shortcomings, and prosperity results not from hoarding but from giving.*

Jesus Christ's life was a divine demonstration of that dichotomy. As creator of the universe He set the tone for His earthly life when He chose a stable for a maternity ward and a feeding trough for his crib. Instead of baptizing, He submitted to baptism. When His disciples should have washed His feet, He washed theirs. Though He was God, He made Himself of no reputation and took upon Himself the form of a servant. He rode a donkey when leaders rode horses and spoke truth when verbal manipulation would have preserved His popularity. When He was falsely accused, He did not justify Himself, and though He had saved others, He would not save Himself. Though King of kings and Lord of lords, His crown was made of thorns. The giver of life, amidst mock and dishonor, laid down His life. Perfection willingly shouldered imperfection as His light was snuffed out by the darkness of sin, and the light of day turned into the gloom of night.

Yet His cross has become for all ages the symbol of hope, victory over evil, and resurrection, and He shall reign forever and ever. Today, 2000 years later when, during Händel's "Messiah," the Hallelujah Chorus is sung, both noble and profane, rich and poor, believer and unbeliever in concert halls around the world rise to their feet in respect and some day shall fall to their knees in submission to Him.

The law of cause and effect, when under the influence of the spiritual laws of the Christian scriptures, brings into play the principle of reverse results. Here causes produce contrary effects, actions invoke opposite reactions, and means serve a different end.

A four-point summary of Jesus' parable of the good Samaritan gives a clear picture of the alternatives confronting us in relationships, as the same aspiration for prosperity and personal contentment is approached from four angles:

1. The robber said, "What's yours is mine, and I'll take it."

2. The priest said, "What's mine is mine, and I'll keep it."

3. The inn keeper said, "What's mine is yours if you'll pay for it."

4. The good Samaritan said, "What's mine is yours, and I'll give it."

In this world of self-seeking and polarization of interests, we are faced daily with difficult choices. Countering the instinct of self-preservation to in honor prefer one another does not come naturally. We must resist conformity to "common sense," and, as individuals, groups, and organizations actively pursue by faith our Lord's uncommon example of self-denial, which will bring about the reverse results of genuine peace, honor, and prosperity.

EPILOGUE

God is and all is well
Henry Greenleaf Whittier

After seven years of reaching out with spiritual and material help, we left Africa in July, 1987. Our departure was reminiscent of that cold and rainy day thirteen years earlier when, shortly after our wedding, Debbie and I had embarked on our hitchhiking tour of West Africa. Then we had looked forward with excitement to the adventures before us, even as our enthusiasm was dampened at leaving her mother distressed over our method of travel. The miserable weather hadn't helped, either.

Now, again, our emotions were conflicting. Parting was not easy. We were sad at leaving our adoptive country and the many friends we had made, and we determined that we would remain in close touch and come back frequently. Now, as we returned to our own continent, we were excited at the unknown that awaited us and happy in the knowledge that family and friends would receive us with open arms, relieved that we had returned safely. Eventually, "snail mail" would be replaced by email, supplemented by the occasional telephone call. Jackson would visit us for four weeks, and, most significantly, the work we had started would not only continue through him and other men we had trained, but expand into another needy place – Rwanda. But for now, our clash of emotions turned to joyful anticipation when we included in our return trip an opportunity we wouldn't have missed for anything.

Situated near the junction of three continents, Israel is hard to by-pass for any world traveler. I had visited it twice as a bachelor and once with Debbie. Now, on our way back, we would stop over as a family. Both of us find no other country as fascinating. Though small – only about the size of Canada's Vancouver Island – it became the one place the Uncaused First Cause chose to visit this planet in human form. Shaped by three cultures and three world religions, it is the historic home of Jesus the Christ, a place of arguably greatest archeological interest in cities and towns dating from the earliest biblical times, such as Jerusalem (Joshua 18:28), Jericho (Joshua 2:1), Beersheba (Genesis:21:14), Acco (Judges 1:31), Qiryat Arba' (Kirjath Arba, Genesis 23:2) and many more. Now, for a small additional expense, we could visit Israel again and enable our children, at ages nine and seven, to get their first impression of this unique piece of real estate.

The history of God's dealings with human kind is widely misunderstood. The multiplicity of Christian denominations and cults contributes to the confusion. So do the failures of the "faithful," especially those who have usurped the name of Christ and, under its cover, have perpetrated unspeakable evil.

But what of God's glorious strategy of reuniting fallen man with Himself? Rejecting His overtures toward us because of the failings of those worse than ourselves is, again, like trying to hide behind an object smaller than we. It doesn't work. It leaves us exposed. And it's hypocritical.

In an effort to bring the history of God's dealings with human kind into coherent form, I wrote a poem over a number of years that, I believe, does just that. I had hoped to get these most important tenets of the Scriptures set to music; see them transformed into a Christian musical, but it was not to be. I include the poem here in hopes that getting it out of my computer file will help bring clarity to a muddled picture.

BORN TO DIE

Before the dawn of all creation
There was no matter, time or space.
The start of all, its destination,
Man's fall and God's redeeming grace

Are in His Holy Word revealed.
God-breathed, it is alive to bless
With truths from science well concealed.
Man's wisdom lauds God's foolishness.

God is the Father, Son and Spirit
In perfect union, Trinity,
Sublime, supreme and without limit
In love, in justice, purity.

His Spirit in a frame all human,
With mind, emotion, and a will,
To understand, to feel, determine.
Thus man was made and stayed, until

The eerie sound of his rebellion
Caused discord in the symphony
And shrieked into God's sweet dominion,
Dispelling peace and harmony.

"Yea, hath God said", the serpent lied,
Thus tempted sinless man to sin.
Man listened, then God's truth denied.
The devil's pow'r had entered in.

The law of Moses was a mirror,
Which God gave us in preparation,
Reflecting unto us our error,
Conditioned us for His salvation.

Since now God's well-known laws were broken,
Exceeding sinful sin became.
God gave in foresight man a token
Of remedy for sin and shame.

As symbol of sin's awful price
Man in obedience to God
Brought lambs and bulls as sacrifice.
Just perfect males would shed their blood.

The High Priest entered once a year
The Inner Court, not without blood.
Behind the veil He would draw near
To mediate for us with God.

When time was ripe God flesh became,
Fulfilling ancient prophecy,
For in His Son He'd bear our shame

As Lamb of God on Calvary.

While women on this earth conceive
And then bring forth, who could deny,
In pain a life that it might live,
God's Son was born that He might die.

And now, O blind, that you might see,
Look back to hist'ry's focal point.
Behold the Man of Galilee.
Perceive this hour in your mind.

For here, amidst a jeering crowd,
For you and me there on that hill,
Christ stands, His head in silence bowed,
Committed to His Father's will.

His brow is crowned with thorns of mock.
They spit into His tortured face.
The blood runs down His beaten back,
And yet His heart is full of grace.

Now stretched out on the cross he bore,
With nails through both His hands and feet,
He prays for those who, just before,
In ignorance performed this deed.

Despised by man, by God forsaken,
With hours passed, He bows His head.
The goal achieved, the vict'ry taken,
The Son of God and man is dead.

The sun's obscured. The dead arise.
The earth revolts, which He had trod.
The veil is torn. A soldier says:
"Truly, this was the Son of God."

O creature, wilt thou comprehend?

This form of flesh created thee.
The One who was omnipotent
At thy hands suffered willingly.

He left His glorious home above;
Laid down His rights as God of all.
He bound Himself with bonds of love
To save us from our sins and hell.

No greater love has mortal man
Than he who for a friend would die.
Yet Jesus was our savior when
We sinners did Him crucify.

Alas, the grave could not conceal
The One who gives us life and breath.
As was His predetermined will,
He was triumphant over death.

And now He lives and reigns forever,
Exalted at His Father's right.
As Lord and King He'll heal, deliver
Those blind, who know they're without sight.

The carpet is rolled out in grace,
Stained red with Jesus' precious blood,
That we, as sinners poor, can face
The boundless riches of our God.

Come knock, repent, and you'll receive
His total pardon for your sins.
If you will with your heart believe,
Then everlasting life begins.

Yes come to Jesus. Freely give
To Him your life, that you might live.

* * *

We booked our flight with El Al, the Israeli airline, from Nairobi via Tel Aviv to Frankfurt, and from Amsterdam to New York. Since El Al didn't have a Frankfurt – Amsterdam flight, we chose Lufthansa for that leg, and Pan American Airlines from New York to Washington D.C., where Debbie's parents would be our first stop in America.

In our seven years in Africa, we had accumulated many mementos – a story, a face, a memorable occasion associated with each one – too many to fit into eight suitcases and eight carry-ons. We had a choice – part with them or pay for them. Neither was appealing. But perhaps there was another way.

We had lived in adverse circumstances in Africa long enough to know that when you can't go over or around an obstacle, perhaps you can go through it. We went "through" El Al. "Dear Sir/Madam, We were missionaries for the last seven years in Africa…" I never believed that, as missionaries, we should expect special privileges. But I must confess that when it came right down to it, I compromised and elected to give El Al the opportunity to decide whether or not it would accord us extraordinary consideration in recognition of the benevolent work the word "missionary" conjures up. And indeed, the airline did; our letter of request met with approval. El Al agreed to carry our seventy-kilo steamer trunk free of charge and sent us a letter to that effect. That was exciting. Serendipitously, it would also turn out to be our rescue from major and costly inconvenience on our way home.

We arrived at Tel Aviv's Ben Gurion International Airport on Sunday, July 19, 1987 after a five-hour flight in business class. We always flew business class to and from Nairobi, not, as you know by now, because we were so well-to-do, but because a Christian organization in Holland paid for the upgrade for all missionaries through the Menno Travel Service in Nairobi. Seeing us with backpacks, duffel bags, and dilapidated luggage at the business-class counter must have aroused some curiosity. Yep, being missionaries did have its perks.

For 24 shekels ($15) a day we put eleven pieces of luggage into storage and breathed a sigh of relief. By 8:30 a.m. on a balmy day on which the sun had turned up for our arrival, we checked into the Christ Church Hospice at the Jaffa Gate inside the ancient walls of the old city of Jerusalem. The place was supposedly booked up, but the friendly staff did have a bright, airy family room for us. We had breakfast in the dining room, whose multi-vaulted ceiling bespoke history and mystery and attended a church service an hour after checking in. Still tired from our overnight flight, we went to bed for the rest of the morning.

The nap refreshed us, and we set out to explore the old city. We walked from the Christian quarter to the Muslim quarter, and, although some shops were closed on Sundays, we had a déjà-vu experience of being back in a soukh in the Middle East: narrow streets for pedestrians only, hawkers trying to attract our attention from small shops with folding metal doors that exposed the whole interior when open – chockfull with merchandise that spilled out into the ancient stone-paved alleys on tables or dangling from coat hangers and ropes – women with the hijab, the traditional head scarves; old men in jalabiyahs or traditional gowns, their heads covered with plain white, black-and-white or red-and-white-checkered kafiyehs, puffing on hookahs (Arabic water pipes) or drinking thick, black kahawa (coffee) from tiny cups; young men pulling two-wheeled wagons full of fruits and vegetables, and vociferous boys playing soccer in the absence of the usual bedlam.

A knowledgeable tour guide, Josef, an Arab Christian, met us early Monday morning and took us through the old city's four quarters – Jewish, Muslim, Armenian, and Christian – ending up on the Via Dolorosa and the fourteen Stations of the Cross. It seems as though a church has been built on every site connected to an event in Jesus' life, be it in the Christian, Muslim, or Armenian quarters. Some stones are identified with his personal touch and become the objects of veneration. I find this peculiar, because the "hallowed" ground Jesus walked lay at least twelve feet below today's streets. Nevertheless, the tour was particularly meaningful because Josef was able to relate some of the sites that had survived countless assaults on the city not only to New Testament passages and events, but to Old Testament events and prophecies, as well.

*   *   *

Near the beginning of this book I related how I came to faith. The Austrian novelist Marie von Ebner-Eschenbach wrote, "In youth we learn; in age we understand." As I grew older, my faith deepened, and I began to understand the impact its historical reality could have on others. And I wanted them to understand also. My business prospered, and I took out full-page advertisements in three major Denver-area newspapers and three college papers in an effort to communicate the impact Christ can have on someone committed to Him. I received many positive responses, but also irrational and angry ones.

In answer to one ad that dealt with the subject of creation vs. evolution, I received a sarcastic letter from a Denver-area scientist. He had taped a shiny new penny as his "contribution" to my effort. Never one to just quietly fade away, I responded, and a friendly email exchange began that lasted several months.

Atheistic scientists, even post-graduate researchers from M.I.T. such as he, have no answer to the question of First Cause – what was there before the Big Bang and the Primordial Soup? What (who?) brought either into being? These questions show that science, which deals only with observable phenomena in organized, repeatable experiments, is not the foundational discipline – philosophy is; philosophy based on truth. This means that if you go back far enough, science runs out of answers and philosophy holds sway. The other day I read about "philosophy of science." But you cannot have it both ways. It shouldn't take a Ph.D. to know that there is no such animal. Science deals with knowledge, not wisdom. (philo = lover – sophia = wisdom)

Here is an excerpt of one of the last letters I wrote to Bill S.:

While I was really hoping to get into some apologetics concerning the existence of God, let me just follow the above thought with a bit of a time warp: It is the year 33 A.D. A skeptical intellectual named Bill and a recent convert to a revolutionary named Jesus Christ, Eb, are sitting in front of a small, cave-like grains and nuts shop in the walled City of David, Jerusalem, sipping chai. Amid the hustle and bustle in the steep, narrow ally we are discussing the events that had the whole city in an uproar just a few days earlier. To you, the subject was buried with the guy. Whatever may have happened to his body is a matter of conjecture – there are all kinds of rumors floating around, each one promoting the philosophical inclination of its perpetuator.

But you bear with me as I challenge you with this question: "Would you submit your life unconditionally to His dominion if 2000 years from now this executed, insignificant rebel carpenter with his small following that went into hiding at the power of Rome, were to be nomi-

nated by a magazine called TIME as the greatest, most influential individual of two millennia, if not of all of human history?"

Before you have a chance to respond, I go on dreaming: "He will split time in two – B.C. and A.D. He will enlist the greatest following, and more people will lay down their lives for Him than for any cause anywhere ever. He will elevate the status of women, promote civil liberties and the dignity of the common man. He will inspire some of history's greatest musicians and artists, give impetus to heretofore non-existent health institutions, will be behind the most far-reaching charitable disaster relief organizations on the planet, and will lay the foundation for free markets and free enterprise. Schools and universities will be founded in His name and scientific inquiry will blossom because of Him. His standards will help prevent his followers from making poor choices, the consequences of which could result in disease and have adverse effects on society. His Word will be the reason for the translation and alphabetization of thousands of languages, resulting in the civilizing of people groups worldwide. A machine will be invented specifically for its multiplication, and its inventor will be named by TIME magazine the most important individual of the second millennium. Sons will be named after His disciples, like Peter, James, and John, while" – I add quietly – "dogs will be named Caesar, Nero, and Rex."

At this point a riot erupts as a group of young rebels attack two patrolling Roman centurions just as they pass by us. Our table, chai and all, gets toppled over, and, amidst the commotion, we join the fleeing mob. I saved my shiny penny that day as I never got to pay, but I also never got your answer. I knew you were a skeptic, but I also believed you to be a man of reason. Somehow, in my heart I knew that it was just a matter of time, and you would be one of us, helping us shape history as you, too, came to believe in His story.

* * *

Bethlehem was served by the No. 22 Arab bus. We looked in vain for the bus stop, only to learn that the locals just wave the bus down anywhere along the way. If you pass the time by walking and talking and don't hear it coming – not to worry! Chances are the ticket collector will spot you, hang out the door of the bus and shout "Bethlehem!" in hopes of attracting another customer or four. Arabs, not unlike Ugandans, are more relaxed in their lifestyle than the better-organized Jews, whose buses run on a schedule and pick up passengers only at properly identified stops.

We got off at Rachel's tomb, Judaism's third-holiest site, within walking distance of Bethlehem. Here, some 3700 years later, Jewish women still bemoan the death of Jacob's second wife. For the uninitiated that can be surprising. I suppose her death symbolizes the suffering and death the Jewish people have endured throughout their history, from exile in Egypt under the Pharaohs to the holocaust in Germany under Hitler.

Fascinating as Israel was, it couldn't halt the march of time. Our departure date came. My sister, Uschi, picked us up in Frankfurt. Four trolley carts piled high with luggage – but where was the fourth person? Seven-year old Misha was dwarfed by her load and could not see where she was heading. But who needs sight when you have faith – in your parents, anyway?

The letter of request for free passage of our heavy, souvenir-laden trunk that I had sent to El Al, I had also sent to Lufthansa in Frankfurt and to Pan Am in New York, but without success. The former had ignored us – fortunately, as it would turn out – while the latter had referred us to another office, and we ran out of time. Pan Am, however, would end up not only carrying the trunk from New York to Washington D.C. at no charge – as it was in transit, I suppose – but delivering it to General Blanchard's house in McLean, since it wouldn't arrive with our other luggage at Washington National (now Reagan National) Airport. That was even more than my letter had requested!

After a week of gourmet food and visits with my half-siblings, Christoph and Petra and with my long-standing friend, Martin Lauth, a well-known architect in that part of Germany, and his wife, Wilma, we were ready for the jump across the big pond. But the excitement of our return to our past and future home was dashed with a huge scare at Frankfurt Airport.

Karsten and Misha still had dual citizenship and were traveling with German and American passports. For the Nairobi – Tel Aviv – Frankfurt leg of the trip, we had used their German passports. For our next flights – Frankfurt to Amsterdam and Amsterdam to New York – we would use their American passports. But where were they? We searched our carry-ons

– nothing. Panic!!! Without visas in their German passports they could not enter the United States. We were in a fix.

The suitcases had already been sent into the labyrinthine recesses of the airport from where the baggage is transferred to the planes. Sympathetic airport personnel escorted us down into a concrete supplier's dream of long ago. It held a maze of conveyor belts, water pipes, electric conduits, and air ducts, and – yes! – luggage carts piled high with suitcases. We quickly found ours. But again our search did not turn up those wayward passports.

We called Uschi, who proceeded to search our rooms and then the rest of the house.

Meanwhile, boarding time rolled around. We decided that I should go ahead to Amsterdam with the children and the luggage. Debbie would follow us on the next flight, which would easily allow her to make the connection to our El Al flight, scheduled to depart in the early morning hours. And Uschi would have enough time to rush the passports, which, surely, she would find, to the airport in Frankfurt before the next flight. It was a plan. Things were looking up.

But it was not to be – Karsten's and Misha's passports were gone! They had either been lost or stolen. Of course, we had a theory that we were hesitant to express. We did not want to make false accusations. But we knew that passports are sold on the black market for terrorist purposes, among others, and when we later reported them lost to the passport agency in Seattle, we voiced our suspicion.

Reunited, we committed again our situation to God. We were totally helpless and had the feelings to go with it. Had we had unlimited funds – time we had aplenty – there would have been no problem. We simply would have booked a hotel room in Amsterdam, taken in a canal cruise while awaiting the completion of the paperwork for our German kids and booked a flight on another carrier – KLM Royal Dutch Airlines, in this case. However, since we didn't have unlimited funds, we couldn't simply kiss our El Al tickets good-bye.

Without their visas, our first problem was not getting the kids into the U.S., but getting them out of Holland. El Al wouldn't allow them to board, risking, as they would upon rejection by U.S. Immigration, not only to have to fly them back at their own expense, but to have to pay a hefty fine on top. To complicate matters further, it wasn't just a matter of getting the visas and hopping on another El Al flight a day or two later.

There was only one flight a week from Amsterdam to New York, and that flight was booked for the next several weeks. Without doubt, we were in deep trouble.

What to do? Well, we continued to pray. And then? We prayed some more.

The secret to our deliverance from the first problem lay in our trunk, figuratively speaking. Had Lufthansa complied with our request for free transport, the trunk would have awaited automatic transfer to our next flight along with our suitcases. As it was, we had chosen to send it with Lufthansa Freight, which was cheaper than paying for excess baggage. That kept it separate from our luggage. Marked with Schiphol Airport as its destination, our trunk was rolled into the transit lounge and delivered to us by Lufthansa personnel. It must have been the biggest piece of luggage ever to grace a transit lounge. We bided our time beyond midnight, trying to get some rest. We still had to get our boarding passes, the first major obstacle as we had to produce our passports for that, and, of course, we still had to check the trunk. That meant leaving the transit lounge, officially entering Holland, and then checking in at the El Al counter.

Then I had a simple idea: I left Debbie and the children with their passports in the lounge – transit-passengers with their proper identification in the transit lounge – rolled our steamer trunk into an elevator, waved good-bye once more as the doors closed, emerged two floors down, entered Holland through customs and immigration, got back onto another elevator, went two floors up and, when the doors opened, there was El Al's own special, extra-secure check-in room. I had never left the building. It was just after 1 a.m., but I was as alert, and my adrenaline was pumping as if I were about to walk a tightrope across the Grand Canyon. Hopefully my mission here would have greater success than that would.

I was greeted in a business-like but friendly manner as I approached the counter. I produced the letter that authorized the trunk to be taken at no charge and presented the airline tickets for the four of us, explaining that my family had remained in the transit lounge. The man in charge studied the letter, then asked me about the contents of the trunk, the packing details, and all the other questions so routinely asked at check-ins nowadays. Two other men put the same questions to me, one right after the other, each observing me for any sign of nervousness and listening for inconsistencies. I must have passed with flying colors, because I did not have to open the trunk for inspection. That was a relief – had they gone through all that stuff, I'm not sure I, or rather they, could have fit it in again.

I remember the first time I left Israel with El Al before other airlines took security seriously. That was in 1974, just before I met Debbie. The security staff had pulled everything out of my backpack, then searched every nook and cranny of the pack itself. When I thought they were done, I made a move to stuff everything back myself. But no way! They handled each piece of clothing a second time as they returned every last one into the backpack themselves.

Now the moment of truth came: The supervisor asked for our passports. I handed him my German one with my green card and explained that I had left my family with theirs in the transit lounge. (That was technically correct, as the kids did have their passports, albeit their insufficient German ones.) Wow! The truth was out. In a second one can think many thoughts, and my mind was racing in different directions, but mostly upward. Would he…?

There wasn't even a moment's hesitation. The official turned to the woman sitting on his right and handed her the tickets. "Make out four boarding passes." It was as simple as that. My face remained as composed and somber as that of one singing in a requiem mass, but inside I was bouncing like a polka dancer. I hoped that security, which had studied my demeanor just minutes earlier, would not detect my disguise.

Why are elevators so slow? On the way I thought up a playful sound bite that was only half true: I said to Debbie: "I got us out of Holland – now it's your job to get us into America." One major obstacle still lay ahead. American immigration officials have no trouble following the rule book. In the process they are serious and businesslike – until you hear the thud of the stamp. Then a smile creases their faces, and you hear those wonderful words: "Welcome home!" Would we hear that? Or would we be escorted into a waiting room and kept there under guard while arrangements were made with El Al to put us on their next flight back, probably bouncing four scheduled passengers in the process?

We weren't home yet by any means, but we saw enough light at the end of the tunnel to have increased faith and hope. We had experienced the goodness of God over many years and in many, sometimes mysterious, ways. We had felt His protection through many dangers and difficulties.

My being alive was testimony to that. Now we were dependent on God's intervention yet one more time.

Just once more, Lord – one more time.

In the arrival lounge at U.S. immigration, as at that of most countries around the world, the "sheep" are separated from the "goats." As a German passport holder with a green card, I joined a long line of other non-citizens. Debbie and I had decided to take our chances with the citizen line for the children. It was out of our view. With a final wave, the three of them disappeared down a pedestrian tunnel, temporarily constructed with two-by-fours and plywood while major renovation was under way. There were the usual signs saying something like, "Please excuse the inconvenience. We are remodeling to better serve you." Yep. We were on American soil, at least unofficially. Americans are so diplomatic! Would they "serve" *us*, and well?

My line moved inversely to my heartbeat, i.e. s-l-o-w-l-y. My heart was racing, but my feet were shuffling. I knew I would enter the country hassle-free. But what was happening now with Debbie, Karsten, and Misha? In Africa, a cute little blond girl like Misha would have opened the door for us without much ado. But we were far from Africa, both in miles and in customs – I mean immigration.

By the time I emerged on the other side, stamped in and legal, I saw a most beautiful sight – my family. I think I ran to get the scoop. They had just walked through. There had been no grave-looking immigration official to examine their passports, shake his head and return them on the next El Al flight to Holland. It was fourteen years before 9/11, certainly. But for the U.S., this sort of lapse was unheard of even in the most peaceful times. For us, it was simply wonderful; the end of a long, long story.

We had a big family hug. We praised God. We were home.

APPENDICES

These six chapters were originally included in the first part of a book I planned to publish under the title "Travels, Trials, and Trajectories." However, there was a consensus that a travel section, full of adventures as it is, would be too distracting from the main story – our experiences in Africa.

The decision to leave these chapters out did not come easily as I knew that any travel buff would find them an interesting read. But, as mentioned earlier, I had learned in my travels that obstacles are there to be overcome. If you can't go around them, try to go through them. And so I opted for the obvious solution – adding the chapters here as a separate entity.

I was told that it's not something that is done. But I've heard that before. And maybe it wasn't.

Having already met Debbie in the book, it will not come as a surprise that she proved to be a derring-do travel companion early in our marriage. She was athletic, had an enterprising spirit, an inquisitive mind, and was linguistically gifted, all of which made her a perfect candidate for adventure travel.

Those qualities were put to the test on our first trip through fifteen countries of North and West Africa. It was challenging physically as well as mentally, with hot, dusty days, long waits between rides, not always the quality food to sustain a weary body, and never selectable comfort for her beauty rest. But she hung in there with me, and together we chalked up many memories.

Here are highlights. Let us go back in time – way back – and get a good dose of armchair travel into some remote corners of the world.

Appendix A

ADVERSITY AND BLESSINGS

Give me health and a day,
and I will make the pomp of emperors ridiculous.
Ralph Waldo Emerson

We were making our way south through Morocco towards Spanish Sahara. We had traversed two-thirds of this fascinating country and had admired the old reddish clay-colored architecture of Fez, looked in vain for Humphrey Bogart in Casablanca, bargained with bronze-faced, caftan-clad vendors with white beards and white turbans in the market of Khenifra, watched snake charmers and shysters in the legendary city of Marrakech, and responded to curious children's friendly attention-seeking "bon jour," all the time watching our steps on donkey, sheep, and goat-trafficked streets throughout the country. At Agadir we enjoyed a campground by the beach with cool ocean breezes and interaction with fellow travelers from Europe and North America. Also at Agadir we got disappointing news: We learned from other backpackers that the road from Tan Tan to the border with Spanish Sahara was closed off and the border itself was closed.

So much for our efficient, well-laid plans. Debbie coped fine with that, but for me it was a major let-down. I loathed the idea of backtracking. Moving onward, discovering new territory, like the Sahara Desert and sub-Saharan Africa beyond – those were my goals. For me, returning was a been-there-done-that nuisance, a time-wasting setback. Always intent on setting new personal records, exploring further and penetrating deeper, I was a stamp collector with no interest in philately. The stamps I collected were put into my passports and opened the world to me. Some may attribute this drive to an upbringing that had deprived me of foreign travel. Perhaps, as a high school drop-out, I felt the need to prove myself "worldly" wise. Whatever it was, I was driven in more ways than one. Debbie, my people-oriented wife, came along not just because she was my better half, but because she had an enterprising spirit of her own.

We neared the end of our time in Morocco, or so we thought, and my two-week visa was running out. Now we had to retrace our steps and return to Spain to find an alternate route. My favorite American needed no visa, and she and I decided that I should return by myself to the capital, Rabat, to get mine extended. She would stay with our tent and our gear next to an older Canadian couple, who had given us a lift in their Volkswagen camper right into the campground. They would keep an eye on her. It would be our first separation since our wedding, but then it wouldn't hurt either of us to remember what we were missing when we weren't together. It was the absence-and-fond-heart thing.

At the Ministry of Foreign Affairs, a maze of dark staircases and cavernous hallways, people were rushing around like army ants on the warpath. I was sent from floor to floor, from room to room,. from Peter to Paul or, better, from Mahmud to Mohammed and back, before I finally came upon an official in the visa section whose job description matched him with my needs.

The Moroccans are a friendly and hospitable people, so I was not prepared for the hostile reception I received. Since the massacre of Israeli athletes at the 1972 Olympics in Munich, the German government had put severe restrictions on visas for Arabs, and, although German tourists were a major source of their country's foreign exchange, the Moroccans reciprocated. No, my visa would not be renewed, and, a government official told me point-blank, if I were to overstay it, I would be arrested. Quoth he, "Ma salama" – "Go in peace", or, more succinctly, "Get out of here."

Wow! I stepped into the blinding sun in front of the ministry as disappointment and uncertainty gripped my gut. My mind was racing in several directions, only to return to the minutes in that office in the ministry behind me in which, as a political pawn, I had given a government pinhead the opportunity the vent his racial animosity. What is it about officialdom that turns people from ordinary fellow human beings into impersonal, self-absorbed and, as in this case, even hostile bureaucrats?

I felt like a beaten dog. What to do? It was not likely that, without incurring major expenses, I could fetch Debbie in Agadir and still have enough time for of us to make it onto a ferry in the Strait of Gibraltar before my visa expired. And, with our tight budget, I was not prepared to do that without exhausting every possible alternative. There's got to be a way out of this predicament!

I examined my visa carefully. I could read Arabic numbers, but it seemed that the expiration date was not legible; the numbers were either too light or totally missing. Is it possible that "nothing," as it were, could solve my problem? My spirits lifted, and I had a spring in my step as I sought to get confirmation of my suspicion.

Young people the world over enjoy interacting with foreigners, if for no other reason but to practice their English. I quickly found a young university-type. Friendly and helpful, he examined my visa carefully and substantiated my hunch. So did a second one. I returned to Agadir relieved. We would not be in a rush to get to Tangier and out of the country. "Was ich nicht weiss, macht mich nicht heiss," is a German proverb, meaning: What I don't know can't bother me; nor would it the agent at the border. My radar homed in on Debbie; after two days, the separation had been long enough.

Still, anxious to put this chapter behind us and to make up for the time we were going to lose, we were up and ready to move at 5:30 a.m. But we couldn't get out of the highly secure campground – the tall, barbed wire-topped gate was locked, and the gate keeper was fast asleep. It was Sunday, alright, but that's an ordinary workday in a Muslim country. The Islamic day of worship and rest is Friday. We bided our time until I finally awakened the man with the key. One of our rides was with the "Marrakech Express", an impromptu fund-raising scheme by two enterprising travelers, a German and an Italian with a minibus. Four dollars a piece took us from Agadir to Marrakech, a distance of 160 miles – at Third World speed in about four hours.

It was close to Christmas now, and, as we headed north, we began to notice people everywhere traveling with sheep. Sheep and goats are the main livestock in this country, but something else was afoot here, no pun intended. It was always just one sheep and never a goat that would be transported in the backseat or trunk of a car, tied up with a board onto the carrier of a bicycle or motorcycle, stowed away on top of a bus amidst piles of suitcases, bulging gunnysacks, beds, and an assortment of other household goods, or led on a leash like a dog. We also knew that Muslims didn't celebrate the birthday of Isa, so there would be no Christmas dinner with mutton. What was the purpose behind this mass movement with single sheep? I finally asked somebody about the meaning of this.

What we learned was eye-opening: Muslims were getting ready to celebrate Eid-ul-Adha, the Feast of Sacrifice, in commemoration of Ibrahim's willingness to slay his son Ishmael and of the sacrifice of a sheep that God provided as a substitute. This is a significant variation from the report given in the Bible and is but one illustration of the gulf that exists between the Muslim and Christian faiths.

According to the Bible, God had promised Abraham and his wife, Sarah, a son through whom all the nations of the earth would be blessed. But as they were getting older and remained childless, Sarah began to doubt that promise and encouraged Abraham to have a child with her servant, Hagar. Ishmael came from that union, and God ordained that his descendants would become a great nation. They are today's Arabs – one mighty ethnic group that, united not only by lineage, but by religion, culture, and language, stretches from the Atlantic coast of Morocco, across North Africa, to the Persian Gulf states.

Several years later, God fulfilled His promise and Sarah, well beyond child-bearing age now, miraculously conceived and gave birth to Isaac. This half-brother to Ishmael became the father of the Jews and thus physically the forefather and symbolically a type of the Messiah. When he, this long-awaited son of promise through whom all the nations of the earth would be blessed, was a young man, God tested Abraham's faith again. "Take your son, your only son Isaac, whom you love, and go to the land of Moriah, and offer him there as a burnt offering on one of the mountains that I shall show you." (Genesis 22:2)

There are several prophetic symbolisms here. In the New Testament, the Apostle John said that "God so loved the world that He gave his one and only Son." That was Jesus, the Son of promise. When Abraham and Isaac left the two servants at the foot of Mount Moriah, today's Temple Mount in Jerusalem and site of the Muslim Dome of the Rock and the Al Aqsa mosque, Abraham instructed them to wait for *their* return. Abraham believed that God would resurrect his son, even as God would resurrect His own Son, the Messiah, forty-two generations later. Although stronger than his father, Isaac voluntarily submitted to his wishes and carried the wood for the burnt offering, just as Christ voluntarily submitted to the will of His Father by carrying His own cross on the way to His crucifixion.

Why did we see individual sheep being moved with every mode of transport in Morocco those few days before Christmas? Because, while at the top of the mountain – the altar of sacrifice built, Isaac lying across it, bound, and Abraham in obedience ready to plunge a knife into his son's heart – God restrained the father of two nations and provided a ram, caught by his horns in the bushes, as a substitutionary sacrifice for Isaac. There is significant prophetic symbolism here because, nearly 2000 years later, Jesus, the "real thing," fulfilled the prophecy as He died on a Roman cross, a substitutionary sacrifice for sinful Jews, Muslims, Christians, and, indeed, all the peoples of the world. It is the answer to this question that separates Muslims from Jews and Christians: Was it Ishmael or Isaac in whose place Abraham sacrificed that ram on Mount Moriah?

*   *   *

When the time came to leave Morocco, we surrounded ourselves with other backpackers. The routine of stamping a group of foreigners out of the country would work in our favor. As we separated, my heart pounded with anticipation. I would go first. If I got arrested, Debbie, who was back just far enough to be out of the immigration officials' line of sight, could step out of the queue and remain in the country, too – she in a hotel and I in one of Morocco's jails. That was not a happy proposition, but at least food and lodging would be free. Fortunately, and much to our relief, it was not necessary to take advantage of the government's hospitality. The illegible date in my visa stood up to scrutiny.

We traversed the Strait of Gibraltar by ferry from Tangier to Algeciras. The salt air was energizing and the stiff wind bracing in that narrow mouth that opened the Mediterranean to the Atlantic Ocean. I felt refreshed and mentally prepared for a new assault on the "black continent". Today was a new beginning. From Algeciras we would go to Càdiz, catch a ship to the Canary Islands and make our way, somehow, from there to Spanish Sahara. It was all Spanish territory, so there must be a lifeline – some connection that would allow us to reenter Africa. So we reasoned. So we prayed. So we hoped.

Part of the adventure in our mode of motion was uncertainty – uncertainty as to our next ride, with whom and how far and what we would see on the way, where and what we would eat, and where we would spend the night. We would learn, we had determined, not only to get along without hamburgers, fries, sodas, and ice cream, but to savor local foods, enjoy local drinks, and appreciate and fit in with local customs. I shall never forget an American lady in Belem, Brazil, who had a dispute with a bank official. She kept saying in her loud and unabashed American [sorry!] way: "Well, we in Ameeerica…," and I had felt like going up to her and saying: "Lady, you are not in Ameeerica." We would not be in "Ameeerica" for months, and we would adjust to the local way of life and make the most of the opportunity for a near total cultural immersion.

Thus, curiosity as to what lay around the corner made our tour all the more exciting. Of course, there were many corners, and spontaneity became the name of the game. Having the mental flexibility to deal with unexpected minor adversities, inevitable in Third World travel as we had already found out twice, can make globetrotting less stressful. I was still trying to learn that. Debbie adjusted more quickly to changes, and to this day I value her positive outlook and even-tempered ability to see benefits in adversity. Failed expectation mixed as little with my rigid German character as oil does with water. But, with practice, I would quickly learn to make the best of every situation – no matter how long it would take.

It was the day before Christmas, 1974, and the disappointment at having been forced to backtrack, in addition to missing the closeness of family at this festive time of year, left us in a melancholy mood.

We always looked forward to receiving mail at the poste-restante counters of main post offices in major cities. (How did we ever manage before email?) At the post office in Algeciras we met the manager for Westinghouse, S.A., Mr. Carson, an American who, like we, had just stepped in to get his mail. A tall man in his mid-fifties with a warm, deep voice, he invited us to his apartment for "a coffee or a cognac."

It turned out to be a lavishly decorated place in an upscale neighborhood. His lovely Spanish wife was still recovering from the flu, but she made us feel as welcome as long lost friends. Her English was fluent, though heavily accented with a typical Latin staccato and rolling "Rs." After brief introductions she disappeared into the kitchen to emerge shortly with delicacies we hadn't seen in over a month: cubed cheese, smoked ham, anchovies, olives and bread. What a treat! We had become accustomed to making open-face sandwiches with sardines in olive oil, sardines in tomato sauce and sardines in brine. Or there was bread with "La Vache qui Rit."

That was a soft, processed cheese made with the milk from a cow that laughed. The occasional splurge took us to a typical, hole-in-the-wall Moroccan restaurant for couscous and mint tea with a ton of sugar.

When Mrs. Carson saw our scantily disguised hunger for her palate-pleasing goodies, she disappeared into the kitchen once more and emerged shortly with a smile, scrambled eggs, bacon, and toast. Wow, talk about dying and going to heaven!

Being kind-hearted and generous, and perhaps missing the opportunity to indulge their own children, if they had any, they invited us over for Christmas Day as well and for a dinner that included chili with tortillas, hot bread, and butter, followed by sweets and plenty of home-made sangria (a cup of Cointreau per liter of red wine, cubed oranges, lemon and banana slices, and sugar to taste – her own special recipe).

We gladly accepted yet another invitation, this one to come back for lunch the day after Christmas to help finish off what was left of the previous day's feast. But as our time for departure was at hand, it was our desire to take our friends out for dinner on our last evening together. They had looked after us as if we were their adopted children. They had read, it seemed, every faint wish on our minds and withheld nothing. We had showered there and even done a load of laundry. By the time we would leave Algeciras, we would be as refreshed as we were the day we left the hospitality of Debbie's parents. So it was our turn to make an attempt at reciprocity. We would take them out that evening. Yes, we would.

Since they knew the area and provided the transportation, we left the choice of the restaurant up to them. Well, they had a surprise in store for us. They took us to the most elegant hotel in Algeciras, the "Reina Cristina" – four-star luxury with a large swimming pool, tennis courts, and orange trees in manicured gardens, and an elegant restaurant with a menu to match. The bill? Never mind. We never saw it. We were told in no uncertain terms that Westinghouse would take care of it. I am convinced that Mr. Carson paid from his own wallet but wanted to avoid a friendly argument. A final drive around the area included a tour of the Westinghouse power plant and the British enclave of Gibraltar.

When it came to good-byes, our vocabulary was inadequate to express our feelings. Life is not supposed to be a one-way street. Relationships are based on mutuality, on give and take, and that isn't supposed to mean that one party just gives, while the other just takes. We don't know what we brought to the table of their lives, but given the fact that we were complete strangers when they took us in and shared so freely of their possessions, we could only hope that, in some obscure way, we had contributed to enriching their lives as well. For us, one thing was sure: Their hospitality went a long way toward making up for what later turned out to have been a false report – the closure of the road between Tan Tan, Morocco and the Spanish Sahara border and the border itself.

*   *   *

The only remarkable experience of our trip to Càdiz was our unsuccessful attempt at hitchhiking. Spain, France, and Italy were not exactly hitchhiker-friendly. And I don't think that fear of getting robbed was a major reason – not in those days. No doubt, many of those motorists were too busy, too preoccupied with their own lives to be interested in our story. I learned long ago that, more often than not, I am more interested in what I have to say than others are in hearing it. That observation has served me well. It has made me more sensitive to the attention span my stories and ideas hold and the level of interest others bring to them. It's not that I have nothing to say, but all of us value the opportunity to express our own thoughts. When the slightest distraction causes others to look sideways, when their eyes get that distant look and they lean against the furniture to keep from falling over, then it's time for me to take a breath and give them a chance to change my monologue into a conversation. This revelation has had the added benefit of making me a better listener.

Of course there are those who are full of questions and can make you feel as though you are an interesting person with a story to tell. (It is for that select group that this book is written.) I remember getting a ride in Austria two years earlier with a woman in her Mercedes. She was just such an individual. She was interested in my travels. When I told her that I was on a round-the-world trip, her eyes got wide with amazement, and she was at once disbelieving and excited for me with a "you-don't-say" reaction. I think our encounter made her day. Not so here in southern Spain, and we finally took a bus for the two-hour and forty-five minute trip.

The ticket agent in the port shook his head. All tickets to the Canary Islands were sold out, or so he claimed. Another disappointment. This extended honeymoon trip was no walk in the park. Black Africa seemed to be an elusive goal. But I was skeptical. Had we not also been told that the road south of Tan Tan was closed? I asked Debbie to pray, while I returned to the ticket counter to talk with el señor. I had learned that persistence in prayer and perseverance in pursuit of a goal can go a long way toward reaching it.

As I pressed the man for two purportedly non-existent tickets, the agent overcame his distant demeanor and exchanged his stiff-routine work hat for a more personable and amiable floppy one. It seemed that the shipping company had an ethically-questionable policy – to sell the more expensive berths before all the lower class tickets are sold out. Most would be willing to fork over the extra cash so as not to be left behind. Understanding now that our budget did not include first-class berths, he softened. And much to our relief, he "just happened to find" two more tickets, and after an overnight trip on the Ciudad de Compostela, we found ourselves on Gran Canaria, the main island of the euphemistically named archipelago. The Canary Islands had no canaries that we could see, and I wouldn't blame them if they shunned the place, given our, admittedly, limited experience of Gran Canaria.

Here is what Debbie wrote into our diary on Monday, December 30, 1974:

> *Las Palmas – Well, we made it! But are we really in Las Palmas, the paradise that we expected? We had to come here in order to get south, but it sure doesn't look like the lush place that one sees on posters. It is warm, but could that be the only thing that attracts so many Europeans to so dreary a place? The city itself claims one of the largest ports around, and it is quite big. People are tan and healthy looking, traffic is horrendous, buildings have a stark appearance, and nothing is green as far as we can tell. We find a pension – Buenos Aires – and start to do our business. We hit the police station for "safe conduct" letters to Spanish Sahara and reserve a place on a boat.*

The ticket agency's hall was about as welcoming as a cross-country bus station in a big city slum – bare, grimy walls, a vinyl tile floor that had seen better days, glaring neon lights, and plastic chairs fastened to each other. Heat, humidity, and a long line of perspiring people made for miserable, close encounters as we moved at about a foot a minute toward the ticket counter that was staffed, despite the press of customers, by a semi-conscious agent going through his routine. But we savored every tick of the second hand, because it brought us closer to a new certainty: Yes, there was a ship headed for Spanish Sahara, and yes, we would be on it. Judging by the line of people, this was a popular route leading to a little-known place in an obscure corner of the world. For only seven dollars per person we would make it back to the shores of Africa.

We decided to stay in Las Palmas for a New-Year celebration with genuine Spanish gusto before we would move on to the campground of Tauro at Melandera Beach. We showed our appreciation for the old year by saying "ciao" with a scrambled-eggs-and-sausage dinner and a bottle of cheap red wine. Near our guesthouse was a small amusement park, where we watched gamblers lose money and ate 12 grapes at midnight – must have been a local custom. The New Year was ushered in with hours of tooting car-horns, boisterous voices, raucous singing and general chaos in the streets. Spaniards do know how to live it up!

With tickets to fresh sea breezes and a return cruise to the African continent in hand, we made our way to the campground. The ship would depart for Spanish Sahara in three days. Despite our poor hitchhiking experience in Spain, we decided to give it another try, and, after about thirty minutes on the busy highway, an elderly couple in a Peugeot station wagon going in the opposite direction honked, smiled, and waved. We smiled and waved back. In short order they pulled up and took us to within a five-minute walk of Tauro.

Tauro fit our budget – it was free – but it was closer to Dante's "Inferno" than to the island paradise of a Somerset Maugham novel. Despite the capital's name of Las Palmas, there wasn't a single tree with the promise of shade from the scorching sun, and a constant wind, rolling down from the hills toward the ocean, swept a fine dust across the desolate beach. Seeking sun and sea, Germans had built self-contained tourist resorts along the beaches further up – creature-comfort-laden digs that offered all the luxuries their customers could afford, including shade under "las palmas", which had been either planted there, or transplanted. Theirs were truly oases in the desert.

We found fulfillment in the camaraderie with our fellow back-packers, some of them with interesting tales of world travel. Rugged individualists they were, who wouldn't trade places with our well-heeled resort neighbors sipping pina coladas at romantically-lit bars by the side of palm-lined, azure-colored fresh-water swimming pools. *A picture postcard from their resorts was all that was needed to tell their story. Their guests would only have to add a greeting and a name. It would take more than one diary to tell our tales*, I mused.

* * *

The ambiance of the León y Castillo matched that of the ticket office back in town. It was a rust bucket of a passenger ship, but the camaraderie of the like-minded would make up for its shortcomings. We were accompanied by eighteen Canadians, a few Americans, Danes, a Dutch couple, two Swiss – one of whom had a black poodle – a German with a German shepherd, and some fifty to seventy members of the Spanish Foreign Legion. Most of the backpackers were going only as far as El Aaiun, Spanish Sahara – today's Laayoune, Western Sahara – to head north into Morocco via the border we had been told was closed.

The legionnaires were being dispatched to Spanish Sahara to fight the Polisario guerillas, who had been formed with Algerian support to fight the Spanish colonists for independence for the parched desert territory. There were several fish processing plants, but the main economic attraction of the province were high quality phosphate deposits discovered in 1947 seventy miles south-east of the capital, El Aaiun. The Spaniards were not prepared to lose the income from their investments in the province – hence the legionnaires. While the more famous French Foreign Legion does not accept Frenchmen, seventy-five percent of its Spanish counterpart were Spanish nationals. The most curious features of their uniforms were small tassels that dangled from their garrison caps in front of their noses to keep pestering flies away.

At El Aaiun the wind was so ferocious that landing proved impossible. We had to anchor for the night. A fine, reddish-yellow dust settled on everything that wasn't stowed away and sealed tightly. It was the same dust carried by the sirocco, a hot, dry, and steady wind, from the Sahara (Arabic for desert) across the Mediterranean to Southern Europe. It gave us a foretaste, quite literally, of what we were to experience shortly.

The trip to La Guera, today's Lagwira, at the southern tip of Western Sahara, was to take three days. The delay at El Aaiun cost us another day. That exacerbated a problem we hadn't anticipated: Like the other thirteen or so deck-class passengers, we had planned to buy food for the three-day journey on Monday morning, the day of departure. That Monday, however, happened to be a Spanish holiday, and shops were closed. Our food ration was insufficient and many of the other travelers had nothing.

Come to the rescue, the legionnaires. They were traveling cabin-class but spent most of their time on deck with us. We mingled with them and got to know some of them quite well. One was a German. I don't remember any particular details about this man, except that I got the distinct impression that he was on the run from the law. The Spanish Foreign Legion didn't pry into one's personal history and, by nature of their soldiering in far-away places, provided a safe haven. As long as you were male, met their age-requirements and standards of physical fitness, you were qualified to apply. Their three-to-four-month training was brutal and accompanied by severe beatings from their training instructors. These men had all that behind them now, as they were deployed to fight as a mercenary force. They were friendly guys and eager to help us. They had brought their own cook, and when they had emptied their plates they went back into line and got seconds or thirds and gave them to a drooling gringo. Inevitably, when mealtime came around, Debbie and I also gravitated toward the big pots. Yum! Muchas gracias al gobierno de España.

Between El Aaiun and La Guera the ship stopped only once, in the port of Villa Cisneros, today's Ad Dakhla, which was the administrative center. Here the legionnaires left us, along with other cabin-class passengers. That meant loss of friends and food. But we were about to replace the latter, so that minimized the loss.

We obtained temporary passes to enter the town. And was it ever dead! It was 4 p.m. and still siesta time. There was a cute little church with stained-glass windows. We meandered down wide, sun-baked streets between simple, single-story houses whose dull-white plaster was sun-baked as well. This place seemed as remote as the dark side of the moon. I don't even remember any cars. With the cooling of the late afternoon, the place came slowly to life. There was – never to be forgotten – a little store, where we stocked up on fresh-baked bread, cheese ("La Vache qui Rit", what else?) eggs, some fresh fruit and a salami-colored sausage, three inches thick and twelve inches long. It was made for the tropics and required no refrigeration. It had enough preservatives to keep us from decomposing for the next millennium. We ate only about two-thirds of it – that was all the preserving we needed.

The next morning we anchored off the coast of La Guera, another desolate place of sun and sand. The beach was lined with onlookers – Arabs, Berbers, Moors, and black Africans. They wore a mixture of traditional and western style clothing – long robes, known as gondoras, or long pants and long-sleeved shirts, probably largely second-hand from Europe. Head-coverings – caps, turbans, or scarves – protected them from the soon-to-be-sizzling sun. Some wore jackets, some sweaters, and one young man even sported a turtle-neck. *Must insulate against the heat*, I thought.

A tugboat pulled out a small barge with four-foot-high sides. We handed our packs to a man inside, jumped in and were towed towards shore. With about a hundred feet to go, a swimmer brought the end of a hawser, and we were hauled in by some ten men, pulling as if in a tug of war. What a scene – some twenty whites and a few Africans hauled in by these strangers. I had mixed feelings about this arrangement. I didn't like my lack of control, and I didn't like the image. It reminded me of the days of slavery. Of course, these guys weren't slaves. They would be paid; but by whom? The boat company? The harbor master? The latter idea seemed preposterous: This looked hardly like a harbor. There were no buildings that I recall and certainly no piers and no cranes. Only a bunch of exuberant guys heave ho-ing us in with a large rope. When 700 miles of coastline have only two navigable harbors, this being one of them, wouldn't you expect to find a bit more infrastructure?

But that's the way it was. *Things are just done differently here*, I thought. Welcome to Africa. You can now set your calendar back 100 years. We passed Spanish emigration and Mauritanian immigration and, voilà, we were in La République Islamique de Mauritanie.

Appendix B

BITING THE DUST

And the cloud that took the form
(when the rest of Heaven was blue)
of a demon in my view.
Edgar Allen Poe

"Ever heard of the Amtrak?"

"Sure, who hasn't?"

"Orient Express? Trans-Siberian?"

"You bet! They are European and Russian long-distance luxury trains."

"How about the TGV and the ICE?"

"Yep. One is the French 'Train à Grande Vitesse', the other the German 'InterCity Express', both high-speed trains that can go in excess of 170 mph."

"Choum train, anybody?"

"Choum train? I've heard of a Choo Choo train, but what's the Choum train?"

We didn't know yet, either, but were soon to find out.

Nouadhibou is Mauritania's northern seaport, just across the border from Lagwira, Western Sahara. At the time of our visit, it boasted some 11,000 inhabitants, ethnically similar to those of Spanish Sahara, but including a higher percentage of tall, lean black Africans. We tourists seemed to be the only Caucasians around.

We encountered Tuareg there, as well, that formerly nomadic Berber sub-group that controlled much of the Sahara, ran their own camel caravans, and taxed those of other tribes. But trucks and trains have now replaced the need for the traditional caravan, and most Tuareg have settled down as shop keepers and tradesmen in towns bordering the Sahara. They are a proud, graceful people with aristocratic bearing. While in the rest of the Arab world most women veil themselves, among the Tuareg it is the men, rather than the women, who cover their faces so only the eyes are seen. Because of their preference for sky-blue and indigo-dyed robes, they are known as the "men in blue". Their society, similar to India's, maintains a caste system that organizes its social order into nobles, vassals, and serfs, and, although they don't keep slaves any more, the Tuareg still employ black Africans for menial tasks.

On the Choum train

The Choum train, as we travelers came to call it, is one of the longest and heaviest trains in the world. It is a four-diesel-engine, 200-wagon, one-and-a-quarter mile long monstrosity that carries 20,000 tons of iron ore from the mines of Zouirat in the northeast to the coastal town of Nouadhibou, Mauritania's second-largest. Here the wagons are emptied by a huge, pincer-like machine, which turns them upside down one at a time, dumping the ore onto a conveyor belt that carries it onto freighters in the port. Emptied and ready to return for another load, this train provides the only mode of transportation to the most westerly of the trans-Sahara routes, locally known simply as "les pistes." This one connects Algeria with Senegal via Mauritania and its small desert capital by the Atlantic, Nouakchott. At Choum, a tiny outpost close to the route of the famous Paris – Dakar rally, rail and desert track intersect.

We reached this serpentine steel caravan and dropped our packs. I walked to the back to examine the only passenger car, counting sixty wagons on the way. For 600 ougias (twelve dollars) you could have a proper seat. But the car had slatted windows, which meant that the passengers would get bathed in the brown iron ore dust of the entire rolling stock ahead. I was not enamored with that idea. I preferred to go all the way to the front, where we would only have to endure temporarily the dust of our own wagon.

It was getting hot quickly, and, by the time I had rejoined the others, I had no desire to drag a forty-five pound backpack 140 wagon-lengths for the sole purpose of avoiding their dust. Neither did anybody else. At that point none of us had an inkling how thick it would get and how long it would last. We climbed into the "Pullmans" before us for the free ten-and-a-half-hour ride to Choum.

We had arrived at 10 a.m., and at 2 p.m. sharp there was a jerk, a clanging of steel against steel – we were moving. This squeaking and sideways-shaking train proved to be to France's TGV and to Germany's ICE what a tool-shed is to the Palace of Versailles – crude and utilitarian versus sophisticated and opulent. I was glad for her sake that Debbie was not the only adventurous female braving this conveyance.

As the speed increased, so did the dust. No matter where we hunkered down, little sand dunes would form against us. Our fellow travelers wrapped their heads with anything that would protect them from the enveloping iron ore particles – T-shirts, scarves, and towels. Apparently aware of what lay ahead, some had stolen pillow cases from the "León y Castillo," which they pulled over their heads. Debbie and I had brought small, collapsible goggles, which worked out well, though we had to remain tight-lipped, as our mouths were still exposed. It became clear to us why the Tuareg wear the "tagelmust", a twenty-foot-long strip of cloth that's wrapped like a turban around the head, but at least one layer covers also the mouth, exposing only the eyes. In a driving sand storm it is indispensable.

But now thirst demanded our attention, not hunger, as before. I had visions of a waiter in a black suit with a bow tie and a neatly-folded white towel over his left arm. "Beer? Coca Cola? Lemonade?" We carried two canteens with iodine-treated water. We took a sip, swished it around, and swallowed. Some had no water, so we had to conserve. We had brought a pound of chewing gum to pass out to border guards – a little gesture can go a long way toward changing a petulant official into an amenable one – children and anyone with whom we came in contact. Since, reminiscent of my childhood, most had no idea what these flat sticks were, we had to persuade them to chew and not to swallow with words they didn't understand and body-language – chewing and spitting out – that left them guessing. That proved a challenge. Now we passed out sticks to our fellow passengers. We didn't talk much, for every time we opened our mouths, we were rewarded with grit between our teeth.

I looked over at Debbie. She sat on her rolled-up sleeping bag, staring at the rusty interior of the wagon while getting shaken from side to side. Reading was out of the question. She was just enduring. This was certainly not an auspicious start to a life together. I was hoping she was not losing her enthusiasm for the adventures ahead that, I expected, would yet make up for current inconveniences. More importantly, I was hoping she was not questioning her decision to marry me, nor her commitment to our union "till death do us part." Surely, the good times would yet roll. Right now and unfortunately a bit early in our marriage, we were, as it were, in the "in sickness" part of our oath. The "in health" part was sure to follow.

An Englishman and I stood most of the time and stared into the distance, though the ever-present dust cloud obscured much of our vision of the vast, empty desert. At one point we passed the carcass of a camel next to the tracks – a sign of life, even in death. Every now and then a head would pop up, the person would do a three-sixty and disappear again. I had expected the movement of matter through the resistant stillness of the air to have wiped every nook and cranny clean of every last stubbornly-adhering dust particle as the train speeded up, but no such luck. What's wrong with physics?

Shortly after midnight we arrived at Choum – well, the engineers did, anyway. We were still about 140 wagon-lengths back. But pick-up drivers collected us free of charge, hoping to make up for the service on the trip to Nouakchott. They hit pay-dirt, as it were, with a handful of travelers who were anxious to get out of this remote and, seemingly, God-forsaken place into friendlier environs. We dreamed of having a hot shower first – why, any shower would do! And a good night's sleep wouldn't hurt, either. We were such a tired, dirty, and disheveled bunch.

Choum's only "hotel" was half tent, half hut. It had no rooms, no beds, no electricity, no toilets, and no water. The toilets were in the desert – anywhere – and the showers were back in Europe or, ahead, in Nouakchott, we presumed. The "beds" were reed mats on the floor.

One of the challenges for Debbie and me was to find a way to shower at the end of each day's journey and keep our clothes clean. Though that never became routine and proved at times challenging, we never failed in that quest. One night, it might be a bucket shower between four walls, another, we might draw water from a well outside and wash by the light of the moon or, less romantically, by the diffused beam of a flashlight. What would we do this night?

By one of only two electric lights in "town" next to the rails, I spotted a tanker car with a leaking faucet. What was trickling over there? Oil? Diesel? French perfume? I held my hand underneath and brought it to my nose. Water! Pure, unadulterated water! The faucet was locked, a sure sign of the preciousness of this commodity in this part of the world, but with patience we collected the cherished fluid in our canteens, stripped to our bare essentials, so to speak, and washed – even our hair. Soon others joined us in our little oasis by the railroad track.

What a sight we must have been! Seven people huddled around a trickle of water in various stages of undress, washing as if with liquid gold, and savoring it more than a Turkish bath in a health spa back home. Though we came from divers countries and diverse backgrounds, we were united in our common search of adventure, and the "Choum" train had been part of it. Now we felt as though we were starting afresh as we rinsed off and returned the now liquefied dust to the earth from whence it had come, retaining only the painless memory of the adventure. The aroma of our own "Safeguard" and other perfumed soaps, sophisticated scents that titillated our senses in this desolate place, created a sense of renewal that helped put behind us the ordeal we had just been through.

Debbie and I looked around for a place to sleep. We came upon a round, one-room hut, empty except for a straw mat on the floor and half a corrugated iron sheet to cover the lower half of the entry. It had no door. At about eight feet in diameter, the hut was just big enough to accommodate us with our luggage. Excited at this clean little place that afforded us some privacy, we rolled out our sleeping bags and tucked our backpacks behind us, away from the entrance. In minutes we were out like a light and slept soundly until we were awakened by a loud, clattering noise early in the morning. Surprise! The hut belonged to somebody! An older, surly Tuareg was rapping with his cane on our "front door" while staring down at us. He was visibly angry, and his gestures, facial expressions, and a torrent of an already harsh-sounding Arabic seemed to indicate that we were desecrating his prayer hut. How do you say "sorry" in Arabic?

After finding our travel companions, we bargained with the driver of a "taxi," a Peugeot 404 pick-up, for a ride for us eleven Europeans (that's Third World lingo for Caucasians) and two Mauritanian merchants, with our packs and their merchandise, to the tiny capital of Nouakchott. His asking price was sixteen dollars each.

Bargaining is a way of life in most of the Third World, and it takes time and patience. I remember when, a year later in Kuwait, Debbie and I sat on a pile of carpets in a little shop in a mall and bargained for a small, finely-knotted Persian silk rug. Yes, the mall was modern, with lots of glass, stainless steel, and fancy tiles, but the ways of doing business were ancient. To the background twang of Arabic music and surrounded with carpets from traditional knotting countries such as Iran, Pakistan, and Turkey, we haggled with the owner for about half an hour without reaching an agreement and walked away. But we passed by the shop once more to give the merchant a chance to call us back with a new offer. He did with a smile and a wave of the hand, and the negotiations resumed. Finally he said "okay," shook our hands with a throaty "mabruk" (congratulations), clapped his hands, and ordered a boy to bring chai so we could celebrate the successful transaction.

I knew there wouldn't be any chai here, but I was convinced we could get the price down to half of the original quote if we stuck together. We could and finally did after three hours, settling on eight dollars each. The driver had come down a dollar at a time and roared off after each refusal. We had more time than money and considered the former well-spent, the latter well-saved.

The trip to Nouakchott began in the heat of day. Our packs, tied above us onto the metal cross-bars that normally hold the canvas that enclosed the back, provided the only protection from the burning sun. We were squeezed like second-class passengers on the Howrah Mail of the Indian railway the day after a strike. I knew that feeling, having once stood on one leg for part of the trip between New Delhi and Varanasi. There simply wasn't enough room for the other. Here, in the pick-up, we sat on the sides, on luggage that hadn't made it to the top, or alternated between standing, squatting, and sitting on the floor of the truck bed. Some time in the middle of the afternoon and in the middle of nowhere, we stopped by a scrawny thorn tree. Our drivers crouched in its imaginary shade, made a little fire, and brewed chai in a small brass teapot – a man's got to have his "coffee break."

Meanwhile we tried to keep (our) cool and wandered around the desert. Making footprints in the soft sand out there reminded me of Neil Armstrong making his imprints on the moon – doubtless nobody's foot had ever stood in that precise spot in the vast desert. Between the discomfort of the heat and the vacuity of our surroundings time stood still. *If that quart of water in that little pot started out at some 110 degrees, why in the world does it take so long to boil?*

Making footprints in the sand

I wondered how one could even think of making a fire in that heat, let alone drink something hot. Debbie and I began to hallucinate - my health-conscious wife of eating a juicy orange, while I tried to convince her that a Baskin Robbins English toffee milkshake would hit the spot. How can one fully appreciate such little luxuries when one has never known deprivation? "The sated appetite spurns honey, but to a ravenous appetite even the bitter is sweet." (Proverbs 27:7)

One of the oddities of nature is the temperature variation between day and night in the desert. After sunset the air got bitter cold. Despite the squeeze, the draft of the cold-night air cut into us like a knife and made us shiver. One of the merchants had a pile of blankets in which some of us wrapped ourselves, until he decided, understandably, that he didn't want to sell them used. Debbie was positively miserable. To this day I don't remember ever seeing her that desperate. "Eb, can't we do something?" In hindsight, I suppose I could have bought one of those blankets. That never occurred to me. Maybe that was good, because under the circumstances I would have paid a premium – time pressure not being conducive to bargaining – and then not have had any use for it again on the rest of the journey. Nor would I have ever realized that the answer to our problem was stashed away in the deep recesses of our packs – the ponchos. They were all that was needed. They blocked the wind and helped us retain our body heat. To this day, when we talk about that episode, Debbie claims that I saved her life. Snuggling a little closer wasn't such a bad idea, either. It saved my life!

The driver and his companion in the front had chosen to go straight through the desert, rather than following the traditional track. They knew this area well. Navigating in this fine sand with a grossly overloaded two-wheel-drive vehicle was tricky. The challenge was finding "islands" of harder than sand-only surfaces, such as stony patches or small stands of closely-spaced mounds of bunch grass, on which one could gain enough momentum to cross the sea of sand to the next one, all the while navigating in the general direction of the destination. If such an island was too small to attain the required speed in a straight crossing, the driver would circle once or twice around its perimeter, pedal to the metal, while looking for the next nearest one to sling-shot off to. It was really less of a science and more of a game – us against the desert. We cheered at every successful crossing and with good reason: Whenever he didn't make it, we had to jump off and push. We didn't cherish that idea, but then, we didn't have much choice. We couldn't just camp out and replenish our supplies at the grocery store around the corner until the number five bus came along. There were no buses, there were no corners, and there was no grocery store. It was somewhat consoling, however, to remember that we had bargained him down to half-price.

The surface of the desert was rough, and there were times when our vehicle bounced over drifts up to a foot high. As if to revolt at stresses for which it had not been designed, the pick-up lost a muffler, suffered a flat tire, and broke a leaf spring that the driver bandaged with multiple layers of tightly stretched rubber strips cut from the inner tube of a truck tire. In the end we made it, arriving at Nouakchott at 11 p.m. It hadn't been your leisurely Sunday afternoon outing, but we had reached our next destination. After the Choum train experience, things could only improve. They had, indeed.

Appendix C

ONE FANCY RIDE!

You call for faith:
I show you doubt,
to prove that faith exists.
The more of doubt,
the stronger faith, I say,
if faith o'ercomes doubt.
Robert Browning

We had one of the most remarkable experiences of our West Africa trip on our last day in Sierra Leône. Unable to obtain visas into Sekou Touré's Guinea-Conakry, we had arrived in Sierra Leône by sea from Gambia. The ship, owned by a German, was being remodeled into a yacht and, while the work was in progress, was used to transport people and goods – to pay for the work, I assume. While at anchor in the harbor of Gambia's capital, Banjul, the captain, also a German, had sent two African cooks into the city to purchase meat. Failing to find the quantity they sought, they returned with two of the skinniest cows I have ever seen. We had just arrived at the ship from the ticket office, early enough to witness an unconventional approach to meat-acquisition. One at a time, the cows were hoisted by their horns onto deck with the ship's crane. The can-do captain, fully regaled in his white uniform and white gloves, though without his gold-oak-leaf-embossed cap, shot them in the head with a pistol and deftly proceeded to butcher them. That little episode helped us believe another event we were to hear about from the engineer: At one point the African crew had threatened a mutiny. The captain solved the tense situation by knocking the ring-leader down for the count, and that had been the end of that.

All passengers were designated deck class. (And I suppose there was no arguing with "Herr Kapitän!") Apart from Debbie and me, they were all

Africans. The engineer, a Spaniard, took a liking to us and gave us a cabin after he had shown us, with a bemused smile, the deck class no-flush toilet – a wooden enclosure protruding on two heavy beams over the stern of the ship. Through the seat one could see the churning waters below.

We arrived in Freetown, the Sierra-Leônean capital named by British abolitionists and designated for repatriated slaves, then traversed about two-thirds of the southern half of the country. Now we found ourselves in the village of Koribundu, just beyond the provincial capital of Bo. It was 10:30 a.m. From here it was only sixty miles to the Mano River that formed the border with Liberia. It would be a cinch to reach – or so we thought.

Koribundu was a typical African village. Set in a lush, green countryside were a collection of grass-thatched mud-huts and a few more permanent houses that had been built with sun-dried blocks made from a pressed mixture of earth, ant-hill dirt, and water, and covered with corrugated iron sheets. These simple dwellings lined both sides of a narrow dirt road and were connected by well-worn footpaths. Interspersed were small shops, which sold bare essentials such as rice, beans, salt, and sugar – all scooped out of 50 or 100-pound gunny sacks and weighed on iron scales. There were also bananas, tomatoes, sweet potatoes, soap, flashlight batteries, paraffin, candles and matches, notebooks and ballpoint pens, and aspirin. The local mini-version of a Super Wal-Mart also offered basic hand tools, plow parts, machetes, cooking pots, thermos bottles, and various utensils. Most of these goods came from China, with brand names such as Flying Swan, Double Happy, and Silver Lotus.

Traffic was mostly of the barefoot or bicycle variety, with a few mopeds or motorcycles that belonged to the more affluent. Women, often with babies tied to their backs with colorful cloth, revealed their activities and destinations by what they carried on their heads: hoes – the field; empty jerry cans or basins – a water pump; firewood – the kitchen; a basket – the store. Many of the men pursued a trade, either in simple workshops that could be locked up at night, or in the open air, perhaps under mango trees, which offer the best shade. There you found furniture makers, bicycle repairers, tailors, and barbers. Some men were just hanging around, talking, playing checkers, or watching others play. Mongrels dodged in and out, goats nibbled here and there, chickens pecked, roosters strutted and, along with loud discussions, laughter and perhaps someone playfully fleeing from a mock would-be attacker, the air was filled with typical African folk music. People were friendly, but not nosy, curious, but not overbearing. It was a peaceful place, and if we had to pick one in which to while our time away, this was as good as any.

We had wound our way to the southeast end of the village to await our next ride but faced two problems: First, a car owner in an African village is king but there was no royalty around; secondly, we were on a dead-end road – the Mano River had no bridge, only rowboats. Therefore, any automobile or truck traffic would have to originate from Bo or before, and would probably go to one of two other villages between us and the border, or to the border itself. From there passengers would cross the river by canoe. In other words, Koribundu, or either of those two villages, while putting us nearer the border, for all intents and purposes brought us no closer to attaining our goal than Bo. At that point, with our heavy packs, we didn't consider walking an option.

By mid-afternoon only one little Fiat had passed with three Italian nuns and their luggage. They stopped to inform us with pleasant smiles and slightly accented English that they were turning off just a few minutes down the road. That was alright; we wouldn't have fit anyway. But it was nice to know that we were not the only foreigners around. Visitors to a foreign land share a bond that is stronger than what at home might separate them. There was also a kind of cultural affinity that I shared, not only with those nuns, but also with Ugandans and Kenyans I would meet later in America. By then I would consider myself, though not quite a Kunta Kinte in Gambia – the "roots" in Alex Haley's book – nevertheless, an "old African," too.

At 3:30 p.m., Debbie ambled back towards the center of Koribundu. "I'm just going to go and have a look around." I stayed with the luggage in the shade of the small front porch where, hours earlier, the friendly African housewife had shown compassion for our weary legs and set out two chairs for us. Debbie's leaving filled me with expectation. I was beginning to respect her intuition. Perhaps she was following it now as she left for a stroll back towards the village center. Perhaps a change from the monotony of a fruitless day of waiting was in the offing, and I hoped that her little excursion would be serendipitous.

She had been gone about 15 minutes when, just slightly concerned, I walked out to the road and looked in the direction in which she had disappeared. There she was, about 200 yards away, talking with a young man – a Caucasian young man! Patrick had approached her, as I read later in her diary and, thinking she was German, had said, "Guten Tag. Wie geht es Ihnen?"

Well, thanks to that meeting she was doing quite well now, thank you, and so was I. I returned to my chair excited. That was the break I had hoped for. What was this guy doing out here so far off the beaten path, at least the path beaten by foreigners, I wondered. Next, I heard the crackling noise of a motorcycle. One of his buddies rode up, turned into the compound and quipped with a welcome American accent: "We've just kidnapped your wife. Hop on! You can leave your luggage here. It's safe." Within minutes Debbie and I had joined three Peace Corps volunteers and the local school principal in his home. While quenching our thirst with a refreshing, ice-cold drink, we listened to a fascinating, if eerie account of West Africa's widespread form of witchcraft, known as Ju-Ju. The hours of waiting for the ride that never came were forgotten.

Ju-Ju is a version of black magic administered by witchdoctors, known here as Ju-Ju priests. It supposedly provides protection from wild animals, accidents, and the evil spells with which an enemy might want to curse a person through another Ju-Ju priest. Even Jerry, who, as school principal, had more education than most in rural Africa, told us that the scars on his arm, made years earlier by a witchdoctor, would protect him from snakes and ensure that he would die a natural death. Well, so far there was no evidence to the contrary, and, for his sake, we hoped it would remain that way.

But, more commonly, amulets – two square-inch black leather pouches, with contents specially formulated by witchdoctors for those desiring protection – are hung by a string around the neck or upper arm. Known here as "gris-gris," they are pervasive in sub-Saharan Africa and worn from cradle to grave. In North Africa, similar charms contain verses from the Koran.

At the time, I found the idea of witchcraft too fantastic to give it much credence. Such hocus pocus belonged into the world of make-believe. My beliefs were backed up by history. But then I read more about it. The book Ju-Ju In My Life (George G. Harrap and Co., Ltd., 1966) was authored by James H. Neal, the former Police Commissioner of colonial Ghana. This man, who was obviously accustomed to distinguish between the legitimate and the spurious, relates how he slowly overcame his skepticism of the effectiveness of Ju-Ju and concludes that, had he known what dangers he was to encounter by way of revenge through witchcraft, he would not have accepted his appointment. Coming, as it did, from the highest law enforcement officer in the land, that was a powerful testimony.

Eventually the conversation turned to us and our hitchhiking adventure. Peace Corps workers are, for the most part, a hearty lot and accustomed to this form of travel to conserve their meager income. But here, all three, as well as the school principal, assured us that this, being a dead-end road, was no place for that. The last six hours would seem to have confirmed their assessment. However, we were confident that there was a purpose for our meeting and that we would get a ride to the river in the morning. They invited us to spend the night and, with their help, we collected our luggage. Our evening together gave us a good opportunity to discuss with them the reason for our faith in the God of the Bible. They were interested in what we had to say. It would appear logical that acceptance of a spiritual force of satanic origin, such as Ju-Ju, would presuppose the existence of a spiritual force of divine origin. Life teaches us that opposites bring each other into focus. There is no light without darkness, no positive without negative, and there are no counterfeit fifteen-dollar bills. If there is a devil, chances are, there is a god as well.

After a good night's sleep and an early breakfast, our new friends took us and our luggage on three motorcycles to the spot where we had waited in vain the day before. There is strength in numbers, and it was never easy to leave the encouraging presence of acquaintances and strike out into the unknown. These guys had received us as if we had been old college roommates. Now it was time, once more, to say our good-byes and follow the call of the road.

There is the saying that the family that prays together, stays together. From the first day of our marriage to this day, Debbie and I have made it a daily priority to read a chapter in the Bible and pray together. We have missed that special time together just often enough to keep it fresh and to keep it from becoming ritualistic and legalistic. I am convinced that this practice of turning our eyes off ourselves and onto God has given our marriage a stability we would not have otherwise enjoyed. For me in particular, it has served as a reminder that, when I let a day's disappointments get me down, it is time to return to the source of my equilibrium. I was about to have that opportunity.

We immediately put feet to our prayers and started to walk. The air smelled fresh, the blades of grass were still laden with dew, and the sun was casting its first rays through the foliage of the trees by the side of the road. It was a new day, inviting us to make new friends and master new challenges. In my craft shop I used to sell a poster with the popular cliché: "Today is the first day of the rest of your life." Yes, this was it. This was that day.

Within fifteen minutes a truck from a non-governmental organization (NGO), hauling sacks of relief food, stopped for us. It was only going to Potoru, the next village, some twenty miles down the road. And, while this ride would provide merely a change in location, not really in progress, as observed before, it would help psychologically.

Two men jumped from the cab to let Debbie in. The three of us got into the back of the enclosed truck and sat on sacks of relief food. Through a little window I could see Debbie and the driver conversing. No doubt she was gathering whatever information she could about the road ahead, the river crossing, the border crossing, and whatever else she could learn from this native son. Certainly, ignorance is not bliss, especially on foreign soil where information can help one avoid unnecessary hassles and where a silly mistake can easily violate local customs and offend those who would be friends. Consequently we made it our habit to learn all we could about the area we would visit and the people we would meet.

Well do I remember a contretemps from my first pre-Debbie trip around the world. How could I forget it? I was guest in a home in Lahore, Pakistan, and ate supper with the large family around a table in the courtyard. I had a slight cold and blew my nose, I thought discreetly, at the table. The second time my host asked me what I was doing. (I thought it was obvious.) He then pointed to a corner in the courtyard and demonstrated with a hand motion that I should blow my nose between my thumb and forefinger and fling "it" away. Repulsive, I thought. Thoroughly chastened and embarrassed, I got up and went to the corner. But I couldn't bring myself to follow his instructions. I still blew into a tissue, wrapped "it" up and carried "it" back with me in my pocket. That sounds gross, too, now that I think about it? Why would one want to carry "it" around? And that seemed to be precisely how they looked at it. Such are the intricacies of foreign customs, or, when analyzed from the perspective of foreigners, of our own as well.

We had been on that truck just minutes when we were passed by three Caucasians in a white Range Rover. I could see them from my perch through that little window. My heart sank. It was safe to assume that in this remote place no driver would refuse a lift to a foreigner. Consequently, I reasoned that if we had only waited instead of accepting this ride with its nearby destination, we might have been at the border within an hour. But, of course, with hardly any traffic on that road, there was little chance that we might be passed on that short ride by someone going further, if indeed he was going further. After all, had we not waited some six or seven hours just the day before with only one vehicle passing? It never occurred to me that the mission of this truck and that Land Rover might be connected. Our spirits weren't lifted by the knowledge that, once across the river, we would be starting out at the dead end of another road.

We thanked the men in Potoru for their willingness to give us a lift, and, after they had moved on, I vented my frustration by beating the dust off our packs with my rolled-up poncho. At least that accomplished something beyond providing a therapeutic outlet. The new day was getting old already. I just wished that the Range Rover had reached us before that truck. But then, wishful thinking has never gotten anyone anywhere. And blaming circumstances was tantamount to blaming God. I recognized and confessed my lapse into frustration and reconciled myself to reality. Then I said something like, "Maybe God is testing us, and if we pass the test, He has something better coming." (Never mind that I had just gotten over failing it.) I had nothing particular in mind. We were not picky. At this point we were a bit like Ronald McDonald in a mad-cow-disease crisis. Anything that would transport us over the final forty miles to the Mano River would be "better."

There might be those who would label our hopes and expectations audacious. "Doesn't your God have anything better to do than to deal with your silly little selfish requests? After all, you put yourselves into this situation, and now you expect some higher being to bail you out?" That's a fair question, especially given my negative attitude at the time. Debbie had maintained her positive equilibrium and her undaunted faith affected me. I have often been in a rush to get to my next destination, and still today, she asks me where the fire is. I then generally point ahead, and we laugh together.

I had barely said "coming," and we heard an engine. We spun around and there, down this same dead-end dirt road on which we had waited in vain for the greater part of the previous day, came not, as earlier in Mauritania, a battleship-gray, overloaded Peugeot 404 pick-up, and not just any car. It was a shiny, black, air-conditioned, chauffeur-driven Mercedes Benz! Wow!

And the driver stopped! And yes, he was going to Zimmi and, beyond, to the Mano River. He spoke English well but didn't initiate any communication. What counted was his "yes," he was going to the river, and "yes," we could go with him. As we left Potoru, we saw the white Range Rover parked at a home – so much for my assumption of its destination. I asked "our" driver the obvious question: "What on earth are you doing with a car like this in a place like this?" His short answer: "I have been sent to pick up VIPs coming from Monrovia." VIPs traveling all the way from Monrovia on a dirt road that ends at a river? It seemed incongruous.

After we had been rowed across the Mano, we spent the rest of the day and all of the following day on the Liberian dirt road that had started at a dead end and led to the capital of Monrovia, named after the fifth president of the United States, James Monroe, during whose presidency the country of Liberia was founded as a home for freed slaves. Since there wasn't much of a village, just an immigration post where we got stamped into the country, we started walking. After about five miles we were picked up by two young men in a pick-up truck. They didn't go far, but far enough to put us into a larger population center with plenty of vehicles. We spent the night in the police station – voluntarily – and pushed on to Monrovia the next day. And no, we never did see any people who resembled VIPs on their way to meet the mystery Mercedes and its driver at the end of a short canoe-ride. Perhaps the passengers he expected to meet had changed their minds and flown, as behooves VIPs, or taken the international road via Guinea-Conakry.

The fact that we had spent hours waiting for the ride that never came at Koribundu and fifteen minutes the next day, stood in stark contrast to the literal second that had elapsed between my statement and the sound of the Mercedes, our last ride in Sierra Leône. An uncanny coincidence? Maybe. An answer to prayer? I believe so. But why would God respond to our trivial request, when many more important pleas go unheard? I don't know. What we do know for a fact is that in all my, and later our, hitchhiking experiences on modern highways between world-renowned cities and financial centers, neither I, nor we, have ever been taken in a chauffeur-driven limousine. It had been, uniquely indeed, one fancy ride!

Appendix D

INTEGRATION AND INTRIGUE

*The world is a great book, of which they
who never stir from home
read only a page.*
Augustine

North Africa is predominantly Arab and Muslim and thus racially, culturally, and spiritually different from sub-Saharan Africa, which is predominantly Negroid and Christian or animist or a mixture of the two, with strong Islamic influence on the east coast. When planning our trip, we had aspired to tour the countries below the Sahel region of West Africa, to meet the people and experience their grassroots way of life. Unbeknownst to us then, this trip would help prepare us for the years we would live in the equatorial regions of this continent.

Debbie and I have traveled extensively in the Arab world and have had three decades of involvement in black Africa. We believe that the Christian heritage and resultant cultural influences we share with black Africans create a closer affinity than does the greater resemblance we share with Arabs. Still, as the following story, not actual but typical, of our interaction with African villagers shows, we in the West live in a much different world.

It has been a long, hot day, but we have made good progress. After waiting once again by the side of the road in the afternoon, bored and fighting off pestering flies, an English-speaking African picks us up in his big truck. We are a welcome distraction from the monotony of a hardtop road that has little traffic, few curves, and stretches through the flat, boring sameness of a dry savannah that is interspersed with sleepy, dusty villages. We have become acquainted with the driver as well as one can in the short time we have traveled together. Now he invites us to spend the night in the family compound. His village is just off the main road. We accept gladly, as we look forward to meeting his family and neighbors; a night on the village, as it were.

His wife and two pre-teen daughters, the older one with her chubby, big-eyed baby brother strapped to her back, clear their one-room mud hut for us and sweep it out with a home-made broom – grass stalks tied together with rubber strips cut from an inner tube. Of the furniture that is left for the evening, several low-slung chairs line the mud walls, which are bare, except for an outdated picture calendar and a black and white photo of our host and his wife in stiff pose and with serious expressions. This is March, and the calendar is dated January of some past year. The picture shows a skier gliding down a mountain in deep powder – an alien activity in an alien land. A simple, rectangular coffee table rounds out the setting. In the kitchen, a separate, smaller hut from which acrid smoke billows through the open door, water is heated in an aluminum pot whose outside is black with soot. The village stove is of the typical three-stone variety, and the fire is fed by long branches that are pushed in between the stones.

While supper is prepared on the same fire, I am taken to a roofless, five-foot-high banana-leaf enclosure with a crushed-stone floor – the shower. A plastic basin of heated water with a plastic cup for pouring and a bar of hard soap on a leaf are awaiting me. On this rough floor the flip-flops Debbie and I share are indispensable. I hang my clothes and my towel over one of the walls (most Africans don't use towels), and, voilà, in minutes the day's dust and perspiration are history.

Ladies first, generally, unless we are in an unfamiliar situation, like here. By the time I return to the hut, I find Debbie surrounded by a group of women in animated conversation. Women the world over, it seems, have the gift of gab and can work around language problems in their own sensitive, intuitive ways. But the next basin of water is already being taken to the shower and, with a bit of prompting from me, she tears herself away.

As night begins to fall – near the equator at about six or seven p.m. year-round – a kerosene lamp faintly illuminates the faces of those near it, leaving those of spectators in the background faintly silhouetted. The atmosphere is charged with curiosity, and the hut is chockfull of onlookers. In the doorway, latecomers stretch on tiptoes and crane their necks to get a glimpse of us over the milling crowd. Some of the older children outside are peeking through glassless windows whose wooden shutters open to the inside. One of the more forward children on my left glides his hand over the hair on my arm, while examining my reaction with an upward glance. African men, like most East Asians, don't grow much hair on arms and legs, so this is an attention-getting oddity. Then, with a few annoyed-sounding words, a wave of the hand, and a disapproving smack of the tongue – the equivalent of our "give them some space" – our host moves the crowd back. A young man plucks a stringed instrument made of the horned shell of an armadillo, then offers it to me to see if I can play it. I can't and wave it off with an appreciative smile. By pointing at us, a mother tries to direct the attention of the baby in her arms to us. Most of the little ones have never seen a white person, and if we were to approach this one, she would start crying.

Somebody draws the eyes of those near him to my rhinoceros belt buckle (see back cover and page 108) – the one about which someone in South America had said, "mire el elefante." Obviously they have neither animal down there, but even here, in Africa, most people have never seen them, either. Everybody admires it. Thumbs point up approvingly – good, very good. Somebody else fingers my Swiss army knife pouch. He looks at me and jabbers something. I take it out. "It's a knife. Here, you see?" I show the various blades and explain their functions with motions. When I open the large blade, somebody moves his index finger across his throat. Everybody laughs, as do we. "No, no! It's for cutting bread and fruit." More pantomime. Some voice their guesses, somebody understands and explains. People nod. Thumbs go up again.

The conversation is halting and appears to be about nothing in particular. It's more a means to an end for those who just want to study us close-up, observing our actions and reactions and my occasional interaction with Debbie. The women are drawn to her like teenagers to a pop star. The men have gravitated towards me. Together, we are to them a live version of People Magazine; we are celebrities. Other than listening to battery-operated radios, there is no contact with foreigners in the African village. Some have shortwave sets and have made it a habit to listen to the BBC, the Radio Deutsche Welle, or the Voice of America. Now the foreigners they are accustomed to hearing from and about are right there with them!

One person is the spokesman for the group but with his heavily-accented French and our lack of fluency, we barely get his drift half the time. That's why we attempt to direct the conversation. I draw a map of the United States to answer a frequently-asked question. Most of the old folks have never seen a map. The spokesman explains, and the others respond with a universal "aaah," which means, "I understand," even when some don't. Someone asks if we are married by pointing at both of us, then placing the two index fingers together lengthwise while enunciating the question in his language.

"How many children?"

"No children? Oooh!"

Now everybody feels sorry for us because in African cultures many children are desirable. They are a couple's security – a type of retirement insurance for old age. Somebody proudly shows us a yellowed, dog-eared photo of himself. Now our thumbs point up. As we return the picture somebody else wants to see it. Our approval has given it new significance.

Between 9 and 10 p.m. is dinner time and most of the visitors disperse. Food is brought, sandwiched between soup plates. There are sweet potatoes, rice, chicken, and peanut sauce. We pull our chairs closer, along with the homeowner and two male family friends. The top plates are removed, and we eat together directly from the plates before us. Our utensils are our right hands, which we have washed again at the table. Smacking is a sign of enjoyment of the food. Two women are sitting on reed mats on the floor, talking in hushed tones to five little ones, ranging in age from two to seven years. There they will also eat with the children after we have finished.

It has been a long day, and by eleven o'clock everybody gets ready for the night. Our hosts watch with curiosity as Debbie and I erect our mosquito tent in our room. Designed to keep flying and crawling insects at bay it is an indispensable item, an adaptation to a design I thought up in my travels through Latin America, but didn't put together until I married a gal who knew how to sew. The sides and flat top are made of no-see-um nylon mosquito netting. They are held up by four six-foot elastic bands sewed to the upper corners of the sides, which we fasten to the tops of two chairs, the top of a backpack, and the upper door-hinge. (The extra length allows us to reach up to twelve feet in one direction – helpful for exterior use.) Two more crisscrossed elastic bands, cut about a foot shorter than the stretched-out tent and sewed from the inside to the outside elastic in the corners, keep the top from sagging. The floor is made of rip-stop nylon and comes up on the sides about three inches. We enter through a four-foot zipper, arrange our sleeping bags and fold up our clothes for pillows under which we stow away our money and passport pouches. (This tent, along with my

Swiss army knife, is still one of our main staples when we visit the African village today. It can be set up on top of a bed, on the floor with mattresses inside or, if they are not clean, on top of the mattresses on the floor.)

As we reflect on the day's events, we realize afresh that the opportunity to participate in such unrehearsed close encounters cannot be bought in travel bureaus or experienced in conventional travel. We end the day with short prayers, grateful for protection and for these villagers, who have so freely opened their hearts and home to us.

In the Ivory Coast we were picked up by a sports journalist named Yoyaga Coulibali. Yoyaga held the 400-meter dash record for his coun-

try for eleven years and had represented it in the Tokyo and Mexico City Olympic Games, a claim, not that I ever doubted it, I verified recently on the Internet for the writing of this book. He was in his early thirties, about 5'8" – a good-looking, muscular man with humble demeanor. He invited us to accompany him to his home in Koundadougou

Yoyaga Coulibali, Olympian

(dougou means village), and, once more, we gladly accepted. We could not have imagined that, before the evening was over, we would be transported, as if in a time-warp, back to the days of the first explorers.

We arrived at about 5 p.m. As usual, this remote village of an estimated 250 people consisted of a collection of mud-huts. But it had one permanent house, his, built with cinderblocks and corrugated iron sheets. He changed from his business suit into the local galabea, a long, lightweight robe. Water was heated for us over an open fire, and we took a bucket shower in his bathroom where a hole in the wall, at the level of the concrete floor, allowed it to drain directly to the outside. The toilet was in a separate room, the kind that is embedded in the floor, like some in Southern Europe and in the Arab world – not suited for serious meditation.

We changed in his bedroom, which he had given us for the night. To our surprise, there was a queen-size bed, side tables, a dresser, and other signs of western influence in this out-of-the-way place. We were impressed, particularly because this was not his primary home. Most of the time he lived with his wife and six children in the city of Bouaké. We joined him for a walk around the village, visiting the chief and all his neighbors. By the time we got back to his house, supper was ready: rice with roasted chicken in a tasty sauce. The table setting included knives, forks, and spoons and cloth napkins, again unusual in an African village.

The sun turned into a red fireball as it set through the haze created by cooking fires across the savannah's vast expanse and emblazoned the horizon with a crimson glow. A pleasant cool had replaced the heat of day. The moon was full and a soft silvery light pushed back the descending darkness. Most of the village had gathered in front of Yoyaga's house and formed a large circle. Something special was about to happen, and we watched the restless crowd as we relaxed with Yoyaga on his porch in big, comfortable chairs.

Of course, we were watched, too. We were a big attraction, especially to the children. They examined us from a distance with shy, sideways looks, embarrassed smiles, and chitchat we didn't understand. The porch was elevated about three feet and created a barrier between us and the onlookers. Yoyaga introduced us now formally to his neighbors and explained to them, as best he could, what we were doing. Most of them had never even visited their capital, Abidjan, so it was difficult for them, if not impossible, to relate to a young couple living on a far-away continent but ending up in their village. The chief and some of the village elders came up and welcomed us again, extending parched, leathery hands for firm handshakes.

Soon the chatter abated. From the distance we heard the approaching sound of drums and people clapping. As they got closer the beat intensified to a reverberating crescendo. It had begun haltingly, as if calloused hands had to get warmed up, but then with increasing speed the rhythmic sound of the African tom-toms filled the air. Now the musicians rounded a nearby hut and came into unobstructed view. Four men accompanied the drummers on small reed flutes. Others kept the beat with wooden rattles. It was as if the airwaves, laden with the pulsation of the big base drums, were resonating through our ears in our torsos, harmonizing with the beating of our hearts. The musicians proceeded to the edge of the circle on our left, while the early arrivals shuffled to the side in a disorderly melee, each reluctant to surrender his front-row place. Unruffled, the band kept playing and settled in without missing a beat.

Eventually a woman threw a scarf over another woman's head and gently pulled her into the circle – an invitation to dance. Perhaps because of the presence of foreigners, there would be token resistance, a bit of shy laughter and a hand partially covering the face self-consciously, but that was quickly overcome. Side by side they stutter-stepped forward in tiny increments, hips and posteriors gyrating, as they shuffled with bare feet and so moved slowly across the twenty-to-thirty-foot-diameter circle. Some of the women ululated with delight and shouts of approval and laughter filled the air.

After a few additional female pairs, it was the men's turn to strut their stuff, and strut they did. They weren't shy at all. Several entered the circle randomly and without partners. In contrast to the women's tiny steps, they flung their legs in all directions. Dust obscured their feet, and their lower extremities were a mere blur as they pounded the ground with amazing speed and agility. Now we knew how Yoyaga had gotten his start running in the Olympics. As the night wore on into the early morning hours, a light fog made the chilly air more palpable. The crowd thinned. Eventually the drums, flutes, and rattles fell silent, giving way to the chirping of crickets and other insects. The squawking of frogs drifted over from a nearby lake. We withdrew to our quarters filled with wonder. It had truly been an unforgettable event.

* * *

That small village was approximately 150 miles from Abidjan and eons, it seemed, from a ship that, seven years earlier, had made history as part of a James-Bond type secret U.S. government mission. We had had the opportunity to tour it, totally oblivious of its unique past. To us it was just a bit of American real estate, of home away from home, and I was curious about the machinery that abounded on deck.

The ship was registered in Galveston, Texas. We asked someone at the rails above for permission to come up and have a look. The Second Mate acquiesced and gave us a tour. He explained that this was a research vessel, and that her current trip was under the sponsorship of the National Science Foundation. Designed for exploration of the ocean floors, she was presently hosting scientists from around the world. There were miles of pipes of all sizes, and stacks of cement in sacks, all part of the equipment and supplies needed for drilling and tapping into underwater oil deposits. There were also cranes and other more specialized pieces of heavy machinery and, after a tour of Howard Hughes' Glomar Explorer, we were thoroughly impressed. That was in early 1975.

But, as we would find out later, there was more to this 63,000-ton ship than met the eye. She had actually been commissioned by the CIA and had been built as a deep-sea salvage vessel with a giant hoisting mechanism for the purpose of raising a Soviet nuclear ballistic submarine that had sunk to a depth of 17,000 feet off Hawaii in 1968. The Soviets had failed in their efforts to locate it. Not so the United States, whose naval intelligence had tracked the ill-fated vessel and, through high-tech, sub-surface listening devices, learned of its demise.

Public records are for public consumption and, more often than not, do not provide access to all the intricacies of international intrigue. In this case they show that the mission had not been entirely successful. Only a 38-foot section of the sub was eventually recovered – or so the story goes.

Appendix E

UNFORGETTABLE ARAB HOSPITALITY

*There is that glorious Epicurean paradox
uttered by my friend the Historian,
in one of his flashing moments:
"Give us the luxuries of life, and
we will dispense with its necessaries."*
Oliver Wendell Holmes

Mini-Foreword

The title of this chapter may evoke negative feelings in some. In a time of Islamic terrorism and effort at Islamic world domination, some readers may wonder how I can devote a chapter of positive musings to Arabs. Well, I can, if for no other reason but that the experiences described in it are true. Fact is, only a minority of Muslims are terrorists. The majority are peace loving members of the global society, if perhaps cowered into silence by their radical fellow-believers. That is not to say that the Koran encourages peaceful coexistence with "infidels." It does not, which is why Islam is not a peaceful religion, as some would claim. But we must be careful to discriminate – yes – between those who are sworn enemies of anything western, and those who respect us as fellow human beings with our rights to choose our own destiny.

* * *

As a young boy in Germany I had read some twenty volumes of Karl May's adventure tales and have been intrigued by the Arab world ever since.

Even today, over fifty years later, I still remember the full name of the Arab hero in several of the books – Hadji Halef Omar Ben Hadji Abul Abbas Ibn Hadji Dawud al-Gossarah.

Our second trip, another six months of thumbing toward distant horizons, took us from Colorado to Germany, then south into Italy. From Sicily we crossed the Mediterranean into North Africa; Tunisia, Libya, Egypt, Sudan. From Port Sudan we flew into Jeddah, hitched across Saudi Arabia to Qatar and back, took a dhow to Bahrain and back, and went up through Kuwait into Iraq, headed west into Jordan and north through Syria into Turkey and back to Europe.

Before the end of the trip, we would bargain for souvenirs with bearded, rotund hawkers in dark but quaint, narrow-alley-ed, colorful, crowded, and noisy soukhs in medinas – old parts of cities that have remained unchanged for hundreds of years. I would walk in traditional Arab style, hand in hand, with a new friend to meet some of his buddies, while Debbie rested in the hotel and was thus, also in traditional style, tucked away in a country where women don't associate with men in public. A common western description for oppressed women – "barefoot, pregnant, and in the kitchen" – isn't far off the mark here. In most of the Arab world women are considered second-class citizens. Now there's something the Women's Liberation Movement could sink its fingernails into.

I believe that this male dominance is at least one reason we did not get to visit many Arab homes. It was, we assumed, a matter of guarding the privacy of family-life. However, on our trip there we benefited from at least two exceptions: One was a wedding reception in a home in Benghazi, Libya, in which Debbie and I were separated – she to be with the women in one room, I with the men in another. The other was a visit to a home in Syria. That visit demonstrated to us again the impressions left by the dissemination – perceived here as deliberate promotion – of loose western morals through the film industry.

We had been treated to a sumptuous meal in an elegant restaurant. On leaving, our host, perhaps assuming that his generosity should be reciprocated in the manner of his understanding of western decadence, asked me in the elevator if he could kiss Debbie. Her opinion in the matter seemed to be inconsequential. I pointed to my wedding ring, wagged my finger, and let him know that that was not in the cards.

My opportunity to challenge his double-standard came when he invited us to his home. It was a modern, spacious house with expensive furniture, which confirmed our impression in the restaurant that this man was well to do. We expected his wife to walk in at any moment with elegant flair, but waited in vain. After some twenty minutes of casual conversation our host asked Debbie if she would like to meet her. His wife was, as it turned out, safely tucked away in the kitchen. Although the question had been obviously directed at Debbie, I gleefully seized the moment. I acted as if he had addressed us both. I slapped my hands on my knees, said "Why, of course!" and jumped up. Now it was his turn to let me know that that did not fall within the parameters of Muslim propriety. *What a double standard*, I thought. *He wants to kiss my wife, while I may not even see his wife unveiled.*

Meeting Arab men, on the other hand, was easy. They were always interested in talking about America, about politics, and about religion. They enjoyed debating and would speak with animated voices, accompanied by hand-gestures and, when operating a vehicle, erratic driving. Consequently, hitchhiking in Arab countries was easy, if at times dangerous. And, again, we encountered a moral double-standard and learned early on that it could be a hassle for Debbie to sit next to a forward driver with me on the outside. Rubbing elbows with westerners, apropos, gave them an opportunity to satisfy their curiosity about the western world and to talk about that favorite subject – religion. In our experience, more than anywhere else a lift would also be accompanied by an invitation to join in a meal, and during our five-month tour we enjoyed some of the most delicious traditional foods in some of the most expensive restaurants and exotic settings with generous hosts. Here are three such experiences:

On December 20, 1975, it was cool and wet some 30 miles south of Gabes, Tunisia. A silver Mercedes 280 pulled up. With a smile on his face and "Tripoli" on his lips Mr. Salama rolled down his window and offered us a ride. And for the next two days he would prove to be a generous gentleman. Born and raised in Sfax, he now had a business in Libya, "Traveaux Publiques" (Public Works), a label that didn't make much sense to us, because he was the private owner. But whatever it was, as we learned later, he must have had a lot of "traveaux," for not only was he warm and humble, he also turned out to be prosperous – an attractive combination.

As usual, we inquired about the country we were about to enter and, like a true businessman, he complained about the high taxes of his adoptive country, the Socialist People's Libyan Arab Jamahiriyah. I have always thought that it must not be easy to be rich in a socialist state where the government wants to divide your money among the poor and conquer with their votes at the ballot box, although, admittedly, that has never been my problem. But Libya was not poor – its oil money even trickled down to the guys with the goats – nor did Libyans have a vote under Colonel Muammar al-Qaddafi. So this country was an oddity among socialist states, of which Winston Churchill once observed: "The inherent vice of capitalism is the unequal sharing of blessings. The inherent virtue of socialism is the equal sharing of miseries." Part two of Churchill's sentiment was reflected by the Vietnamese Foreign Minister from 1982 -1987, Nguyen Co Thach, when he defended his country's economy: "We are not without accomplishment. We have managed to distribute poverty equally." In socialist Libya, the poor were the guest workers from Egypt, who were still more affluent than their countrymen back home.

With most of the day gone, we spent one more night in Tunisia and left the next morning for the nearby border. As it turned out, our friend, Mr. Salama (Arabic for peace), was also a patient man, as he willingly waited almost two hours for us while we filled out lengthy forms, waited in slow-moving lines, and shuffled from one office to the next. His delay made me feel pressure to get through this border quickly, but that made time pass all the slower – officialdom the world over just cannot be rushed. Passing the border had taken him, as a native son, only about fifteen minutes. Now he was cooling his heels somewhere out of our sight, probably fingering his prayer beads, though that wasn't getting us through any faster.

That slo-mo border crossing was a political statement. It was rooted in the same attitude that had earned me the visa problem and threat of imprisonment in Morocco. We were pawns in a political chess game. The Libyans were suspicious of us, as of any "decadent" westerner, and Qaddafi, ever the Arab-cause-promoting visionary along the lines of his idol, Egypt's late Gamal Abdel Nasser, and agitating for greater recognition of and respect for the Arab world, was not about to let us in without putting us through our paces. This became evident when we first applied for our visas. Our passport information had to be translated into Arabic by an embassy-approved interpreter. The last page of the passport – the first for right-to-left-reading Arabs – was stamped with a form, which was then filled out with the translated information. All this for a fee, of course, and only in then-West Germany's capital, Bonn. The attitudes of Arab governments toward foreign tourists don't always reflect the attitudes of their citizens, though, as we had already learned in Morocco and as demonstrated here by our host. In our opinion, Arabs are among the most hospitable, welcoming people in the world and that welcoming is extended towards Americans, as well.

We found a two-dinar-a-night ($6) hotel in Tripoli later that afternoon. However that price came at a price. Our room was on the fifth floor and the elevator was kaput. The hotel was clean, but, apart from the Choum Hotel, more basic than any I have ever seen. But this place, at least, had rooms – living spaces made private by walls. They were bare walls, and a single bare light bulb hung from the ceiling. There were two beds, a chair, and a night stand. The sheets were clean. It would do for a couple of nights.

Except for some restaurants, the city was beginning to shut down. With just two days before Christmas, the sad ambience of our room was made sadder by the fact that there were no Christmas lights anywhere in sight. That did not come as a surprise in one of the world's strictest Muslim nations. But then, Debbie didn't miss the commercial hoopla of an American Christmas anyway. I was never bothered by it, I admit, but emphatically agreed that Santa Claus and the reindeer, and all they have come to mean, should never usurp the spotlight from Jesus the Christ on His birthday.

The operative word above is "restaurants," because, after we had first parted in Tripoli, it was not to be the last time we would see our friend of 200 miles and a day and a half. He collected us that evening and took us to the "Sindebad," the finest restaurant in all of Libya, whose second claim to fame was a visit the year before by Muhammad Ali, the American boxer. The owner, Mr. Hassein, was Mr. Salama's friend – short, stout, and amiable. Between the two of them, we were treated to a feast fit for a sheikh. What made the treat even more special was the alternative – a longer night in our dull hotel room.

But then our hosts did not deem our sumptuous dinner sufficient. There was more to come as entertainment was about to follow. Our next stop was an alcohol-free bar, the "Benoasis," also owned by Mr. Hassein. Alcohol-free bar may sound like an oxymoron to a westerner, but in the strict, teetotaling Muslim nations of North Africa and the Middle East that was all you got. The atmosphere was bar-like, with dimmed lights, elegant wall decor, a counter with barstools, and round tables with cushioned chairs, most of which were occupied by people dressed for a night on the town. The drinks were served in fancy glasses, with orange slices or lemon wedges, mint leaves, and long straws. There was a stage, and if we had been blind we might have thought that we were in England – Liverpool, to be precise. For on stage was a group of musicians giving amazingly authentic-sounding renditions of the Beatles. And that in Colonel Qaddafi's strict Islamic Libya. Imagine!

*   *   *

Saudi Arabia did not issue tourist visas except to relatives and friends of its foreign workers and that only in response to letters of invitation from within the country. The Saudi government, guardian of Islam and Islam's two holiest cities, Mecca and Medina, was, though more restrictive, like Libya reluctant to expose its citizens to the corrupting influences of western societies. The Sharia law was enforced to the tee. Theft was punished by amputation of the right hand. That meant that the thief henceforth had to eat with his unclean left and was therefore socially an outcast. Murder was punished by beheading and adultery by stoning of the woman only, after prayers on Friday in Riyadh's "Chop Chop Square" – so nicknamed by expatriates. Curiously, the most famous beheading of modern times was that of a Saudi prince, Faisal bin Musad, who had been a student at the University of Colorado in Boulder. Great grandson of Ibn Saud, after whom Saudi Arabia was named, his head was chopped off with a golden sword for the assassination of his uncle, King Faisal, in Riyadh in 1975.

Western culture inevitably accompanied western expertise, which had started the country's oil industry and was required to keep it going. Hence, compromise was essential, but strictly controlled. We hoped that letter of invitation from family friends was awaiting us at poste restante in Cairo. But it was not to be. The request had gone out early enough and they would be excited to see us. But in the Arab world things move at a more measured pace. Here, IBM stands for "**I**n sha'Allah," which means "if Allah wills," or, often more accurately "if I feel like it," "**B**oukhra," which means "tomorrow," and "**M**alesh," which means "Who cares?" or "Never mind." Our chances for success, once again, were slim.

I have had difficulty learning that embassies the world over are not particularly visitor-friendly. Short hours on just certain weekdays and long waits don't give the impression that the government is rolling out the welcome mat for you. We found ourselves at the Saudi embassy just after the doors had been locked for the day. A throng of people, unwilling to give up, pressed tightly against them. So, when in Rome... I grabbed Debbie's hand. As suspected, when the door was opened just wide enough to let somebody out, there was a great big shove, and next thing we knew, we were inside.

The consul had been stationed in Germany on a previous assignment and, perhaps thinking that in me he had a captive audience that would show sympathy in deference to his authority, vented his frustrations with my country. But I remained true to my convictions, and we got into a friendly argument. Maybe he appreciated that I stood up for my country (at that point I was still a German citizen), even when the levers to Debbie's and my further progress were in his hands. We left visas in hand. The tongue-in-cheek lesson: When trying to get into a closed country, arrive too late at the embassy and get into an argument with the visa-issuing officer.

*   *   *

We didn't generally hitchhike in cities, but exceptions make the rule. Sudan's desert capital, Khartoum, was not a big, noisy, bustling metropolis. It struck me more like a sleepy provincial capital, boasting just a handful of tall buildings, unpaved parking lots and wide, tree-lined thoroughfares with little traffic; an ambiance conducive to hitching. And that was to result in an interesting encounter before we would leave the city.

We spent four days in Khartoum, camping with a number of other foreigners in the yard of a youth hostel for $1.30 a night. We had to do quite a bit of work and started early the first morning, before the cool of night would give way to oppressive day-time heat. We had to get a permit for overland travel within Sudan, pick up our mail at the American embassy, pick up a letter of endorsement for our Kuwaiti visa application from the German embassy, and try to get visas for Kuwait, Iraq and Syria. The Jordanian visa would be no problem.

It took four trips to the Kuwaiti embassy before our persistence was rewarded. But Iraq and Syria were another story. In Kuwait City several weeks later British friends took us to the Iraqi embassy, assuring us that we were going in vain. "Getting a visa for Saudi is one thing, getting one for Iraq is quite another. It would be a miracle." Not by my definition. We had heard the same about the difficulty of getting a visa for Saudi Arabia. An American consul informed us that no American had been issued an Iraqi visa in two-and-a-half years. Still no miracle by my definition. We emerged visas in hand. No doubt it helped that we had entered Saudi Arabia, Qatar and Bahrain and were applying for our visas in Kuwait, Iraq's neighbor, but prayer must have helped, as well.

We also visited Omdurman, the biggest village in the world, then and now. Situated opposite Kartoum on the west bank of the Nile, it was a dusty, busy, and loud place. It is the burial place of the Madhi, Sudan's most popular political figure, who drove the British colonial power out of most of the Sudan and killed General Gordon when he overran his fortification at Khartoum in 1885. Omdurman had a huge, non-touristy market full of portly, bearded men with large white turbans, long robes and pointed shoes that were open at the heel. There was also a separate camel market with railed stalls and that distinctive camel odor. Today, at around 1.5 million, Omdurman, though still considered a suburb of Khartoum and still exhibiting a village atmosphere, is Sudan's largest city.

Hitchhiking was easy among the friendly Sudanese (of the seventeen countries we had visited in North and West Africa, we put them on par with the Ghanaians on the friendliness scale) and made that our only form of transportation. At one point we were picked up by a well-dressed gentle-man in an aqua-colored Volvo. He introduced himself as Mustafa. He was the director of the large sugar factory in Khartoum. He invited us into his office for a cup of chai (with sugar). We took care of one more errand first, then stopped by. As we sat in front of his imposing desk with the obligatory picture of the president behind him, I noticed a striking similarity between them. Mustafa's English was excellent; he had probably studied overseas. We enjoyed the break from the heat between our errands in his air-conditioned office. But my eyes kept wandering from his face to the picture of General Jaaffar Numeri behind him. I finally expressed my surprise at the likeness between him and the president. He craned his neck as he slightly turned in his chair and looked back and up as though he had never seen the picture before and remarked that he thought to have removed the resemblance when he shaved off his beard after the hadj, the Muslim pilgrimage to Mecca.

Before we left, Mustafa set up a time to collect us at the Youth Hostel to take us on a sight-seeing trip of the city. What an opportunity to get such a tour from a native son! But he had more in mind. He took us to several gift shops to treat us each to a souvenir of our choice. To our hesitation he insisted, using the word "must." There were small stuffed desert animals, leather goods, silver filigree jewelry and assorted trinkets. Unlike Debbie, I can still remember what I selected: A leather-strapped choker with two elongated pieces of bone, rimmed with silver.

But that wasn't enough. Mustafa collected us that evening and treated us to shish kabab at the elegant German Club of Khartoum. We sat in the meticulously-tended gardens, the rustle of palm leaves audible in the cool evening breeze. It was such a respite from the heat, dry though it was. The setting might have been in Germany on a late-summer evening except for an unexpected reminder that we were still in the Third World. A little boy at the table next to us needed to use the bathroom. No, he didn't, because his mother let him urinate right next to the table at which she was seated with a number of guests, who didn't seem to notice.

We don't know why Mustafa Numeri at first eschewed being identified with his brother, as Jaaffar Numeri was a popular president. But he did own up to the relationship that evening in the course of our conversation. Given the fact that on a continent where nepotism permeates most governments, his independence was admirable.

* * *

In Saudi Arabia a white-thobe-clad businessman with his white ghutra headdress, held in place by the black ring known as agal, had two seats for us in his Mercedes. In typical Bedouin fashion he had smartly tossed one side of the ghutra over the top of his head. He looked sharp and his English was excellent. We had just spent a week with Jack Peterson, a retired army general. Jack lived with his wife, Bea, in a beautiful villa in a suburb of Riyadh. I don't know what impressed us more: his beautiful digs on a steep, rough, unpaved road with a narrow open sewer running alongside, or the swimming pool in the flowered garden in a country where water was more expensive than gasoline. Bea was visiting family in America, but Jack had welcomed our company and had spoiled us with a wonderful R&R. We had savored typical American food, played tennis, caught up on the latest news with Newsweek and the Herald Tribune, taken in a movie or two, gone to parties in other American homes, and washed our clothes in a real washing machine. And we found out that Jack had, indeed, sent that letter of invitation. When the time came to say good-bye, he drove us to the highway, snapped our picture, there were hugs, and we were off.

Yes, that American hospitality had been spectacular. But then, Jack and Bea were close family friends. This Saudi gentleman didn't know us from Adam and Eve. He had likely shed a western-style business suit in favor of the more comfortable and cooler local garb and left his air-conditioned house in Riyadh to spend the weekend in his tented camp in the vast, sand-carpeted expanse of the desert. Then he came upon these two backpackers by the side of the two-lane, black-topped highway, arms extended, thumbs up, their eyes peering in his direction.

His fluency in English with a slight American accent led us to believe that, like so many Saudis, he had probably studied in the United States. He was going to his desert dwelling, and would we like to join him? Another wonderful opportunity to experience local hospitality and to get the inside scoop on a still somewhat secretive culture. We accepted gladly on condition that he take us back to the road later.

Soon, two big tents and a small one appeared in the desolate distance. "This is winter, and I am a son of the desert, so I have to come here," he said with obvious pride. In the small tent, the kitchen, a servant prepared a large, round platter of mansaf, an Arab feast of rice with raisins, nuts, and spices, and half a roasted lamb spread across the top. We sat cross-legged on a floor bedecked with Persian carpets. Apart from a sideboard and a chest of drawers, the tent was empty. In Africa, India, and the Middle East the right hand replaces the fork, and soon the servant approached with a kettle of cool water, which he proceeded to pour over our hands, catching it in a basin below.

And so we feasted on a succulent meal in an unforgettable Lawrence-of-Arabia-style setting. As if that hadn't been enough, following another washing, a second platter piled high with apples, oranges, and bananas was served, and that in a country that has little more than sand, oil, and dates – almost everything else had to be imported. We could not figure out for whom all this food had been prepared. It was more than we could eat, and we hadn't even been expected.

Afterwards our host led me outside. I remembered that we were in a man's world. Debbie, my "women's libber" of yore, was sensitive to the culture and remained in the tent. The air was still, the sun had the sky all to itself, the temperature was a pleasant seventy-five or eighty degrees, and not a sound could be heard. I could see the attraction of escaping from the pressures of business and the noise of city life to the tranquility of this place. *It would help though,* I mused, *to have a sound system for some classical music, a TV to keep up with world news and sports, some news magazines, and maybe a chess computer, or better yet, a wife to play chess with, although that would be unlikely in this society.*

But soon that tranquility would be interrupted. He did have a toy. From somewhere he produced a handgun and inquired matter-of-factly, "You want to shoot my pistol?" We came from different backgrounds and cultures, but we were men, united, perhaps, by the hunter-gatherer instinct of centuries earlier and thus sharing the same interest in things that go boom. About a dozen tin-cans were strung up from a clothesline behind one of the big tents. There were camels in the distance. In jest I pointed. "The camels?" He smiled and pointed to the cans. And so we did our target practice, enjoying what we had in common like two big boys at play in this empty vastness of the desert.

Appendix F

REVERSALS IN ASIA

Some men see things as they are and ask why.
Others dream things that never were and ask why not.
George Bernard Shaw

Our third trip took us around the world (finally!). We arrived in London the day Jimmy Carter was sworn in as president of the United States. The news, I thought at the time, was good, the weather was pristine, and the world lay before us. What more could we ask for?

London is a traveler's paradise. There are numerous travel organizations and clubs that facilitate low-budget international travel, offering discount flights, hotel-bookings, overland travel for the more dauntless, visa services, and the like. The overland trips will go as far as South Africa and India. For the former there are four-wheel-drive Bedford trucks pulling trailers that contain tents, canned and dry goods, cooking gear, and other supplies. The passengers sit in second-hand airplane seats in the open back that can be covered with canvas for protection from the elements. For the India-trek there are "Rotels," rolling hotels using buses and trailers or single units with claustrophobic sleeping cubicles. Not my way of losing sleep.

We flew to Thailand after visits in Germany and England. Bangkok International Airport was socked-in with a heavy fog, and the pilot made two 360s before abandoning the idea of landing. He took us to the Thai air force base at Udon Thani, near the Laotian border – a wise decision, I'm sure. It's been said that a third effort at landing is the most dangerous, because the pilot will feel added pressure to set down in unfavorable conditions. When we left the landing pattern for whoknowswhere, I was relieved. Flying, let alone landing, under instrument flight rules is not terribly reassuring to a passenger who, while getting jostled around, looks out the window and sees nothing but a milky soup. When I was in my late-twenties, I earned my visual flight rating and soloed some 150 hours. But before I went for the instrument flight rating that would enable me to fly by instruments only, I realized that for one hour of flying I could go one day skiing. So I skied. Then I discovered that for one day of skiing I could travel internationally for one week. And I have been traveling ever since. But no matter the learning – weather-related accidents prove that flying by instruments only is still a risky business, particularly for the private pilot. Encapsulated in his cockpit with no focal point outside, he can easily experience vertigo. If, then, he trusts his feelings more than the instruments he will crash. It is widely believed that that's how John Kennedy, Jr. and his wife, Carolyn Bessette, died.

We disembarked and waited on the tarmac. It was hot and humid, but bearable for Thailand. At a discreet distance, several armed soldiers stood guard to keep us from wandering off in, what I presumed to be, a restricted-access installation. We stood around in small groups, conversing, stretching and shaking off stiffness and fatigue from the long flight. Soon, banana-leaf-wrapped rice dishes were distributed to sate our hunger while we waited for the fog to lift for our return flight to Bangkok.

Maybe we should have taken the hint and skipped it. Why face the inevitable? We had barely arrived when we learned that Air Siam, the carrier that was to take us to Los Angeles with several stop-overs in between after our traipsing around South East Asia, was on the verge of bankruptcy. The government of Thailand was squeezing it out of competition with its own airline, Thai International Airways – or so rumor had it. Naturally, that bit of information was not terribly reassuring. But what were we supposed to do? Call our trip off and jump on the next plane? Do our thing and hope Air Siam will hang on long enough to carry us back? Hope another airline will honor Air Siam's tickets?

We had bought them through our travel club in London – World Expeditionary Association (WEXAS). Our hope was that, if all else failed, WEXAS would come to the rescue because they had chosen the airline and, we reasoned, bore some responsibility. But we had better save enough money in the event we would have to pay for our return ourselves. Thailand is a beautiful country and a prime vacation spot for Europeans, Americans, and Canadians alike, but like they, we had just come to visit, not to resettle. Yet we never considered scratching our tour for an early return. Always playing it safe can make life boring, while taking calculated chances can be exhilarating. Like those incorrigible sports fans who, eternal optimists that they are when it comes to their teams' dim prospects for winning, throw reason to the wind and bet on the underdogs, we thought that, surely, our airline would stay solvent long enough for us to complete our three-month tour around South East Asia. Yes, that's what we thought. We kept a positive attitude about it and, eventually, even forgot that a problem could be awaiting us on our return.

*   *   *

As usual, our backpacker-style of traveling allowed us to meet interesting people in far-off places. In the remote jungles of Borneo, the world's third largest island, divided between Malaysia (East Malaysia) and Indonesia (Kalimantan), we became acquainted with an American missionary.

Having made it a habit to learn about Christian mission activities wherever we went, we had met many missionaries in our travels up to that point and had found them to be particularly friendly, informative, and outgoing in their hospitality. We had stayed overnight with many of them and remained in contact with some long after our return. In several cases we had the opportunity to contribute to their support and experienced vicariously the satisfaction of their work and the truth of Christ's words, "It is more blessed to give than to receive." (Acts 20:35)

But this man was uncharacteristically uninterested and distant. We were stymied. Here was a man who, far away from his own country, had spent years teaching a simple people about the life and death of Christ, who was anything but aloof. As other missionaries, he might go on a three month home furlough every two years, but be shut into relative seclusion from the outside world the rest of the time. There was no regular mail service, and he didn't have a telephone whose sweet ring might bring good news from a far country. *That's not necessarily negative,* I thought. *It's good to bloom without distraction where you are planted.* But it seemed that there was no affinity with those of his own background, and for us that was difficult to comprehend. Besides, I would think that an individual, whose life's work is people-oriented, would be more welcoming, especially toward those who share his faith and come from his own country so far away.

Despite our cool reception we were interested in this man and his work. As we sought to get to know him better, his life and work among the indigenous people, we discovered a chink in his armor. There seemed to be a void, a measure of homesickness that he filled by listening regularly to the Voice of America Breakfast Show via shortwave radio. At that time, that was the most widely-received radio program in the world. It appeared as though that was for him the daily version of the World Series, Super Bowl, and NBA Playoffs all rolled into one. That was his daily fix that seemed to make other contact with home unnecessary.

It so happened that Pat Gates, the lovely hostess of the program, was also a friend of Debbie's parents. We had met her several times and had talked and laughed with her. What's more, she had interviewed us on her program after one of our trips. "We have with us today a couple of world travelers who…"

When he learned about that connection, his attitude toward us changed faster than you can say "Yankee Doodle Dandy." His stern mask fell, and, like a reporter closing in on a scoop, he plied us with questions about her. Eventually he went beyond that and expressed genuine interest in us, as well, and we experienced a fellowship we would have not thought possible just hours earlier.

* * *

As I was writing this story for this book some thirty years later, Debbie and I had a chance to tell Pat, long since retired in the Washington D.C. area, of our encounter with him. She was pleased at our testimony of her effectiveness in her work so long ago, of course, and she told us her secret. She said that, because the medium that connected her to her audience was radio and not television, her listeners shared with her the inability to see one another. This handicap helped her reach out to them in a more personal way. That explanation made sense to us. It had obviously been her road to success, and that missionary had been a faithful pilgrim on it.

* * *

From Sandakan to Tawau, two port cities in Sabah, one of two East Malaysian states, a trip by ship would be $50, excluding food and drink. There were no connecting roads that could ease the strain on our wallets. With our tight budget we didn't even bother to inquire about flights. But we decided to check out the harbor for any freighters going in that direction. Maybe we could hitch a ride on one of those. Debbie was skeptical, but then, "we've got the time and one never knows." In fact, as it turned out, there was one, Tawau-bound. A verse in the New Testament says, "You do not have because you do not ask." But that's easier said than done when you deal with fallen human beings. It's one thing to approach an invisible God whom you perceive as loving, merciful, and forgiving; it's quite another to face the possibility of encountering an ornery, gruff sea-captain who might blow pipe smoke into your face. Still, we were cautiously optimistic.

The harbor was busy with locals coming and going, buying and selling, loading and unloading, and I was thinking, *Who in the world has ever heard of Sandakan, a tiny spot on the map, yet a real place with real people who have real interests and concerns? Don't they deserve to be acknowledged in their remote isolation from the world where the movers and shakers work and play? Maybe I should display the Southeast Asian version of a popular bumper sticker in my home area in the western part of the United States. "New York – London – Tokyo – Sandakan."*

My mind wanders on such uncharted waters, but never quite finds a place to anchor, and if it did, I wouldn't know what benefit there was in having arrived. The world is so diverse and so full of contradictions. The combined assets of the three richest people on this planet are worth more than the GDP of the forty-nine poorest nations. In India you find luxury and squalor side by side. Rio de Janeiro has its Ipanema and Copacabana beaches and hotels for affluent tourists and its favelas for the down-and-outers. Some Arabs nations, such as the United Arab Emirates, have more oil money than they know what to do with. That leads them to think up hitherto unheard-of projects, such as a seven-star hotel – up to $7000 a night – when there aren't even any six-star ones anywhere in the world and a man-made island chain in the form of a palm tree full of hotels, golf courses, and other play-things for the super rich. Meanwhile their brethren, the Palestinians, linger in refugee camps in abject poverty. Why all this inequity? What is it about us that makes us so selfish that we can live in the lap of luxury while others suffer deprivation?

But I could be lost in my dream world only so long. Reality was knocking, and we had a job to do. There was a gangway leading up to our possible escape from this piece of real estate locked in by the South Pacific.

It took a bit of courage just to climb on board. We were not interested in emulating the questionable method we had used two years earlier to enter a restricted harbor in Spain in hopes of finding a private vessel that might sail to the Canary Islands and have room for two more bodies. Then we had walked at an accelerated, purposeful pace as if in a hurry. We had been deep in conversation, gesticulating as we went, acting as if we were well-acquainted with the place. At the precise moment we were about to cross an imaginary line that divided "out" from "in" near the guardhouse, I had lifted my arm and checked my watch, even as I continued concentrating on our uninterruptible discussion. I mean, would you have dared to stop us? Neither did the guard. Nevertheless, that effort had been in vain, and, with a more sensitive conscience now, I have to confess deservedly so. There had been no boat going to the islands. But, perhaps we would be more fortunate here.

A deck hand directed us to the captain's cabin. We knocked – nothing. We knocked again. After about fifteen seconds the door was yanked open and a sleepy-eyed, angry captain bellowed that we had awakened him, and no, whoever we were, we weren't welcome. Yep, that was one gruff sea captain alright. We were disappointed, but not disheartened at having tried. Fear of failure, speak pride, is one of man's greatest hindrances to success.

As we started to leave we ran into the radio-officer, a Burmese Christian we found out later, who engaged us in conversation and of his own initiative – "Just wait here." – took up our case with the captain. When he emerged from his quarters he brought us welcome news. The skipper had reluctantly agreed that, if we could obtain written permission from the harbor master and the shipping agency, he would take us.

That struck me as a daunting task. Shipping agency? I could picture an office between sea-going containers and stacks of fifty-five-gallon drums with an apathetic secretary buried in a pile of papers and telling us that she would have to check with the head office in Jakarta and that that would take at least a week. Harbor Master? Where in the harbor would we find him? And why should he care? And, even if he did, would he be willing to give his okay in writing?

I was reminded of the story in which, late one night, a driver in the mid-western plains had a flat tire and no jack. He saw light in a farmhouse off in the distance. As he started toward it, he muttered to himself that these people might be getting ready to go to bed and wouldn't want to be disturbed. Getting closer, he wondered if the farm dog would make a big racket and the farmer would view him with suspicion and chase him off. Then, just a few yards from the house, he feared that he might even get shot. Still, he persevered the last few yards in his quest, made it to the front door, and rang the bell. When the farmer opened, the stranded motorist, now thoroughly disgruntled, blurted out: "I don't want your old jack any-way!"

Since I was the man of the house or whatever, the petitioning fell on me, while Debbie played the housewife and did our laundry. Two hours later the laundry was clean, and we had been cleared by both authorities, and the captain, as promised, had no objections. We boarded the ship the night before the departure and were given our very own cabin. At six a.m. we set sail for Tawau. Wow is right! What a blessing! We were excited. We were grateful.

Contrary to our initial impression, the captain turned out to be per-sonable as he warmed up to our presence. We concluded that he must have been suffering from a nightmare when we had awakened him, maybe one in which we were the ghouls. During the journey he had a sailor bring us coffee several times. But it was the radio officer who really took to us. He was young, married only one year, and homesick, and the fact that we shared the same faith was an encouragement to him. He appreciated our presence on board so much that he made every effort to make us comfort-able. At suppertime he brought us a vegetable curry and supplied us with milk and sugar during the twenty-four-hour journey. It was one of those special experiences that puts a smile on your face and remains with you for the rest of your life.

*   *   *

From sea to air; a similar change of fortune occurred just three days later, when we sought to get on a flight with an oil-company plane from Tarakan to Samarinda, both cities in the eastern part of Kalimantan. Again, there were no roads between them, and we had already suffered through one voyage on a Chinese junk off the coast of Sarawak, East Malaysia's southern state. After that experience we knew how that type of boat had earned its name. We had no stomach, literally, for another five days of put-ting up either with the unappetizing food or the seasickness that came with the rolling of the small ship. What had made the latter worse was the fact that it made us taste the former twice – but we don't want to get into that. A trip by ship would take five days for the 300-mile journey with numerous stops, no doubt.

We learned about an international oil company based in Tarakan, which had a weekly flight to Samarinda with its small company aircraft. The executive in charge, an American named Dick Pickens, had a large, air-conditioned office with a slightly smaller desk. If piles of papers on a desk are indicative of the busyness of a man, then Dick Pickens was very busy indeed. It was Monday morning when we went to see him – not the best time to drop in on somebody who is trying to get another week started. He was civil but gave us a cool, business-like reception and told us that Wednesday's flight was already full. We were disappointed but accepted the alternative – not that we had any choice – namely a junky slow boat with junky food and stops in half a dozen or so harbors in between.

But we were interested in this Texan and spent a few more minutes asking him about himself, his family, and life at the end of the world. He opened up. His family had remained in the States, but he was able to see them regularly. His son-in-law, an Australian who normally flew DC-3s out of Singapore, was filling in as the company pilot. By the time we were ready to leave he said, "Well listen, why don't you stop by tomorrow morning and see if any seats have become available."

It's amazing what a bit of reaching out beyond ourselves, a bit of personal interest in someone else, can effect in that person. We had no reason to believe that there was still a chance to get on that flight. But when, irrespective of that, we showed selfless interest in the man and his concerns, he opened up and reciprocated our interest. And so we did stop by, and yes, seats had become available. We could barely hold our excitement in check. Avoiding the hassle of "junk-travel" and saving money to boot while flying on a company plane – that was special. It turned out to be a nine-seat twin-engine Islander with three other passengers, a box of ham and cheese sandwiches and bottles of Seven-Up. What a treat!

The ride was smooth and we had a good view of the inlets in the uneven coastline. We also flew over jungles, mountains, and a few isolated villages. Samarinda is big timber town, and we began to see logging trucks as we got closer. Just two hours after leaving Tarakan, we arrived at our destination. What a blessing! Another rocking-chair story tucked away into the memory bank to be relived when life slows down and the body isn't quite up to doing somersaults any more.

* * *

As I mentioned earlier, like hopelessly biased sports fans we had thought that, surely, Air Siam would beat the odds and still be in operation to take us home at the end of our three-month tour through Malaysia, Singapore, and Indonesia. Yeah, just like the college kids of the 1982 American Olympic ice hockey team at Lake Placid would beat the vaunted Russian professionals!

When I was a boy, my father had told me to "leave thinking up to horses. They have a bigger head than you." I should have listened. For, although the Russians would be defeated, we arrived back only to discover that Air Siam had folded and that our tickets were now worthless.

There would be a "miracle on ice" in Lake Placid, but there was no "miracle" in steamy Bangkok. Not yet, anyway. No airline would accept our tickets.

At Air Siam's sprawling headquarters in Bangkok the electricity was still on, the air-conditioners were still humming, and the telex machines were still in operation when Debbie and I walked in. But the headquarters of the defunct airline that occupied the whole floor of a high-rise, looked like a "left-behind" office. In addition to the manager, only two or three staff were still around. It resembled more the office-equivalent of a ghost town than the nerve center of an international airline.

The manager was both friendly and helpless. He told us that, to the best of his knowledge, none of thousands of booked passengers had had their tickets replaced at no charge. We also learned that some Japanese ticket-holders had been so angry they had come close to practicing their jujitsu on the innocent staff. That would have been, of course, a misplaced use of energy. The poor staff had nothing to do with the airline's demise nor, therefore, with that of the Japanese passengers. The drama of stranded and angry Air-Siam customers must have played out quite a bit earlier. There was no sign now of anyone with worthless tickets in hand. We may well have been the last stragglers.

As I talked with the manager amidst a full complement of office equipment now sitting unused, I said something like: Actually, any of this should belong to us, up to the price of our tickets. Of course, the implementation of that would have been unrealistic, but, at least, it expressed their indebtedness to us. In recognition of that, the manager had agreed to do the only thing left in his power: to send telexes for stranded passengers anywhere in the world at no charge, and he was willing to do the same for us.

Mike Skinner, a young Canadian who was celebrating his acceptance into a highly competitive law school with a round-the-world trip, had already been wired money by his father to buy tickets for the final leg with Korean Airlines. Having already discussed spiritual issues with him, we divulged to him that we were talking to "our Father which art in heaven" about getting us back. We felt that WEXAS owed us replacement tickets but, given the failures of others, believed that only God could persuade them. Mike, as one might expect, was skeptical and told us that, if He did, he would submit his life to God.

Dependence on the Almighty was easy to claim—after all, we had set aside enough money to buy new tickets. But after a week in "The Atlanta," our backpacker hotel – air-conditioned but cheap and nicknamed the Hippy Hilton – and two rejections by WEXAS, our reserves dropped below the lowest airfare. Now we were stuck. We had clung firmly to our conviction that God would step in. Now, our faith was confronted by a new reality. And, going by the experience of thousands of eye-witnesses, our situation looked bleak.

Mike's commitment was equally easy to make – why should Eb and Debbie beat such considerable odds? Well, we couldn't. This was out of our hands.

Today, thirty years later, I look back and think that we had allowed ourselves to be put into a more precarious and vulnerable position than ever before. Our dependence on God had remained undaunted even after WEXAS had rejected our first two telexes. To top it off, we had allowed our funds to drop below the lowest price of new airline tickets. When does faith become presumption?

We did not want to be presumptuous. Since time immemorial the world has faced problems infinitely greater than our relatively trivial ticket situation – problems that could use a generous dose of divine intervention. But we cannot dictate to God. That *would* be presumptuous. We can only entrust ourselves and our world to Him as a wise and loving Father who delights to reciprocate selectively by His criteria our dependence in faith on Him, i.e. within the parameters of His sovereign will.

A third and final telex from us resulted in a third and final telex from WEXAS. "Fresh tickets in post today." Our friend Mike was profoundly affected and, with whatever else might have been transpiring for him, his life changed course. He eventually became a leader in the Christian Fellowship of Law Students at the University of British Columbia.

Some will credit our persistence with WEXAS for our eventual success – while others might have given up after the first telex, we had sent two more. The old adage, God helps those who help themselves, is valid if accompanied by trust in Him. There is the story of a man who prayed that he would win the lottery. After praying day in and day out, he was stopped one day in the middle of his prayer with a voice out of the clouds saying, "John, why don't you meet me half way and buy a ticket."

Others would call us foolhardy, audacious, and lucky. Maybe they're right. Maybe we were dreaming, but, at least, it wasn't a nightmare. What we do know is that odds that were stacked against us turned in our favor. We have not drawn our conclusions in a vacuum, as the context would seem to support them. It does for us, and we can live with that. In our home is the framed telex communication as a testimony to our experience. It was indeed remarkable.

*   *   *

But there is another "rest-of-the-story" story, as Paul Harvey is wont to say. About six months after our return we received a letter from the president of WEXAS stating that the replacement tickets had been issued in error, and would we kindly agree to refund half their cost. We did. Since WEXAS had met our needs when it counted, then approached us with a request rather than a demand and we were now in the financial position to be generous, we were happy to acquiesce.

Final Thoughts

Reversals are part of life – mine, yours, everybody's. I wrote about mostly positive ones in these chapters. There is enough negative news in the world, and a good share of it is just plain heart-wrenching. But there is an organized pattern to our personal lives that is based on reciprocity. It is a universal maxim that we reap what we sow. One doesn't sow oats and reap wheat; one doesn't plant a plum tree and harvest cherries. When we examine the dysfunctional world of much of the glitterati, we discover bitter fruit. They may flaunt their wealth, revel in their status, and exhibit their destructive anything-goes behavior amidst flashing lights to adoring crowds. Role models they are, whether we like it or not, and their nihilistic influence via sleazy tabloid journalism degrades our culture. But self-absorption is shallow and devoid of meaning and rarely results in a fulfilled life. And at the end of their rainbow is a bucket of amassed disappointments. It has been said that someone all wrapped up in himself makes a small package. That goes for megalomaniac tyrants as well; some of the most powerful, selfish individuals ever to walk on this planet. You read the names of some of them on page 92.

But in an almost contradictory way and in keeping with God's character, we esteem humility, we honor sacrifice, and we admire selfless courage, and those qualities carry their own rewards in this life. I have hinted at this in my musings entitled "The Principle of Reverse Results." The information in Ecclesiastes 7:2 is designed to remind us of those enduring values. "It is better to go to the house of mourning than to go to the house of feasting, for this is the end of all mankind, and the living will lay it to heart." That, too, is the reverse of commonly accepted thought. Consider the contrasting lives of Elvis Presley and Albert Schweitzer; of Marilyn Monroe and Mother Teresa; of Mike Tyson and Martin Luther King; of Caligula and Christ.

Jesus, the God-man, said that it is more blessed to give than to receive. My own experience testifies to that. I wrote about buying materials in Kenya for the roof repair of a church in Uganda and delivering these goods at the job site during my commutes. I expected nothing in return; I was happy I could help without being much inconvenienced. But shortly afterwards, my family and I were to benefit disproportionately and directly through that service to the tune of tens of thousands of dollars over the next four years.

I mentioned earlier that my father-in-law had commended us for serving in Africa while our contemporaries were building their nest eggs back home. I wrote also that we lost out on nothing, as our work was deeply satisfying. And it still is today, as it continues under African leadership. What I didn't say is that the business I started so far exceeded our expectations, that we were enabled to participate in mission outreaches at home and in various parts of the world. You can't "outgive" the One who said, "Give, and it will be given to you. Good measure, pressed down, shaken together, running over, will be put into your lap. For with the same measure you use, it will be measured back to you." (Luke 6:38)

We are grateful that our travels led us into meaningful involvement with the needy. As I matured from a footloose and fancy free and largely self-absorbed world traveler to a family man and missionary with a mission, I grew in spirit and became a little wiser. By God's grace, our mission was effective and our work grew. Much credit goes to the wise leadership of Alfred and Carney Farris and to our African point man, Epaphras Edaru. In our work with church leadership, Jackson Mugerwa was the pepper that pairs with the salt. Even more credit goes to the stick-to-itiveness of Debbie, my affectionate, devoted wife. But most of the recognition belongs to the overarching care of a loving Father and His guidance through the Scriptures. At the end of his compositions, the magnificent composer Johann Sebastian Bach routinely penned the letters S.D.G. – Soli Deo Gloria (To God alone the glory). Of Bach, one no less than Ludwig van Beethoven said that he was the greatest composer of all time, and Bach, fittingly, praised God for the talent entrusted him. I praise God for the protection He granted me throughout our time in Africa – on dangerous roads, under the gun, and amidst intertribal conflict. To Him be all the glory. Yes indeed, S. D. G.!

ISBN 142511939-5